Restoring Trust in Higher Education

Restoring Trust in Higher Education

Making the Investment Worthwhile Again

Aneil K. Mishra, PhD, Editor

Foreword by J. L. Stimpert

PRAEGER™

An Imprint of ABC-CLIO, LLC
Santa Barbara, California • Denver, Colorado

Library of Congress Cataloging-in-Publication Data

Names: Mishra, Aneil, editor.
Title: Restoring trust in higher education : making the investment worthwhile
    again / Aneil K. Mishra, PhD, editor ; foreword by J. L. Stimpert.
Description: Santa Barbara, California : Praeger, 2017. | Includes
    bibliographical references and index.
Identifiers: LCCN 2016052128 | ISBN 9781440843358 (hardcopy : alk. paper) |
    ISBN 9781440843365 (ebook)
Subjects: LCSH: Education, Higher—Aims and objectives—United States. |
    Education, Higher—Economic aspects—United States. | Universities and
    colleges—United States—Administration. | Educational change—United
    States.
Classification: LCC LA227.4 .R474 2017 | DDC 378.73—dc23
LC record available at https://lccn.loc.gov/2016052128

ISBN: 978-1-4408-4335-8
EISBN: 978-1-4408-4336-5

21 20 19 18 17   1 2 3 4 5

This book is also available as an eBook.

Praeger
An Imprint of ABC-CLIO, LLC

ABC-CLIO, LLC
130 Cremona Drive, P.O. Box 1911
Santa Barbara, California 93116-1911
www.abc-clio.com

This book is printed on acid-free paper ∞

Manufactured in the United States of America

Contents

Foreword

I was delighted to be asked to write the foreword to *Restoring Trust in Higher Education*. The book project has given me an opportunity to reconnect with Aneil Mishra, a colleague I first met as I was beginning my teaching career at Michigan State University, and to join the distinguished group of scholars and practitioners Aneil has gathered as contributors. I am also pleased to be a part of a book on higher education that speaks to so many audiences. We need books like this one that broaden the conversation across constituencies.

The landscape of higher education is the scene of profound change. Once widely respected, colleges and universities are now bombarded almost every day by a critical news story, editorial, radio or television program, or social media sound bite. Schools are criticized for being too expensive, for having bloated cost structures, for not offering a relevant curriculum, for not requiring our students to study and learn more, for not doing enough to make our campuses welcoming and inclusive, for going too far to make our campuses welcoming and inclusive, for having graduation rates that are too low, for not helping our students obtain internships and jobs, and for many other shortcomings. Some of these criticisms are fair and deserved, but, in their quest for headlines, the media typically ignore the positive impact colleges and universities have on the lives of their students.

Other changes include less support for public universities, dramatic socio-demographic shifts in the traditional college-age population, rapid growth in the number of nontraditional college students, an unusually long period of little or no growth in family incomes and, as a consequence, new challenges in making college affordable. In response to all of these changes, colleges and universities are evolving so that higher education is now in a critical period of transformation; higher education is not what it was, but it is also almost surely not yet what it is likely to become. We have never needed more new thinking and creativity. As Rollo May noted, the need for creativity in a profession is in direct proportion to the amount of change that profession is experiencing.[1] Fortunately, colleges, universities, and the entire higher education "industry" are full of bright, creative people, so we have the capacity and talent required for change and renewal.

Restoring Trust in Higher Education gathers the best thinking of many talented individuals in the higher education profession to focus on several of the most important challenges in our industry. The contributors offer many valuable insights about the current state of higher education and the ways in which colleges and universities can and should evolve to restore trust and confidence. Here, I'll briefly highlight a few of the book's most important topics and contributions:

The Transforming Power of Higher Education

Colleges and universities are not magicians, and those of us in higher education can't be expected to cure all of society's ills. But, the public should have high expectations for our schools' educational programs because we can and often do have a transforming impact on our students. Over the years, I have shared with many students my own experience as a first-generation college student attending a college just 12 miles from my family's farm and how those college years opened a whole world of possibilities for me. This happened because faculty and staff members and fellow students showed an interest in me and my development; they encouraged me to take advantage of opportunities; they gave me the confidence to move outside of my zone of comfort. This same transformative work is occurring for thousands of students every day at colleges and universities across the land.

Our colleges and universities offer opportunities to educate the whole student—the intellect, most certainly, but also the physical, social, emotional, moral, and spiritual dimensions as well. Our best faculty members awaken curiosity and creativity in their students. Participation in clubs, activities, sports, and other co-curricular activities develops our students' leadership skills and their ability to work collaboratively. Because our society is so economically and racially stratified, most of our students find their college or university campus to be the most diverse environment in which they have ever lived. These living and learning environments can model for our students the best aspects of life and vital participation in a democratic republic. Our students can also use their college years to understand their talents and gifts and to find a calling where they can make the greatest possible contributions to the organizations where they work and the communities in which they live.

How We Teach and How Students Learn

For some time now, we have had sufficient research evidence to know how students learn most effectively—what have come to be called "high-impact" learning practices. We know, for example, that students learn best, and best learn how to learn, when they are active participants in the learning process and not just passive spectators. It's no surprise, then, that many faculty members are coming to see that content is overrated. It remains important for our students to acquire knowledge, but in such a dynamic world when so much knowledge is just a Google search away, learning how to learn and how to interpret, synthesize, and communicate knowledge is much more important than acquiring knowledge content. As a consequence, many colleges and universities are adopting innovative new approaches to teaching and learning that feature first-year experience programs, writing requirements, off-campus study opportunities, and culminating senior research projects. Schools are also realizing the value of community service projects and internships, acknowledging that students who have opportunities to apply their learning become more engaged and motivated learners.

Small liberal arts colleges with their low student-to-faculty ratios and a highly personal approach to education have taken the lead on many of these initiatives, but new approaches to teaching and advances in technology are also allowing large universities to offer their students many of these high-impact experiences. We also have an almost unlimited array of opportunities to collaborate with partners beyond our campus boundaries. For too long, colleges and universities have had a "we have to do it ourselves" mentality. But, the educational value our students derive from civic engagement, participation in community-based learning projects, and internships demonstrates that we have much to gain from collaborating with organizations beyond our campus borders.

Above all, our most important task is to make a difference in the lives of our students. Too often I worry that we are content to admit good students, offer them an interesting experience during the next several years, and then graduate good students. Some authors, such as Arum and Roksa, in their book, *Academically Adrift*, have been highly critical of college curricula that require only minimal work and study from our students.[2] Beyond the media headlines this and similar books generate, we need to consider seriously and respond meaningfully to research suggesting that it doesn't really matter where students go to college—that the differences in student learning within different types of colleges and universities are greater than the differences across different types of schools.[3] These research findings are a special challenge for liberal arts colleges like my own because we boldly assert that our highly personalized approach to higher education offers students special benefits; we have to deliver on these claims.

Access and Affordability

Access and affordability are also important topics that deserve far more consideration and conversation than they get in media headlines. It's true that the cost of higher education has grown much more rapidly than family incomes, especially over the last decade. But, the incomes that accrue to college graduates and the return on investment in higher education have never been greater. Moreover, colleges and universities, and especially small private colleges, have focused vast resources on access so that financial aid is the largest item in many college budgets. Loans and student indebtedness get a lot of media attention, but average student indebtedness is around $30,000, which should be quite manageable when average starting salaries for college graduates now approach $50,000, and the highest debt burdens are carried by graduate students (who are responsible for over 40 percent of all student loan debt).[4]

We also need to focus not solely on cost but also on quality, value, and student outcomes. Prospective students and their parents should ask about job and graduate school placement rates and the salaries earned by graduates. (These data need to be considered carefully because colleges that have more graduates going into teaching or other lower-paying occupations will not have the same average starting salaries as colleges that graduate more engineers.) Prospective students and their parents should also study college and university graduation rates and the average time to graduation. A liberal arts college may have a higher "sticker price," but, especially after financial aid is included in the analysis, a student graduating from a liberal arts college in four years may incur less cost than a student who needs five or more years to graduate from a public university, and this analysis doesn't even take into consideration the lost earnings due to spending another year or more in school.

In addition to the topics I've introduced here, *Restoring Trust in Higher Education* includes chapters on many other important and timely topics in higher education. Read the book with interest and share the book with others. Most important, join the conversation and offer your own perspectives and ideas.

J. L. Stimpert
Hampden-Sydney College
November 2016

Notes

1. Rollo May, *The Courage to Create* (New York: Bantam Books, 1976).

2. Richard Arum and Josipa Roksa, *Academically Adrift: Limited Learning on College Campuses* (Chicago: University of Chicago Press, 2011).

3. Sara Lipka, "Does It Matter Where You Go to College?" *Chronicle of Higher Education* 55, no. 12 (2008): A30.

4. Many sources provide data on student indebtedness. See for example: https://lendedu.com/blog/student-loan-debt-statistics.

Acknowledgments

This book is inspired in part by the example of my late father, Vishwa Mohan Mishra, who was a journalism professor at Michigan State University, and who encouraged me, or rather *expected* me to earn a PhD, and whose example and insights I continue to draw upon to this day. This book is the result of how I have preferred to work in academia: gather diverse minds to focus on important problems and opportunities and work collaboratively to find solutions to them. Much work in higher education is done in a solitary fashion, and I have treasured the quiet time that such work affords in a world that gets noisier each year. Nonetheless, I have also sought to create a "merry band of brothers and sisters" with whom I can charge up the hills that make a difference in our students' lives while also prevailing through the occasional valleys and deserts as well.

In addition to my fellow contributors, this book would not have been possible without the help of the several academic leaders we interviewed and our students who shared their formative experiences with us. I want to thank Tom Arthur for his financial support through my professorship, which allowed me to take on this project. I'd like to thank my colleagues at East Carolina University, with whom I've had many useful conversations over the past two years that have provided grist for the mill. I'd also like to thank my graduate assistant Kelly Reburn, who helped with the gathering of chapters and edits as the deadline for completion loomed. Finally, I'd like to thank my wife and frequent coauthor, Karen Mishra, who has made this book as well as my other professional and personal achievements so worthwhile.

This book is dedicated to the late William G. Bowen, former president of Princeton University when I was an undergraduate there, and who led Princeton from 1972 to 1988. His quiet, thoughtful, and compelling leadership style is a role model to which I continue to aspire.

CHAPTER ONE

Higher Education in Crisis: The Importance of Rebuilding Trust

Aneil K. Mishra

Courage is the most important virtue, because without it you cannot practice the others.

—Aristotle

Student has contacted Student Affairs about not being able to graduate. Because this is an academic matter we have referred her back to Academic Affairs. Her GPA is 1.994. She has attempted 212 hours, passed 144 hrs.

—North Carolina Central University administrator

My motivations for this book are many, but one of the most important is my experience as associate dean for the School of Business at North Carolina Central University (NCCU), a historically black college or university (HBCU). I read widely and so considered myself knowledgeable about the challenges facing higher education—and those faced by African Americans in particular—before joining NCCU. However, what I experienced there in my 15 months as an administrator was searing. I witnessed some of the most vulnerable college students in America having to learn in substandard classrooms with outdated technology. Many were unable to afford textbooks or computers, and they flunked courses repeatedly, with no tutoring or other remedial help, spending six, seven, or eight years without earning degrees. By the time these students reached my office, they were begging for one more chance to complete their degrees and to be readmitted to the university that was expelling them for either poor academic performance or failing to earn a degree in a timely fashion. In advocating for these students, I was routinely criticized by university administrators when I requested that they be allowed one more chance to graduate. The administrators were more concerned with university policies than with the individual students who had not only been failed, literally, by their professors but also by university administrators and staff who had not provided them with the tutoring and other assistance they needed to succeed academically. My experience at NCCU also starkly contrasted with my experiences as a professor at Penn State, Wake Forest, and Michigan State, where we had had the resources to help students in academic difficulty far earlier in their academic careers.

An example should prove illustrative. Soon after joining NCCU as associate dean, it became my responsibility to regularly review appeals by students to be reinstated to the university following dismissal for "excessive credit hours" or GPAs that had fallen below 2.0. "Excessive credit hours" was a term I had never encountered in the previous two decades I had served as a professor and sometime university administrator. In essence, students were being dismissed before earning a degree because of having *too many* credits rather than too few. How this could actually happen had to be explained to me. When a student flunked a course or earned a D in a course in which he or she needed to earn a C or better, the student would have to repeat that course, but the credits for the initial D or F would still accumulate in his or her total credits.

When considering such appeals at NCCU, I often reviewed cases in which the student had flunked the same course more than once, had never received tutoring during his or her initial or subsequent efforts to pass the course, and then had been dismissed, even though he or she had spent several years trying to earn an undergraduate degree. Indeed, I reviewed one such student in the second month of my time there who had already been dismissed twice for excessive hours and three times for a low GPA. More than a year later, and right before I departed NCCU for East Carolina, she was still trying to take another course in which she needed to earn a grade of B or higher to attain a high enough GPA to graduate.

Well before I entered higher education as a profession, my upbringing shaped my expectations and preparation for college. My Indian father, a "Tiger father" before "Tiger moms" became well-known, immigrated to the United States in 1957 on a Rotary International Foundation scholarship to attend graduate school at the University of Georgia. He went on to earn a PhD at the University of Minnesota and became a professor at Michigan State University. He wanted me to follow in his footsteps by also earning a doctorate. In the summer before sixth grade began, he took me to school and introduced me to the principal, Mr. Jarrett, saying that he wanted me to be able to attend Harvard when I finished high school. Mr. Jarrett took this request seriously and made sure that I was able to get the teachers I requested throughout middle school, which set me on a path that enabled me to attend Princeton as an undergraduate (when I didn't get admitted to Harvard).

My professional journey since then has provided me with what may be a unique perspective on what works in and what ails higher education. After graduating from an Ivy League university, I then worked for General Motors for several years before earning a PhD from the University of Michigan. I then taught at major public and private universities, left academia for a time to help develop and launch of an online MBA program, and then returned to academia to serve as an associate dean at an HBCU (historically black college or university), North Carolina Central University (NCCU), in Durham.

Why Write Another Book on Reforming Higher Education?

The simple reason for this book is that higher education still needs significant reform. Perhaps the most important reason for writing this book is that our economic future depends on reforming higher education. Even though the additional lifetime earnings for those with a college degree over those with just a high school degree are over $1 million, just over 10 percent of 17- to 24-year-olds in the United States have completed college or earned an advanced degree.[1] Average hourly earnings for high school graduates have also declined since 2000, and in 2016, 3.2 million disadvantaged youths between 16 and 24 are not in school and do not have jobs.[2] The lost economic potential and the social cost of this wasted human capital are immense. Indeed, in 2012, it was estimated at approximately $1.69 trillion in additional burdens for taxpayers in the form of lost tax revenue, and $4.75 trillion when the costs of additional crime and lower economic growth are factored in, for the cohort of 16- to 24-year-olds.[3] "College graduates are healthier, happier, more likely to remain married, and more likely to be engaged parents and more likely to vote."[4]

Indeed, I would argue that our very representative form of democracy is at stake. Higher education should contribute to a better-informed citizenry that is more likely to vote based on rational rather than emotional appeals. Thus, restoring trust in higher education will also be critical to restoring trust in society's other critical institutions, including government. In contrast, people who are denied the opportunity for a college education because of high costs or lack of information about financial aid or who drop out may even make our republic unstable and susceptible to politicians who take advantage of their ignorance. As Robert Putnam, a Harvard University political scientist, wrote in *Our Kids: The American Dream in Crisis*:

> An inert and atomized mass of alienated and estranged citizens, disconnected from social institutions, might under normal circumstances pose only a minimal threat to political stability, with any menace muted by the masses' very apathy. Government under such circumstances might not be very democratic, but at least it would be stable. But under severe economic or international pressures—such as the pressures that overwhelmed Europe and America in the 1930s—that "inert" mass might suddenly prove highly volatile and open to manipulation by antidemocratic demagogues at the ideological extremes.[5]

Moreover, failing to attain college and advanced degrees could result in people permanently or at least highly unable to ever move up the socioeconomic ladder. It's not just the "1 percent" that has benefited from the economic recovery following the Great Recession of the last decade:

> Stephen Rose, an economist at the Urban Institute, finds in new research that the upper middle class is larger and richer than it has ever been, expanding to a record 29.4% of the population as of 2014, from 12.9% in 1979.
>
> "Any discussion of inequality that is limited to the 1% misses a lot of the picture because it ignores the large inequality between the growing upper middle class and the middle and lower middle classes," said Mr. Rose. The Urban Institute is a nonpartisan policy research group.
>
> There is no standard definition of the upper middle class. Many researchers have defined the group as households or families with incomes in the top 20%, excluding the top 1% or 2%. Mr. Rose uses a more dynamic method, similar to how researchers calculate the poverty rate, which allows for growth or shrinkage over time, and adjusts for family size.
>
> Using Census Bureau data available through 2014, he defines the upper middle class as any household earning $100,000 to $350,000 for a family of three: at least double the U.S. median household income and about five times the poverty level [see tables 1.1a and 1.1b]. At the same time, they are distinct from the richest households. Instead of inheritors of dynastic wealth or the chief executives of large companies, they are likely middle-managers or professionals in business, law or medicine with bachelors and especially advanced degrees.[6]

The focus of his book will be on four-year colleges and universities, for which the editor and contributors have the greatest amount of expertise.[7]

Table 1.1a Share of the U.S. population in each income class (2014) (based on annual income for a family of three).

Rich ($350,000+)	Upper Middle ($100,000–$349,999)	Middle ($50,000–$99,999)	Lower Middle ($30,000–$49,999)	Poor ($0–$29,999)
1.79%	29.36%	32.01%	17.08%	19.76%

Table 1.1b Share of the U.S. population in each income class (1979) (based on annual income for a family of three).

Rich ($350,000+)	Upper Middle ($100,000–$349,999)	Middle ($50,000–$99,999)	Lower Middle ($30,000–$49,999)	Poor ($0–$29,999)
0.10%	12.90%	38.80%	23.90%	24.30%

The situations these institutions have been dealing with over the past two decades is much different than it was in the century before that. As the president of the American Council on Trustees and Alumni, Anne Neal, noted,

> In the last 20 years or so, colleges and universities found themselves competing for limited resources, something they had not had to do before. Faced with limited resources, growing demands from policymakers and greater competition from new delivery modes in the higher education space, many colleges and universities really had no choice but finally to assess what they could and should not do.[8]

Intractability of Reform due to Poor Information and Low Student Engagement

Despite the plethora of books on higher education's endemic problems, innovation in and reform of this sector has lagged all other sectors, including health care, with which it shares several critical characteristics, including unacceptably high costs and ambiguity in connecting means and ends. In other words, does higher education lead to positive results, including individuals with greater critical thinking and problem-solving abilities or higher incomes than those without similar education attainment? Acquiring a college degree also entails significant vulnerability on the part of its consumer. For example, wrong choices can lead to lower-than-expected life satisfaction, employability, and income over decades, if not a lifetime; educational debts that cannot be repaid.

I believe that one reason that it has received inadequate attention is that education, like health care, is a good that is jointly produced by both the service provider (i.e., the institution and its faculty and staff) and the consumer (i.e., students and their parents). Just as poor patient compliance with treatment regimens will lead to poor patient outcomes, poor student engagement will lead to less-than-optimal student outcomes. No matter what the institution does to increase students' engagement, it will still be up to the students as to how much time and effort they devote to studying and attending classes. This appears to be a significant challenge, as "one study of University of California undergraduates found that students spend 13 hours a week studying, some three times fewer hours than they devoted to socializing with friends, watching television, and exercising."[9] In 2003, full-time students at four-year colleges in the United States spent 10 hours less per week studying than they did in 1961, from 24 hours to 14 hours per week.[10] To the extent that students are devoting less time to studying and attending classes, the costs associated with educating them are increasing. Indeed, it is possible that colleges and universities may contribute to higher costs because they expend resources to increase engagement among a student body that has ever-increasing distractions from social media and entertainment technologies, cocurricular activities, and a drinking and partying culture that is even more prevalent than it was when I attended college more than 30 years ago.

Trust and Higher Education Are Inextricably Intertwined

Trust is defined as a willingness to be vulnerable to others based on the prior belief that those others are reliable, open and honest, competent, and compassionate.[11,12] *Compassionate* here means having the other party's best interests at heart. Reliability, openness and honesty, competence, and compassion are the four key dimensions of one's trustworthiness, or what we call the *ROCC of Trust*.[13] Second only to health care, perhaps, higher education involves significant uncertainty and risk, resulting in a high degree of vulnerability for students and their families. Whether students will succeed in completing their degrees and whether the investments of time and money toward that effort will be worthwhile—that is, whether graduates will be able to pay back their loans or pay back their parents who have borrowed money on their behalf, especially given that the unemployment and underemployment rates for college graduates are higher than they have been in previous decades, as noted earlier—are hardly guaranteed.

Information asymmetry compounds this vulnerability. Administrators, professors, and instructors know more about the educational processes and outcomes than the students and their families. As David Yaskin, the founder of Starfish Retention Solutions, told me,

> I believe that colleges need to provide consumers, students, and parents more information about how long it takes to go to college, the probability of success, and what's the cost associated with that. Whether it's through a government mandate or an individual school's goodwill and marketing, or an accrediting group's approach, the more that you can have information about what works and what doesn't for which kinds of students, you need that kind of transparency to build trust.[14]

Although more is known about the financial and career payoffs (e.g., incomes, jobs) from education than the educational process itself, it is still very difficult to obtain comparable data on institutions. Even then, such data typically do not control for, except in gross ways, the quality of either inputs, that is, the composition of the matriculating students, or through-puts, and how an institution transforms those students through its educational process. In terms of input quality, some colleges report the percentage of matriculates with 4.0 GPAs, the percentage of the student body who were in the top 10 percent of their high school graduating classes, or average or median SAT or ACT scores. When it comes to throughputs, static indicators are often provided by institutions, for example, faculty-student ratios, size of endowments or libraries, or the percentage of students who elect various majors. Institutions may also provide qualitative descriptions of throughputs, including the availability of career, graduate school, or professional school development resources; freshmen seminars; and study-abroad programs. In any case, measures of effort are not collected, making evaluations of educational quality and career prospects even more troublesome, even though there are some rankings as to the *lack* of seriousness with which students take their educations (e.g., rankings of best party schools, etc.).

Compassion Failures: High Costs and Unsustainable Student Debt

Prices for a college education continue to rise much faster than inflation and incomes, even as quality and results are difficult if not impossible to evaluate by "consumers," that is, students and families. The trend lines became unsustainable years ago. As a personal example, the approximately $8,500 Princeton charged me in 1980 for tuition, fees, and room and board would be about $24,500 in 2016, not the $60,090 that Princeton states these items will cost in total for the 2016–1017 academic year.[15] Moreover, the price I paid in 1981, "strategically set" at $9,994, represented a 133 percent increase over the previous decade.[16] Since then, annual price increases in the United States for a college education have continued to exceed the inflation rate. "From the 1983–1984 enrollment year to the 2013–2014 enrollment year, the *inflation-adjusted* cost of a four-year education, including tuition, fees, and room and board, increased 125.7 percent for private school and 129.0 percent for public school (according to the College Board) (emphasis added)."[17] Price increases in tuition and fees above inflation have only accelerated over the years, with average increases during the period 1995 to 2015 more than three times general inflation rate among private national universities and almost six times the general inflation rate among public national universities according to *U.S. News and World Report*.[18] "Even in the best-performing states, college is less affordable than it was in 2008, and low- and middle-income families face significant economic barriers that limit their ability to invest in education."[19] First-generation, low-income, and underserved minority students may even be disproportionately discouraged from applying to highly selective schools with high list prices (list prices are the published prices before scholarships and other financial aid are awarded).[20]

Not surprisingly, student loan debt is at an all-time high, $1.3 trillion, and continues to grow apace:[21]

> Using the Survey of Consumer Finances, Fry (2014) shows that in 2010, 37 percent of the nation's households headed by an adult younger than age 40 owed money on student debt, a proportion that has more than doubled since 1989. For households with student loan debt, the average amount was $26,682 in 2010, and the median was $13,410.[22]

As of 2016, 7 million student loan borrowers are in default, with millions more apparently on the same path to default.[23] These levels of student loan debt have meant that graduates are increasingly deferring purchases of homes and even getting married. According to a 2015 survey by Student Loan Hero, one in seven Americans have delayed marriage due to student loan debt, and one in five delayed starting a business.[24] Although the percentage of respondents who say they have had to postpone parts of their lives due to borrowing money for college differs depending on the survey, it is clear that deferring major life events such as marriage, having children, and saving for retirement are all adversely affected by student loan indebtedness.[25]

Indeed, I graduated from college in 1984 with $20,000 in student loans.[*] My father's consulting business had suffered as a result of an economic

---

[*] Approximately $46,000 in 2016 dollars.

recession almost as severe as the one of 2007–2009. I had $7,500 in federal guaranteed student loans (GSL) and the balance in personal loans from my stepgrandfather, which carried the same terms as the federal GSLs, a seven-year repayment term at 9 percent interest. Unlike the GSLs, the interest accumulated while I was in college. My wife, Karen, and I were married in 1985, right after she graduated from Albion College with her own $5500 in GSLs.* Our marriage so soon after graduating from college was in keeping with many of our college classmates. However, our waiting 13 years before purchasing our first home was not. This is because we had to first pay off our first and second "mortgages," that is, our students loans. (We were still paying her loans from her MBA when we bought our first home.)

Federal government programs will reduce student indebtedness, but only at taxpayer expense. For example,

> The Obama administration moved to wipe out $7.7 billion in student debt for hundreds of thousands of severely disabled Americans, responding to years of complaints of bureaucratic snafus that led to some borrowers' disability checks being improperly garnished. Federal law entitles such people to have their federal student loans discharged—removing any obligation to repay—because they are "totally and permanently disabled," the Education Department said.[26]

There are many reasons for this highly significant price inflation of higher education, some of which are discussed in detail in other chapters in this book. One reason is declining state government support. States are collectively investing 17 percent less in their public colleges and universities, or $1,525 less per student, since 2007, in inflation-adjusted figures.[27] As a result, tuition has risen by an average of 33 percent over the same time period.[28] Indeed, according to one study, declines in state government support for higher education account for 79 percent of the increase in tuition between 1991 and 2011 at public colleges and universities. Higher construction costs another 5–6 percent, and increases in health care costs account for much of the reminder, with increases in "administrative bloat" being a relatively insignificant percentage.[29] Another reason is that online technologies may actually increase certain costs while reducing others. Having helped lead the development and launch of the online MBA program, MBA@UNC, for the University of North Carolina at Chapel Hill and having taught online undergraduate courses at East Carolina University, I know firsthand that cost savings are not a necessary result from

---

* Approximately $12,300 in 2016 dollars.

moving from face-to-face to online venues. Initial course development can be costly. Although savings can result from not having to utilize physical classroom space, until rigorous studies comparing learning outcomes of identical courses taught in both face-to-face and online formats are conducted, any projected cost savings should be viewed with suspicion.

Reliability Failures: Students Take Longer and Are Less Likely to Complete a Degree

As discussed below, it's bad enough that prices have risen so significantly, but at least if the process of and results from earning a college education had improved in line with price increases, we could say that we're getting our money's worth. Instead, students are taking longer than ever to complete their undergraduate degrees, with the six-year completion rate for students who began college in 2009 at 53 percent, a decline of two percentage points from the cohort the year before, and continuing a pattern of decline in completion rates.[30] At the same time, global competition in the higher education sector continues to increase, and the United State lags its competitors in the developed world. "U.S. college graduation rates are among the lowest in the developed world, with fewer than two-thirds of students who start full-time at a four-year college earning a degree from any college within six years of initial enrollment."[31] This additional time to complete a degree has high economic costs. "Every additional year that a student spends at a public four-year college costs approximately $68,000 (nearly $23,000 in cost of attendance and $45,00 in lost wages)."[32]

Competence Failures: Poor Job Prospects

Moreover, students are finding the job market to be lackluster, and they are increasingly working in jobs for which a college degree is not necessary. "In 2000, 36 percent of employed college graduates age 22–27 worked in jobs that did not require a college degree"; this figure was 38 percent in 2007, and it rose to 46 percent by 2014.[33] According to the Economic Policy Institute, "for young college graduates, the unemployment rate is currently 7.2 percent (compared with 5.5 percent in 2007), and the underemployment rate is 14.9 percent (compared with 9.6 percent in 2007)."[34] Perhaps one positive way to view these dismal statistics is that at least college graduates have better employment prospects than those who have only earned a high school degree. "For young high school graduates in 2014, the unemployment rate is 19.5 percent (compared with 15.9 percent in 2007), and the underemployment rate is 37.0 percent (compared with 26.8 percent in 2007)."[35]

In addition, earnings prospects don't necessarily improve upon acquiring additional education when examining the same students over time:

> Among (nonprofit college) students who enrolled in 2005, on average only half graduated from such institutions within six years. On average, nearly four in 10 undergraduates at those schools who took on student debt earned no more than $25,000 in 2011, the same as the typical high school graduate. Other research shows similar dropout rates at public colleges and universities.
>
> Along with the weak job prospects, most of these students are now severely behind on their payments, damaging their credit and limiting their ability to borrow for homes and cars. More than a fifth of all student debt is at least 90 days delinquent, according to the New York Federal Reserve, and federal data show dropouts are three times more likely to default than degree earners.[36]

Only 38 percent of college students believe that their "college education/ experience has been very helpful in preparing them for a professional career," and only 21 percent of college students believe that they are "very prepared for a professional career."[37] It is not clear what accounts for the drop-off between their evaluations of their colleges and universities and their self-evaluations, but the relatively low scores for each measure indicate that much could still be done for colleges and universities to help their students be prepared for the world of work.

Even efforts by higher education to demonstrate that learning takes place are often limited in their scope and validity. For example, the Assurance of Learning (AOL) that must take place at business schools accredited by the largest and most influential accrediting body, the Association to Advance Collegiate Schools of Business (AACSB), typically is conducted on only a subset of courses offered and on a limited number of measures, all of which must be agreed upon by faculty and administrators. Based on my experience at several business schools as both an administrator and faculty member, the percentage of courses evaluated is very small indeed, the number of criteria used quite few, and the efforts to refine such criteria exceedingly cumbersome and time-consuming. Most importantly, the evaluations are conducted by faculty and staff, not by such external stakeholders as employers or parents. I deliberately left out government institutions, as the failure of even the Obama administration to introduce rigorous evaluations of the efficacy of higher education and the increasing antagonism between state legislators and higher educational institutions mean that both the federal and state governments are unlikely to be accepted as evaluators anytime soon.[38]

Trust in Higher Education Needs to Be Rebuilt

The irony is that any possibility for the reform of higher education won't work unless the key stakeholders trust each other. Parents and students need to be able to trust that their significant financial and temporal investments in higher educational institutions will be worthwhile. Faculty members need to be able to trust that administrators' strategies and resource allocations are both smart and equitable. The staff that support the faculty in the educational process have to trust that their input will be respected and incorporated into key decisions by both the faculty and executive administrators. Parents and students need to be able to trust that faculty are both qualified and motivated to provide them with the best possible opportunities for learning. In turn, faculty need to be able to trust that students will make the most of these opportunities and not waste the time of their instructors or their peers.

Although indicators of trust among these various stakeholder pairs are not readily obtainable, there are some worrisome indicators. According to the annual National Survey of Student Engagement, 31 percent of first-year college students in 2015 "seriously considered leaving their institution in the current year," and of those who did, 25 percent did so "to improve their career prospects" and 26 percent to "obtain a better quality education."[39] These two reasons for wanting to leave a college or university are evidence that at least the competence-based trustworthiness of colleges and universities has suffered in students' assessments.

Available evidence does show that trust between faculty and their college or university administrations is suffering and perhaps deteriorating. Recent no-confidence votes and unionization efforts are evidence of increasing faculty-administrator distrust and the failure of traditional faculty governance mechanisms to address concerns about ever-greater reliance on part-time instructors, deteriorating campus climates, and budget cuts. No-confidence votes at U.S. universities have been increasing in recent years, with 7 in 2012, 10 in 2013, 21 in 2014, and 14 in 2015.[40] The past year has provided several additional noteworthy examples of deteriorating faculty-administration relationships. The University of Minnesota faculty in January of 2016 called for an election to form a union, driven in part by the shift to low-paid instructors.[41] Both the president of the University of Missouri system and the U-Missouri chancellor of the main campus in Columbia were forced to resign in late 2015 over their inability to "address racism and other ugly incidents on campus."[42] The University of Wisconsin-Madison faculty voted "no-confidence," and the University of Wisconsin-Milwaukee faculty voted unanimously so, in the U-Wisconsin system president and board of trustees in May of 2016 because of their failure to "mitigate $250 million in budget cuts over two years" by Governor Scott Walker and the Republican legislature as well as weakening shared governance and tenure provisions.[43]

Who Guards the Guardians?

Although it is not direct evidence, the growth in both oversight by the federal government and regional accrediting bodies and ratings/rankings by various publications all attest to deficiencies in trust in colleges and universities by those who pay for higher education and their elected representatives. The Obama administration has asked accreditors of colleges and universities to "focus more on enforcing standards that measure student achievement and to consider additional scrutiny for colleges with significant problems."[44] This is in the context that accreditors have often failed in their basic duty to assure that colleges and universities are fulfilling their basic mission: educating their students in a timely fashion. In 2015, the *Wall Street Journal* found that "nearly 350 out of more than 1,500 four-year colleges now accredited by one of six regional commissions have a lower graduation rate or higher student-loan default rate than the average among the colleges that were banished by the same accreditors since 2000."[45] The *Wall Street Journal* also found that the "U.S. government sent $16 billion in aid (in 2014) to students at accredited colleges with graduation rates of less than 33 percent."[46] In addition, the Center for American Progress has criticized the accreditation system for being inconsistent across colleges and universities because accrediting agencies vary in how they apply their negative sanctions and how long an institution is under review once it has been found to be out of compliance.[47]

The federal government itself bears some of the responsibility for accrediting agencies not serving as proper watchdogs:

> The department can't require accreditors to set so-called bright line standards, such as by dropping accreditation and federal aid eligibility for a college or academic program with a graduation rate below a certain percentage. For that to happen, the U.S. Congress would have to lift its ban on specific requirements for accreditors.[48]

Indeed, taxpayers will increasingly pay the price for the failure of accrediting agencies and government agencies to ensure that colleges and universities provide a decent education:

> As of early May, 19,657 borrowers alleging illegal practices by their schools had applied to the Education Department to be relieved of repaying their federal

student loans. Under a decades-old law, borrowers are entitled to have loans forgiven if they prove their schools used deceptive advertising and recruiting.

That total represents a surge in such requests. As of January, the agency had received about 7,500 applications for forgiveness from borrowers owing an aggregate $164 million.

Most of the debt forgiven under the program is likely to be absorbed by taxpayers.[49]

Hope for the Future

Even amid very difficult circumstances, there are compelling examples of success within and across higher educational institutions that have not been given adequate attention. One example is Paul Quinn College, an HBCU in Dallas, Texas, led by President Michael Sorrell. When he was asked to be president after serving on the board of trustees for several years, he had to turn around a broken institution:

> It's the hardest job I've ever had. It is brutally difficult. It was the most broken institution I've ever seen in my life. There was no time to play around. We were in a crisis situation. When you are in failing situation, you cannot do the same old thing the same old way. It was very interesting—people don't tend to believe what they've never seen before. You have to be willing to try anything. You have to send a message that you are serious. The first thing we did was cut the football program.
>
> One of the things I've discovered is you can find tremendous inspiration for the future if you're willing to look to the past but not become a prisoner to it. We subscribe to that Marcus Aurelius quote, "Choose the harder right over the easier wrong without apparent regard for self." Everyone was held accountable. Everyone was taught and told, "Look: this is who we're going to be. We're going to do things the right way. We're not going to take short cuts. We're going take the hard times to get to the great times."
>
> Some of the hard times were hard. There was a point where I had to cut salaries. I cut my own 25 percent. I'd already taken a 40–45 percent pay cut to take the job. I cut the VP's 20 percent, the executive directors' 15 percent, and the faculty 10. Everyone had to take something. We had to do everything possible to put ourselves on sound fiscal footing. I appreciate that colleges are places of learning, but they are in the business of learning. If your business doesn't work, the learning cannot work.
>
> You can control how you are perceived. We instituted a dress code. It has allowed us to create a Clothing Closet. So our students can go in, get whatever they need for free. That gave us a chance to get into churches, to get into businesses, and tell our story. In the process of telling the story, people began to really engage. It also gave us the opportunity to do some donor cultivating, right? Because if you were a donor in the Clothes Closet,

we treated you like you were a donor of cash, and the way we gauged donor capacity was by the caliber of clothes you donated. So if you donated Armani suits, that was a little bit different than donating Levi jeans.

At the end of the day, it's a special place. Why shouldn't under-resourced students have an extraordinary institution that makes them feel nurtured and safe and warm? Our ultimate goal is to become one of America's great small colleges. But to do that with the same target demographic: students who are Pell-Grant-eligible.[50]

This book seeks to share this and other examples and to identify some of the ways in which they could be expanded within the contributors' own institutions or adopted by other colleges and universities. This book will also provide examples of innovations that have taken place outside of higher educational institutions but which nonetheless benefit students both academically and professionally when they graduate.

Notes

1. Jaison, R. Abel and Richard Deitz, "Do the Benefits of College Still Outweigh the Costs?," Federal Reserve Bank of New York, *Current Issues in Economics and Finance* 20, no. 3 (2014): 1–11. https://www.newyorkfed.org/medialibrary/media /research/current_issues/ci20-3.pdf; Patricia Cohen, "It's a Tough Job Market for the Young without College Degrees," *New York Times*, May 10, 2016. http://mobile .nytimes.com/2016/05/11/business/economy/its-a-tough-job-market-for-the-young -without-college-degrees.html?smid=tw-nytimesbusiness&smtyp=cur&referer=.

2. Cohen, "It's a Tough Job Market."

3. Clive R. Belfield, Henry M. Levin, and Rachel Rosen, *The Economic Value of Opportunity Youth* (Washington, D.C.: Corporation for National and Community Service, 2012). Figures quoted in Robert D. Putnam, *Our Kids: The American Dream in Crisis* (New York: Simon & Schuster, 2015), 353.

4. David Leonhardt, "College for the Masses," *New York Times*, April 24, 2015. http://mobile.nytimes.com/2015/04/26/upshot/college-for-the-masses.html?emc =edit_th_20150426&nl=todaysheadlines&nlid=64467426&_r=0&referrer =; Philip Oreopoulos and Kjell Salvanes, "Priceless: The Nonpecuniary Benefits of Schooling," *Journal of Economic Perspectives* 25, no. 1 (2011): 159–184.

5. Robert D. Putnam, *Our Kids: The American Dream in Crisis* (New York: Simon & Schuster, 2015), 239–240. Kindle edition.

6. Josh Zumbrun, "Upper Middle Class Sees Big Gains, Research Finds," *Wall Street Journal*, June 21, 2016; Stephen J. Rose, *The Growing Size and Incomes of the Upper Middle Class* (Washington, D.C.: The Urban Institute, June 2016), 8.

7. Although community colleges and graduate and professional education are also in need of significant reform, it is beyond the scope of this book to address those areas comprehensively.

8. Transcribed telephone interview with Anne Neal, past president and Senior Fellow of the American Council of Trustees and Alumni, April 7, 2016.

9. Jeffrey J. Selingo, "Many Colleges Are Failing to Prepare Students for Their Working Lives," *Washington Post*, October 15, 2015. https://www.wash ingtonpost.com/news/grade-point/wp/2015/10/15/many-colleges-are-failing -to-prepare-students-for-their-working-lives/?postshare=4511444911304722; Stephen Brint and Allison M. Cantwell, *Undergraduate Time Use and Academic Outcomes: Results from UCUES 2006* (Berkeley, CA: Center for Studies in Higher Education, 2008). http://www.cshe.berkeley.edu/publications/undergraduate-time -use-and-academic-outcomes-results-ucues-2006.

10. Philip Babcock and Mindy Marks, "Leisure College USA: The Decline in Student Study Time," American Enterprise Institute, *Education Outlook* 7 (August 2010). http://www.aei.org/publication/leisure-college-usa.

11. Roger C. Mayer, James H. Davis, and F. D. Schoorman, "An Integrative Model of Organizational Trust." *Academy of Management Review* 20 (3): 709–734, 1995.

12. Aneil K. Mishra and Karen E. Mishra, *Becoming a Trustworthy Leader: Psychology and Practice* (New York: Routledge, 2013).

13. Aneil K. Mishra and Karen E. Mishra, *Becoming a Trustworthy Leader: Psychology and Practice* (New York: Routledge, 2013).

14. Transcribed telephone interview with David Yaskin, founder and former CEO of Starfish Retention Solutions, August 28, 2015.

15. Laurie Johnson, "The $10,000-a-year College Education Has Arrived," *New York Times*, February 19, 1981. http://www.nytimes.com/1981/02/19/nyregion /the-10000-a-year-college-education-has-arrived.html; CPI inflation calculator, U.S. Government Bureau of Labor Statistics. http://data.bls.gov/cgi-bin/cpicalc.pl ?cost1=8495&year1=1980&year2=2016; https://admission.princeton.edu/finan cialaid/fees-payment-options.

16. Johnson, "The $10,000."

17. Alyssa Davis, Will Kimball, and Elise Gould, "The Class of 2015: Despite an Improving Economy, Young Grads Still Face an Uphill Climb," *Economic Policy Institute*, Briefing Paper #401, May 27, 2015. http://www.epi.org/publication/the -class-of-2015.

18. Travis Mitchell, "Chart: See 20 Years of Tuition Growth at National Universities," *U.S. News & World Report*, July 29, 2015. http://www.usnews .com/education/best-colleges/paying-for-college/articles/2015/07/29/chart -see-20-years-of-tuition-growth-at-national-universities.

19. Institute for Research on Higher Education, *College Affordability Diagnosis: National Report* (Philadelphia: Institute for Research on Higher Education, Graduate School of Education, University of Pennsylvania, 2016). http://www2.gse .upenn.edu/irhe/affordability-diagnosis.

20. Dian Schaffhauser, "Perceived Rise in College Tuition Hits 'Access' Students Disproportionately," CampusTechnology.com, May 31, 2016. https://campustech nology.com/articles/2016/05/31/perceived-rise-in-college-tuition-hits-access -students-disproportionately.aspx?admgarea=News.

21. Serena Elavia, "Why 2016 Will Be a Big Year for Student Loans," Fox Business, December 30, 2016. http://www.foxbusiness.com/features/2015/12/16/why -2016-will-be-big-year-for-student-loans.html.

22. Davis, Kimball, and Gould, "The Class of 2015."

23. Josh Mitchell, "College Loan Glut Worries Policy Makers," *Wall Street Journal*, June 5, 2016. http://www.wsj.com/articles/college-loan-glut-worries-policy -makers-1465153138?mod=itp&mod=djemITP_h June 5.

24. Student Loan Hero staff. "2015 Student Loan Burden Report: One in Seven Americans with Student Loans Have Delayed Marriage due to Crushing Burden of Student Debt," StudentLoanHero.com, August 28, 2015. https://studentloanhero .com/press/2015-student-loan-burden-report-student-loan-hero.

25. Janna Herron, "Survey: Student Loan Debt Forces Many to Put Life on Hold," Bankrate.com, August 5, 2015. http://www.bankrate.com/finance/consumer -index/money-pulse-0815.aspx; William Elliott III and Melinda K. Lewis, *The Real College Debt Crisis: How Student Borrowing Threatens Financial Well-being and Erodes the American Dream* (Santa Barbara, CA: Praeger, 2015).

26. Josh Mitchell, "Obama Administration to Forgive Billions in Student Debt for Disabled Americans," *Wall Street Journal*, April 12, 2016. http://www.wsj.com /articles/obama-administration-to-forgive-billions-in-student-debt-for-disabled -americans-1460488542?cx_navSource=cx_picks&cx_tag=contextual&cx _artPos=7.

27. Mikhail Zinshteyn, "States Have Cut Money for Higher Education 17 percent since the Recession, Report Finds," *Hechinger Report*, May 19, 2016. http://hechinger report.org/state-cut-money-higher-education-17-percent-since-recession-report -finds.

28. Michael Mitchell, Michael Leachman, and Kathleeen Masterson, "Funding Down, Tuition Up: State Cuts to Higher Education Threaten Quality and Affordability at Public Colleges," Center on Budget and Policy Priorities, May 26, 2016. http://www.cbpp.org/research/state-budget-and-tax/funding-down-tuition-up.

29. Robert Hiltsonsmith, *Pulling Up the Higher-ed Ladder: Myth and Reality in the Crisis of College Affordability* (New York: Demos, 2015), 15. http://www.demos .org/sites/default/files/publications/Robbie%20admin-bloat.pdf.

30. D. Shapiro, A. Dundar, P. K. Wakhungu, X. Yuan, A. Nathan, and Y. Hwang, *Completing College: A National View of Student Attainment Rates—Fall 2009 Cohort* (Signature Report No. 10) (Herndon, VA: National Student Clearinghouse Research Center, November 2015). https://nscresearchcenter.org/wp-content /uploads/SignatureReport10.pdf.

31. The Education Trust, *Tough Love: Bottom-line Quality Standards for Colleges* (Washington, D.C.: The Education Trust, 2014), 1; Organization for Economic Cooperation and Development, *Education at a Glance 2013*, Chart A4.2 (Paris: OECD, 2013).

32. Ronald M. Berkman, "Helping College Students Finish What They Started," *The Hill*, January 29, 2016. http://thehill.com/blogs/congress-blog /education/267375-helping-college-students-finish-what-they-started.

33. Jaison R. Abel and Richard Deitz, "Are the Job Prospects of Recent College Graduates Improving?," *Liberty Street Economics* (blog of the Federal Reserve Bank of New York), September 4, 2014. http://libertystreeteconomics.newyorkfed.org/2014/09/are-the-job-prospects-of-recent-college-graduates-improving.html#.VUt7TvlVhBc.

34. Davis, Kimball, and Gould, "The Class of 2015."

35. Ibid.

36. Mitchell, "Obama Administration."

37. *McGraw-Hill Education 2016 Workforce Readiness Survey* (New York: McGraw-Hill, June 1, 2016). http://www.mheducation.com/news-media/press-releases/2016-workforce-readiness-survey.html.

38. Michael Stratford, "The Non-ratings Future," *Inside Higher Ed*, August, 15, 2015. https://www.insidehighered.com/news/2015/08/12/ratings-fight-over-education-department-prepares-launch-new-consumer-tool.

39. Center for Postsecondary Research, Indiana University School of Education, "National Survey of Student Engagement: 2015 Topical Module: First-year Experiences & Senior Transitions" (2015). http://nsse.indiana.edu/2015_institutional_report/pdf/Modules/NSSE15%20Module%20Summary-First-Year%20Experiences%20and%20Senior%20Transitions.pdf.

40. Education Advisory Board, "No-confidence Votes Spreading across the Nation," May 5, 2016. https://www.eab.com/daily-briefing/2016/05/05/no-confidence-votes-spreading-across-the-nation.

41. Maura Lerner, "University of Minnesota Faculty to File for Union Vote," *Star Tribune*, January 16, 2016. http://www.startribune.com/university-of-minnesota-faculty-file-for-union-vote/365851061.

42. Susan Svrulga, "U. Missouri President, Chancellor Resign over Handling of Racial Incidents," *Washington Post*, November 9, 2015. https://www.washingtonpost.com/news/grade-point/wp/2015/11/09/missouris-student-government-calls-for-university-presidents-removal.

43. Patrick Marley, "No-confidence Vote by UW Faculty Passes Overwhelmingly," *Milwaukee-Wisconsin Journal Sentinel*, May 2, 2016. http://www.jsonline.com/news/education/no-confidence-vote-by-uw-faculty-passes-overwhelmingly-b99717701z1-377877451.html; Colleen Flaherty, "No More 'Job for Life,'" *Inside Higher Ed*, May 11, 2016. https://www.insidehighered.com/news/2016/05/11/wisconsin-governor-and-university-system-president-anger-professors-comments-tenure.

44. Paul Fain, "Monitoring the Gatekeepers," *Inside Higher Ed*, April 25, 2016. https://www.insidehighered.com/news/2016/04/25/education-department-tells-accreditors-focus-more-troubled-colleges-and-standards.

45. Andrea Fuller and Douglas Belkin, "The Watchdogs of College Education Rarely Bite," *Wall Street Journal*, June 17, 2015. http://www.wsj.com/articles/the-watchdogs-of-college-education-rarely-bite-1434594602.

46. Ibid.

47. Antoinette Flores, "Watching the Watchdogs: A Look at What Happens When Accreditors Sanction Colleges," Center for American Progress, June 21, 2016. https://www.americanprogress.org/issues/higher-education/report/2016/06/21/139529/watching-the-watchdogs.

48. Fain, "Monitoring the gatekeepers."

49. Josh Mitchell, "Surge in Americans Applying to Have Student Debt Canceled," *Wall Street Journal*, May 26, 2016. http://www.wsj.com/articles/almost-20-000-americans-apply-to-have-student-debt-canceled-arguing-they-were-deceived-1464279054.

50. Transcribed telephone interview with Michael Sorrell, October 20, 2015.

CHAPTER TWO

The Marketing and Business of Higher Education

Christopher P. Puto

The title for this chapter contains two words that are often problematic for those in the academic community: "Marketing" and "Business." For different reasons, college and university administrators, faculty, students, prospective students, and parents are often uncomfortable or skeptical when these terms are mentioned. In keeping with a goal of this volume—making higher education respected and relevant to our society and helping students and parents to know that the human capital and financial capital investments they make in education will pay off—this chapter provides a grounding to help *all* constituents in the higher education process reach good decisions in choosing the most suitable institution for a given student to pursue for his or her college education.

We begin with a brief review of the circumstances that produced today's challenging higher education environment. This is followed by an introduction to the roles of marketing and business concepts in higher education and then some guidelines designed to help all constituents—college and university administrators and prospective students and their parents—use this information to enhance the success of choosing the right college or university for their educational goals.

A Brief Historical Perspective

For over 350 years, higher education in the United States mostly operated inside its own cocoon. From Harvard's founding in 1636 to the turn of the millennium, the "marketplace" of U.S. colleges and universities was surprisingly little understood. Reputations were based largely on word-of-mouth transmissions: somebody famous or notorious "went there" and so it must be "good" or "not good." Sometimes, the reputation came from personal contact with alumni who had shared their positive (or negative) experiences. Finally, cost and selectivity contributed to a school's reputation, with expensive, highly selective schools perceived as being "better."

In the 1960s, tuition at an Ivy League school was approximately $1,500 per year. Room and board and expenses added another $1,500, for a total cost of $3,000 per year—$12,000 for a four-year degree.[1] Fast forward to 2016, and the same figures are $50,000 for tuition and $12,000 for room and board, for a total published cost of $62,000 per year—$248,000 for a four-year degree.[2] Note that these are the so-called published tuition prices; scholarships and other forms of financial aid may reduce the actual cost to something less. Even so, a 2,000-plus percent increase in 55 years can create considerable consternation and confusion in what was heretofore a relatively stable marketplace.

How can a 17-year-old student—and his or her parents—accurately judge the *value* of one school's educational offering versus another's? How can a college or university effectively describe and communicate its value and potential fit so that students can make good decisions on college choice? Bad decisions are costly for all parties. Students who make the wrong choice suffer emotional and financial stress and the challenge of starting over if they elect to continue at another college, or they may even decide to forego college. Colleges must deal with the discomfort of dissatisfied students and the foregone revenue for the remaining years as well as the loss of a potentially supportive alumna or alumnus. It is in everyone's best interest to foster good decision making when choosing a college. Here is where marketing and business join the process.

The Business of Higher Education

We first explore the business aspect of higher education and then describe the role of marketing in enhancing the effectiveness in choosing the "right" college. There are countless definitions of the term *business*. Essentially, a business is an organization or entity that provides goods and services to satisfy market needs in exchange for payment (money). A "good" business identifies a genuine need in the marketplace, produces a solution that surpasses existing offerings at a competitive price, provides a safe and respectful work environment with a fair and equitable wage for its employees, and respects the physical and societal environments in which it functions.

When a business's costs regularly exceed its revenues, it typically ceases to exist; that is, it goes out of business.

Most colleges and universities clearly fit this definition of business. They provide services (educational experiences typically leading to degrees/certificates) for payment (tuition). Indeed it is quite reasonable to believe that they are "good" businesses in that they seek to serve a genuine need with a superior offering at competitive prices; pay fair wages with a safe, respectful work environment; and seek to be sensitive and attentive to the physical and societal environments in which they operate.

The concept of *profit* must also be addressed. A for-profit business is typically owned by a person or persons who expect a monetary return (profit) for the funds they have invested in the business. For-profit businesses pay taxes on their profits, and the owners typically pay personal income tax when the business profits are distributed to the owners. Nonprofit businesses follow a set of rules and conditions set by the U.S. government and administered by the Internal Revenue Service in which surplus revenues are not ever distributed to the owners but rather retained as reserves and often used to defray future expenses, thus reducing the costs or increasing services for their users. In the case of colleges and universities, it is extremely rare for many such institutions to generate surplus revenue. Most such surpluses are the result of accounting policies; for example, depreciation is a noncash expense that should be placed in a reserve fund to provide for future maintenance and repairs. Given the vast amount of "deferred maintenance" noted on so many college campuses, former "surpluses," however generated, are now going toward covering regular operating expenses.

In this context, colleges and universities are clearly businesses. Most U.S. colleges and universities are nonprofit enterprises. In the reminder of this chapter, the focus of discussion will be the traditional nonprofit college or university. These generally fall into two broad categories: private and public. Public colleges and universities are state owned and receive a portion of their financial support from the state in which they operate. State government financial support for these institutions has shrunk significantly over the years, with the remaining support coming from individual student tuition and other sources to be discussed subsequently. Private colleges and universities are owned by independent entities represented by fiduciary boards of trustees. The bulk of revenues for private colleges and universities come from individual student tuitions plus other sources to be discussed below.

Public and private colleges and universities also fall into two broad descriptive categories: research institutions and primarily teaching institutions. Research institutions typically have a significant amount of resources (staff and physical plant) engaged in the discovery of new knowledge, such as science, engineering, and medicine, and they compete for and receive large grants from the federal government and certain major corporations. Our country has benefited tremendously from the results of this research (e.g., better disease treatments, better technology, deeper understanding of economics and societal challenges), and when managed well, some of the funds from the research grants also cover a portion of the institution's overhead.

In general, American colleges and universities have the following sources of revenue: tuition, alumni donations, endowment earnings, research grants, and income from facilities rental and nondegree program offerings. Their costs include salaries for faculty and staff, operating expenses (utilities, maintenance, insurance, health care), interest on debt, and depreciation. The minimum goal is for the revenues and the expenses to be in balance, that is, to break even. Ideally, the revenues would exceed the expenses, and the surplus would be placed in a reserve account for unexpected contingencies. It is important to note that when nonprofit colleges and universities deplete their reserves, they become wholly dependent on current revenues, and their existence is threatened. With this basic understanding of the business of higher education, we now turn to the issue of value and the seemingly endless escalation in costs.

As noted in the introduction, the stated tuition, room and board, and expenses at an Ivy League college in 1960 were $12,000 for a four-year degree and $248,000 for a comparable degree in 2016. But are these costs truly comparable? Here, it may be constructive to consider a different analogy. Consider a 1960 top-of-the-line Chevrolet Impala four-door hardtop sedan that had a sticker price of $2,768.[3] Compare it with its 2016 equivalent top-of-the-line Chevrolet SS with a sticker price of $48,870.[4] The 2016 model is larger, more comfortable, safer, more powerful, more efficient, and contains more technology than its 1960 counterpart. Yes, it costs far more. Indeed, the sticker price increase is a whopping 1,765 percent, but it is also far more automobile. Who today would pay the inflation-adjusted cost for a "brand-new" 1960 automobile versus the price of its 2016 counterpart?

Now consider the 1960s educational expense versus its 2016 counterpart. The 1960s classroom had a chalkboard, no technology, no air-conditioning, and a knowledgeable professor who stood in the front of the room and delivered a lecture covering much of the material the students supposedly read the night before. Students resided in mostly unair-conditioned dormitory rooms, often with bunk beds, and single-gender communal bathrooms and showers at the end of the hall. They ate in institutional dining rooms with single-menu cafeterias. They studied in libraries with no technology and often without direct access to the book and periodical "stacks." They were also responsible for their own health care—whatever that might be.

Now consider the 2016 college student. She or he sits in a classroom laden with audiovisual technology, most likely with electric power outlets at every seat for laptop or tablet computers, and taught by a professor who is expected to operate at the intellectual leading edge of his or her academic discipline and with whom the individual student has virtual 24/7 communications access. Internet access is available everywhere on campus. The student resides in an air-conditioned residence hall in a single room or in a "pod" unit with a shared bath and living room facilities among only the pod residents. The technology in the residence halls has access to all modern media, including cable and video downloads from Netflix and the like. The dining facilities offer extensive on-campus sites and feature every form of menu option, typically offered on a prepaid, unlimited choice and amount basis. The library has extensive technology and computer printing resources. Almost any book or periodical can be electronically accessed should a traditional physical version not be in the library's collection. The reference librarian is a highly skilled technician who can guide the student to whatever resources he or she might need to complete a project. And, consider all the campus amenities (swimming pool, bowling alley, physical workout areas) present in 2016 versus 1960.

It is also important to note that for most colleges and universities, administrative costs have risen considerably as part of the cost of doing business. Life in the 1960s was just a great deal simpler for higher education institutions. Today, campus safety, often taken as a nonissue years ago, is now an appropriately high priority, but also an added cost. Similarly, regulations such as Title IX, a very reasonable approach to assuring gender equity (and more recently also protection for sexual assault on campus), have increased the cost of college through providing nonrevenue sports and other forms of administrative support to assure regulatory compliance.

Interestingly, both the automobile in the example above and the college education have been subjected to a variety of hidden cost factors that are not necessarily within the control of the provider but which also contribute to price increases. For example, the automobile is subjected to emissions controls and safety and fuel economy mandates that all increase the cost of manufacturing. Similarly, the college education is subject to added administrative costs for meeting countless new regulations for privacy and safety; none of which are implied to be negative, but they do increase the cost of delivering the education.

Even so, who among today's college-bound youth would choose a school offering the equivalent of a 1960s educational experience at inflation-adjusted tuition versus the experience currently offered in 2016? Very few indeed. This suggests there may be a value perception gap, which brings us to exploring the role of marketing in the college decision process.

It is noteworthy that there is a small but emerging trend of what the experts have labeled "tuition resets," in which a college or university lowers its published tuition by a substantial amount and correspondingly reduces the number and/or the dollar amounts of the scholarships and tuition grants it offers. Two such institutions are Concordia College in St. Paul, Minnesota, and Utica College in New York. In retail-market vocabulary, consumers know this as "everyday low prices." Such a strategy is not without its risks. First, it presumes that more students will be attracted to the institution, and thus it will be able to at least sustain its revenue if not increase it. For expository purposes, assume that College A has a published tuition of $40,000, but it has been giving scholarships of $20,000 to virtually every admitted student. By resetting its tuition to $20,000 and eliminating most scholarships, the college may be able to attract students who otherwise would have considered it to be unaffordable and never even applied. The accompanying risk, however, is that price (tuition) can be a surrogate indicator of value, and the institution with the reset tuition may be perceived as having lowered the value of its degree. Second, by only awarding scholarships that are funded by "real" dollars (e.g., endowment earnings or gifts), students who no longer receive a scholarship offer may feel as if they are less desired at that institution. Importantly, all of this must be tested in the marketplace to see which of these outcomes is actually manifested.

The Marketing of Higher Education

Although there are numerous definitions of the term *marketing*, we define it as a process of identifying needs among individuals or organizations, creating solutions (products or services), communicating the existence of the solutions to those who need them, and making the solutions available at a price, time, and location accessible to those having the need. A *customer* is an individual or an entity that has a need the business can fulfill *and* who is willing and able to exchange something of value in exchange for the solution (good or service).

Marketing is *not* selling. It is *not* advertising. It is *not* promotion. It is *not* the design of the solution (product or service). Rather, *all* of these are subcomponents of marketing. A key objective of good marketing is to facilitate buying decisions in which a mutually beneficial exchange of value occurs between the provider of the solution (good or service) and the acquirer (customer). To put this squarely in the context of higher education, the prospective student (e.g., a high school senior) and, most likely, the parents are the customer; the need in search of a solution is the knowledge and skill to achieve success as a contributing member of society; the possible solution is an undergraduate educational experience; and the provider (business) is a college or university. One can readily imagine an enormous number of combinations of high school seniors (prospective students), trade schools, community colleges, and four-year colleges and universities all seeking to match the best solution to a specific need. This is where marketing can play a significant and constructive role in facilitating a good fit between student needs and the educational solution.

The process begins with the prospective student assessing his or her general life goals and capabilities and exploring the educational solutions that connect to these capabilities and support the goal achievement. For example, a high school student may have a goal of becoming a physician. If so, he or she must have an affinity for and a capability of succeeding in the sciences, particularly biology, chemistry, and anatomy. A high school student with a goal to become an engineer should have an affinity for and a capability of success in mathematics and physics. Teachers, guidance counselors, parents, relatives, and family friends in the profession can all offer helpful insights to guide the student's selection of colleges that offer educational solutions to the student's goals. In the above cases, the recommendations would include colleges with good premedical programs or good engineering programs. None of this is marketing, but all of it is part of the college-selection decision process that can be affected positively or negatively by marketing.

While parents and their children spend considerable (and appropriate) time and effort in identifying and choosing a college, they are also vulnerable to distractions that are not always key elements of the college education. Going to a residential college for four years is indeed an educational experience and is more than just "book learning," which can be achieved in numerous other ways (e.g., online or as a commuter student not living on campus). However, overweighting the aspects of the amenities and not attending sufficiently to the impact the college has on its students' successes can lead to a suboptimal choice of college. It is important to sift through the distracting elements and focus on the core value the institution delivers to choose the college that best matches a student's needs and intellectual capabilities. This is where genuine marketing can have a positive effect.

Marketing is manifested in the college's efforts to understand and facilitate the student's decision process. Given its importance to assuring the best fit between the individual student's needs and the college's or university's educational offering, the marketing function should report directly to the president and be assigned the responsibility for identifying groups of students (also known as segments) whose needs the institution can fill with its current program offerings; understanding fully the processes students follow in learning about and deciding on specific colleges and universities to pursue (apply to); developing communications strategies, media, and collateral materials that enable the admissions staff to connect with students who potentially fit with the institution; and presenting the institution's offerings with sufficient accuracy and clarity to enable the students to effectively judge the appropriate fit between their goals and capabilities with the institution's programs, culture, and environment. In certain circumstances, this also includes the marketing function's responsibility to suggest program alternatives not currently offered but worthy of vetting through traditional institutional academic processes.

Merely as an example, my college has noted a significant increase in the health care sector among students, but not everyone is ideally suited to the demands of a premedical school curriculum. By taking a closer look at the emerging career choices in health care, our faculty determined that careers in allied health sciences, such as physical therapy, physician's assistant, nurse anesthesiologist, and the like, offer many additional opportunities. Using this as a guide, they created an undergraduate major in health sciences, which prepares graduates to access these emerging growth career opportunities. Similarly, a new major in health care administration at the undergraduate level can open doors previously reserved for people holding graduate degrees. Other schools will have similar examples of how attending to emerging market conditions provides new opportunities for their students.

Putting marketing into practice effectively requires the ability to thoroughly research high school student decision-making processes, to understand and utilize appropriate communications media and messaging, and to fully analyze competitive offerings and how prospective students and their parents perceive them. The marketing function must utilize this insight to create a marketing strategy that includes specific groups of prospective students for whom the institution's program offerings and overall education experience are a good fit. This is also where the institution's brand is refined and used to distinguish it from other educational offerings. A *brand* is the set of characteristics, emotions, and feelings that customers associate with a given institution. Thus, as the nation's oldest and perhaps best-known university, Harvard has a well-defined set of charac-teristics, emotions, and feelings that it evokes in the minds of prospective students. A school seeking to imitate or transfer those same characteristics, emotions, and feelings to itself might then describe itself as "the Harvard" of (some geographic region other than the Northeast, where Harvard is located).

By knowing the characteristics of the competition, the educational goals of the students it seeks to enroll, and its own special characteristics, an insti-tution can create its own brand statement describing the values it delivers and the reasons to believe it. This then becomes the heart of the marketing strategy, identifying those students the institution is best suited to serve and preparing a complete package of visual, verbal, electronic, and personal communications that effectively delivers the institution's brand promise.

As an example of this, I have challenged my marketing staff to more closely examine those aspects of Spring Hill that make it a distinctive col-lege educational experience for students of varying backgrounds who are motivated to achieve a purposeful life. In response, they have identified several important characteristics of the Spring Hill brand. We are one of just 28 Jesuit colleges and universities in the United States. Founded by Ignatius of Loyola in the 16th century, the Jesuits have a 450-plus-year his-tory of crafting a complete educational experience for their students. The basic tenant of a Jesuit education is that knowledge is not something to merely be acquired as a possession, but rather it is to be used by the newly educated person to go out into the world and make it a better place for all. One's discipline could be medicine, science, education, business, the arts, the social sciences, or the behavioral sciences, but in each instance, our graduates use their knowledge to improve the circumstances of those with whom they engage. More than just teach, more than just educate, Spring Hill College forms students to become morally responsible leaders in the service of others.

While we are a small (1,300 students) liberal arts residential college where faculty are mentors and students make lifelong friendships in a sup-portive learning environment, we are also a national liberal arts college, drawing students from 36 states and 11 countries and with alumni in all 50 states and numerous countries. Our pristine campus environment, located in the heart of the Deep South, provides the ideal complement to the classroom and cocurricular experiences that make us distinctive. Couple that with the successes of our graduates who are leading or have led national organizations and who have advanced medicine and led social change and we offer a powerful value proposition to prospective students and their parents. We are but one example of how colleges and universities can utilize sound marketing practices to create an educational offering that resonates with the goals of young people seeking to achieve the best start as they journey into being productive members of society.

Obtaining the Best Educational Value

This chapter is not a how-to treatise for academic marketers. There are many sources for that. However, it does seek to inform academic leaders of the importance of using good marketing to facilitate students' abilities to identify and choose an educational institution that provides the best fit for achieving their educational goals.

At the same time, some colleges seek to take advantage of unsuspecting students and of confusion in the marketplace by making promises they cannot fulfill. The U.S. Department of Education is taking serious steps to ferret out those schools that promise career openings that never material-ize, that misrepresent faculty qualifications, or that have inordinate drop-out rates, all of which detract from what should be a powerful growth experience for their students.

For students and their parents, the goal of this chapter is to offer insights into what to look for in identifying potential colleges and how to utilize the college's marketing resources to obtain the information needed to judge which college will provide the best educational experience your resources will allow you to undertake. First, do the best job you can in identifying the broad goals you hope to achieve through your educa-tion, consistent with your capabilities. Then carefully search for potential schools whose brand promise matches those expectations. Visit as many schools as you can, seeking to interact with students similar to yourself. Ask them to describe their experiences, and push them to further explain why they either like or dislike a particular experience or aspect of the school. Always ask "why" because their goals and values may not perfectly coincide with your own. See if you can find alumni who are living the careers you hope to have, and ask them the same questions about their college experience.

Finally, be comfortable in applying to a range of schools that provide a measure of fit with your educational goals but may have different pub-lished costs. Do not initially exclude a school because of its perceived cost. Wait until you learn whether you have been admitted. Then rank order the admitted schools according to your sense of the best fit, and integrate any scholarships or financial aid you are given by each school. Choose the best-fitting school that your resources will support and then commit to doing your very best as a student there.

Notes

1. University of Pennsylvania archive (www.archives.upenn.edu) rounded slightly to facilitate calculations and comparisons.
2. Ibid.
3. NADA Guides (www.NADAGuides.com).
4. Kelley Blue Book (www.kbb.com).

CHAPTER THREE

Building Trust through University Assessment

Leah Katell

In recent years, assessment has gone from being a buzzword within business schools to being its own department for some AACSB-accredited schools. The Association to Advance Collegiate Schools of Business (AACSB) is the internationally accepted accrediting body for business schools. The AACSB accredits 777 business schools in 52 countries.[1] An assurance of student learning is a major component of the accreditation process for AACSB schools. Assessment is the tool that measures the student learning in their programs. This is the base component of the model of accountability and continuous improvement that all AACSB schools around the globe seek to embody.

Assessment of student learning begins with programmatic goals that embody the mission, vision, and values of a college. The goals should be overarching as to include the major competencies that any student graduating from a program should possess. For example, in business schools, a bachelor of science in business administration (BSBA) will have students from many different disciplines, such as accounting, finance, marketing, management, management information systems, and supply chain management. Students graduating with a concentration in entrepreneurship should have comparable critical thinking and written communication skills as a student graduating with a concentration in accounting. Their knowledge from their concentration courses will obviously vary depending on the chosen field, but for AACSB, the core goals apply to all of the BSBA students.

Based on the programmatic goals, assessments should be developed that best showcase the abilities of the students based on each goal. Multiple-choice questions can be used in a test to measure a student's ability to employ ethical decision-making skills when faced with a business problem, but assessment professionals have determined that they can get a much better idea of students' comprehension of ethics by presenting them with a business case problem and a series of short-answer questions addressing the issue(s) embedded within the case. When evaluating students' written work or presentations, assessments are scored with rubrics. The rubrics are general enough to be used on different assignments from different courses, but they adequately examine the skills and knowledge of the students completing the assignment. For example, a written communication rubric should be general enough to be used on any written assignment from any business course but should adequately measure the student's ability to write professionally. Based on my experience, the rubrics should be developed by the faculty within the college to ensure that the skills deemed to be most important are what are actually being assessed. Although this participative approach is more time-intensive, it is essential if faculty are going to accept the assessment process and view it as a valid way in which to evaluate the degree to which a business school truly educates its students in a consistent and competent way.

The methods used for assessment can either be course embedded, like a quiz, or part of a program but independent from a class. Course-embedded assessments have generally provided better data as they are typically associated with a grade. If there is no incentive for students to take an assignment seriously, they typically will complete the bare minimum.[2] An article on *Inside Higher Ed* discusses this motivation phenomenon. A study conducted by the Educational Testing Service (ETS) concluded that students with a personal motivation to do well performed better on an assessment exam than students that were not told that the exam scores would be shared with their faculty or potential employers. The easiest way to ensure student motivation is to have the assessments embedded in courses with grades attached. In many instances, the students do not even know that the assignment, test, or quiz is being used for assessment. The professor will use the item as a grade and, oftentimes, score it again for assessment. The assessment data will then be gathered, sometimes across many different sections, courses, and semesters, and aggregated. Pedagogical and curricular programmatic changes are based on the results from the aggregated data. For example, if the results from a written communication assessment show that the students are having trouble with grammar in their written assignments, the faculty may decide to make changes in a few courses or throughout an entire program.

One of the current best practices for written communication, based on a large southeastern University's written error elimination policy, is the implementation of a written error policy throughout a program. These policies typically require less than five grammatical errors on any page and no more than 20 total errors in an entire document. Once the error count exceeds the maximum allowed, the faculty will quit grading and return the assignment back to the student. The student then has a set amount of time to correct the document and resubmit it to the professor. A resubmission document will be docked a letter grade. This type of pedagogical change and consistency throughout a program reinforces the importance of written communication and assists students in knowing exactly what is expected in the program. This type of improvement takes time and commitment from the faculty in an environment where faculty and administrators are having to do more with less time and funds.

Of course, the idea of using course grades for assessment purposes seems appealing and simpler at this point. The issue with this course of action is that a course grade involves more information than whether a student can write professionally. For example, we could look at two students who both earned a B in a course. This particular course could have a written project, two exams, and multiple quizzes. The first student could perform poorly on the exams and quizzes but perform spectacularly well on the written project. The second student might excel on the exams and quizzes but not perform as well on the written assignment. Both of these students received the same course grade, but one displayed professional written communication skills while the other did not. The course grade does not indicate how well a student can write and includes too many other factors to be used for assurance of student learning.

Once learning goals have been agreed to, assignments for assessment have been identified or developed, and the data have been gathered, the faculty should then analyze the data. Assessment data should give a snapshot glimpse into the program using data from multiple sources. Faculty routinely argue that many students are unable to learn particular skills or acquire requisite knowledge in their courses. Assessment then puts actual data to these concerns. The evidence gathered from the data about deficiencies in student learning in a program should help drive positive change. If the students have trouble with oral presentations, for instance, faculty can, as a group, decide to add presentations to more courses in a program. More practice and more feedback should increase how well the student body presents as a whole. If all the faculty are on the same page and know what is going on in other courses, it is beneficial to everyone. Discussions about assessment results are a systematic way for faculty to continue a dialogue about the entire program.

Some schools publish their assessment results on their Web sites. This publication forces the faculty to own the data and to make substantial pedagogical and curricular changes to increase student learning and thus increase the assessment results year after year. The accountability increases faculty involvement in the assessment process as external stakeholders as well as the accrediting bodies would be able to view the longitudinal data easily. The transparency provided from publishing the data increases ownership of the process, provides motivation to conduct assessments correctly, and drives innovative programmatic changes in a mature assessment process. Understandably, schools might be hesitant to publish such data. If the students are not performing well on certain goals, they would not want to make that public knowledge. But, if they can provide data showing improvement in the program and student learning, sharing this information can be beneficial for stakeholders and recruitment of students.

A newer buzzword in academia is "continuous improvement." This buzzword will not be going away anytime soon. Programs have been continuously improving since the beginning. There are very few courses on a college campus that are taught the same way now as they were 30 years ago. Advances in pedagogy research and technology have driven many of these changes. However, every semester, faculty will tweak their courses to better assist the students. Perhaps the students did not understand a business concept as well as anticipated, so the professor may add a new case to the course. These small changes happen constantly in courses, and assessment facilitates changes at the programmatic level.

The issue with continuous improvement is that continuous improvement models are sometimes misconstrued to mean that changes need to be made every year. This can be viewed as change for the sake of change, especially by the faculty. The accrediting bodies do not require that changes be made every year based on every assessment conducted, though some school have interpreted the requirement that programs continuously make changes for every goal assessed each year. This creates a culture within faculty of making "unnecessary" changes despite what the assessment data reveals. It is also difficult for actual improvement to be effective unless it is incorporating new technologies or major curricular changes. For example, the addition of a couple more presentations throughout the program have not had a major impact on the oral communication skills of the students when leaving the program. On the other hand, moving the résumé requirement from the junior year to the freshman year has substantially increased the quality of the résumés that the students use during their mock interviews their junior year. But when the university requires some pedagogical or curricular change be made every year, the changes that faculty claim to make are akin to extra class time or discussion of a particular subject. These are not meaningful changes for the students or the faculty. These are the types of requirements that programs should shy away from to have a valuable assessment process.

Once changes are decided on and implemented in the program, the gathering of assessment data must be done again. This is called "closing the loop." The second set of assessment data should be compared to the first set to assess whether the implemented changes were successful in increasing student learning. The cycle then continues from there: make pedagogical or curricular changes based on the most recent assessment data and then assess again. In a mature assessment process, this is just part of the culture, and the faculty own the process. Using the written communication example again, two years ago, the students scored a 1.7 out of 3 on the grammatical portion of the written communication rubric. The faculty analyzed the results and implemented a written error policy throughout the program last year. Written communication was reassessed this year, and the students improved to 2.3 out of 3 on grammar. The students could still improve their grammatical skills, so the faculty will meet to discuss how to further improve student learning and written communication skills for next year. This should be an ongoing cycle.

In a perfect world, assessment would be done in multiple courses across the curriculum. Ideally, assessment would only be done using rubrics based on student work and assessed by other faculty, not just the professor teaching the course. The data from each assessment would be compiled and disseminated to the faculty. The faculty would then make pedagogical and curricular changes across the program based on the data. In my experience, a full cycle would ideally be three years. This would mean gathering data the first year; compiling the data, reviewing the results, and coming up with actions based on the data the second year; and then implementing the changes in the third year. The cycle would then begin again the fourth year.

Some of the improvements may take up to three years to make it through the cycle. For instance, a change in a freshman-level course would not affect the data for three years if a school is only assessing at the senior level. A way to combat this is to complete pre- and posttesting. Most schools do not have the resources to assess in this fashion at this point. It is costly and time consuming to test students at the beginning of the program and then to track them to assess them at the end of the program. There is also the issue of how to assess the students using course-embedded assessments at the end of the program as they most likely will not be in the same courses together again in a large program. The best way to complete pre- and posttesting is with a business knowledge exam. While unnecessary and costly, assessing all of the students entering into the program, whether as freshman or transfers, and then when they are leaving would be the most comprehensive way to gather this data. There are many different external companies that conduct these types of assessments.[3,4,5] Their questions are statistically valid, and they can track the students. But these exams can cost around $30 per test. With the budget cuts of the past few years, this is just not a feasible option for many universities.

Assessment should build trust both within a college and with its outside constituents. The problem is that there is no trust within the system in many colleges as of yet. It has been my experience that faculty do not trust assessment and see it as a "checking boxes" exercise for accreditation purposes. There are worries that if students do not perform well on an assessment in their course, that specific professors will be judged on their teaching abilities. This is simply not the case. Assessment measures the amount and extent that a student learns the skills and information that we deem to be important in our programs. Many programs expect their students to have critical thinking skills, oral and written communication skills and to display ethical decision-making skills when they graduate from a business program. If an assessment is pulled from the capstone course and students cannot think critically or write professionally, it is not the capstone course professor's failing. This implies that as a program, we have deviated from our mission to teach students these skills much earlier in the program. For assessment to be done well and correctly, a foundation of trust in the assessment, the system, and the process must be established.

If the faculty buy into the assessment culture, we can then involve the students. In some schools, the students expect to see the rubrics that will grade and score their assignments. If the students are exposed to the assurance of learning goals and rubrics from the beginning of the program, they will have a clear understanding of what the college deems important. They can then make the connections within courses regarding how the entire program is put together and can understand the bigger picture from the beginning. I have heard of a program where the students will actually ask to have the rubrics used on their assignments so they can see how they have improved over time. As the goals and assessments are based on a college's mission, vision, and values, the students will then embody those principles that we hold dear.

To truly integrate the students in the assessment process, the faculty have to be open with the students when assignments are being used for assessments. When appropriate, the faculty should share the rubrics being used to score the assignments. This gives the students a clear picture of what is expected from them. It could also be helpful if faculty were to list the learning goals that their courses address on their syllabi. If the students start seeing and hearing about assessment in all of their classes, it follows that they will understand the importance of assessment.

Once the faculty and students are embodied in the assessment culture, we then can start bringing in outside constituents. Employers, boards of governors and trustees, and the community at large will begin to know what important principles and skills our graduates possess. Of course, employers know the skills their employees developed from our program, but assessment makes this more concrete and formalized. A college can post their results and changes made based on the data in a very mature assessment culture. It becomes a bragging right, if you will.

Involving external stakeholders in the assessment process is something many schools deem to be imperative, but they have struggled with the actual implementation of inclusion. Employers have the utmost interest in the assurance of student learning, and many of them are involved with the faculty and students by volunteering their time to assist with mock interviews and business etiquette events. As the employers are interacting with the students in a one-on-one manner, it would be a simple request to have them fill out an assessment on each student. This ensures that they have a formalized voice in the assessment of the students and the improvements within the programs.

Including alumni is a slightly more difficult feat. At this point, many universities send out surveys to their alumni. These surveys can help uncover the areas in which the alumni feel that their training and education in business programs is lacking. Perhaps they have found that, as students, they would have benefited from more formalized presentations in their current careers. The information gained from alumni can be invaluable, but it is difficult to collect. Without some incentive, many people will not willingly fill out and return a survey. Typically, the responses will be from the most satisfied and the most disgruntled people. This is a problem assessment professionals discuss at length anytime they convene as a group. As difficult as it is, alumni information is imperative to the continuous improvement of business programs.

All of this begins with trust though. The ROCC of Trust, in *Becoming a Trustworthy Leader*, includes reliability, openness, competence, and compassion.[4,5,6] When assessment is done correctly, it embodies all of these principles.

Assessment ensures the reliability of our business programs. As faculty, accreditation requirements, and processes within a college change through the years, sometimes programs become less cohesive than they were at first. New professors teaching slightly different things in courses through time will add up to major shifts in focus from where the program and specific courses were first aligned. For example, if a professor changes a test from short answer to multiple choice, the students will lose a chance to practice writing. This does not seem like a major issue, but imagine if this happens in 10 or 15 of their courses. Courses change and morph over time, so this is to be expected. The problem arises when many small changes in multiple courses add up to massive shifts in student learning throughout the program. Assessment is the best way to keep student learning consistent over time. It forces the faculty to use data to take a critical look at the programs in their entirety on a consistent basis. This ensures that if a shift in courses is happening, it is going in the direction intended by the college. The open dialogue between faculty and instructors throughout a program is essential for reliability over time, and assessment is central to this process, if done correctly.

Universities need to become more transparent to survive. The rising cost of tuition, the recent news stories of students receiving grades for courses that never met, and other reasons including distrust of government entities, has increased the call for openness and transparency in academia. These have become such issues that accrediting bodies are insisting that schools increase their transparency both with the organization and facing the public.. Students and families want information as to how good a program is compared with other colleges and universities. With so much information on the Internet, universities need to find a way to make themselves stand out to retain enrollment numbers. Posting assurance of learning goals and the results from the assessments is a very effective way to showcase our programs.

Once students are in a program, posting the assessment information publicly helps students and their parents feel good about the program, especially if the assessment results increase over time. The assurance that the students are getting better throughout their tenure in our programs is essential to getting and retaining students.

Openness within the faculty body is also essential. Assessment ensures that faculty can see where students are deficient in our programs so that they can make an effort in their individual courses to help increase student learning. If students are found to have deficiencies in professional writing and multiple faculty add just one more written exercise in each of their courses, the overall impact of the written component of a program increases substantially. Assessment of student learning helps keep faculty on the same page on how the students are doing and creates on ongoing, open dialogue within a college.

The process of assessment, when conducted well, undeniably increases the competence of the students. Once faculty pinpoint deficiencies that the students possess at the end of a program, the changes based on the results of an assessment that are designed to increase comprehension will increase competency. The process of closing the loop is meant to increase competencies within a program and ultimately does so over time. Students must display competencies in their respective fields when they graduate or the university educational system has failed miserably. There is also the competence of the faculty. Instead of complaining that students are not as proficient in a skill in their course as they should be, assessment provides concrete data to substantiate the claims. It also provides a data-driven basis for affecting change in a program. Any improvement in a program will increase student learning and competence. It can be argued that more competent students (i.e., better students) will attract more competent faculty. A more competent body of faculty will better prepare students for their careers. This is a cycle that definitely manifests a continuous improvement cycle.

It can be argued that assessment increases faculty compassion toward students. When faculty can definitively see the areas in which students are struggling, making changes to help students become better is undoubtedly a compassionate practice. While a few faculty primarily care about their research, in my experience, most care deeply about the students and the education being provided. Faculty will routinely do just about anything to help a student better understand the material and master the skills that are pertinent to their future successes. Assessment is a systematic process that keeps compassion at the forefront of what a college does, and this begins a domino process. When students perceive compassion from their business faculty and other school officials, they are more likely to be compassionate managers in their careers as business leaders. It is typical for faculty and instructors to allow extensions for extenuating circumstances or for students to miss one test or assignment for any reason. Faculty and administrators understand that life happens, and it is human nature to want to be compassionate and help others when possible. While faculty are compassionate on a more personal level with students, assessment can aid in the compassion of teaching knowledge and skills.

The goals of a university are to educate students, to externally increase knowledge in every field with advances in research, and to serve their local and wider communities. Assessment can be an imperative tool to achieving these goals if done correctly within the right culture. Assessment can establish and maintain trust within the faculty, the students, and the outside constituents. While it may have started as a buzzword, assessment is a major component of any educational system and will continue to be an integral part of universities and business schools in the future.

Notes

1. "AACSB-Accredited Schools Worldwide." *AACSB International.* N.p., n.d. Web. 21 Nov. 2016.

2. Scott Jaschik, "Tests with and without Motivation," *Inside Higher Ed,* January 2, 2013. https://www.insidehighered.com/news/2013/01/02/study-raises -questions-about-common-tools-assess-learning-college.

3. One such testing service is Peregrine Academics. They may not be the most widely used service at this point, but they are unique in that they provide schools with the raw scores of the students. Other testing services only provide how well the students of a program measure against other schools. While this is valuable information, I find student-level data to be more beneficial for assessment purposes. Peregrine also has the ability to track students that have taken assessment exams more than once. This makes pre- and posttesting an easier process.

4. Aneil K. Mishra and Karen E. Mishra, *Becoming a Trustworthy Leader: Psychology and Practice* (New York: Routledge, 2013).

5. Aneil K. Mishra and Karen E. Mishra, "The Research on Trust in Leadership: The Need for Context," *Journal of Trust Research* 3, no. 1 (2013): 61–71.

6. Aneil K. Mishra, "Organizational Responses to Crisis: The Centrality of Trust," in *Trust in Organizations: Frontiers of Theory and Research,* ed. Roderick Kramer and Thomas Tyler (Thousand Oaks, CA: Sage, 1996), 261–287.

CHAPTER FOUR

How Faculty Can Increase Student Engagement

Linda Quick

Two key issues facing higher education today are the increasing cost of higher education and competing incentives for universities to provide job outcomes and produce a well-rounded, educated student who is prepared to be a lifelong learner. To restore both the students' and the public's trust in the higher education system in the United States, these two issues need to be addressed by universities. Costs of higher education have continued to increase since the mid-1980s, even when adjusting for inflation, making it more difficult for students from less privileged backgrounds to access the advantages of higher education.[1] From 1985 through 2015, public four-year colleges and universities have increased their tuition by a minimum of 10 percent every five years, based on inflation-adjusted dollars.[2] See tables 4.1 and 4.2 for detailed information regarding the changes in tuition rates and room and board versus inflation at public and private four-year universities from 1975 through 2016. First-generation college students and underrepresented minorities can be hit especially hard by these increasing costs.

One effect of these increasing costs is higher student loan debt. This higher student loan debt has drawn national attention, as many feel it is unsustainable as a model for higher education in the future. The student debt problem has even given rise to nonprofit organizations such as Student Debt Crisis with a mission to reduce higher education costs.[3] While this nonprofit organization has gathered feedback and personal stories

Table 4.1 Average tuition and fees in 2015 dollars, 1975–76 to 2015–16, selected years.

Year	Private Nonprofit Four-Year	Five Year % Change	Public Four-Year	Five-Year % Change	Public Two-Year	Five-Year % Change
1975–76	$10,088		$2,387		$1,079	
1980–81	$10,438	3%	$2,320	–3%	$1,128	5%
1985–86	$13,551	30%	$2,918	26%	$1,419	26%
1990–91	$17,094	26%	$3,492	20%	$1,658	17%
1995–96	$19,117	12%	$4,399	26%	$2,081	26%
2000–01	$22,197	16%	$4,845	10%	$2,268	9%
2005–06	$25,624	15%	$6,708	38%	$2,665	18%
2010–11	$29,300	14%	$8,351	24%	$3,002	13%
2015–16	$32,405	11%	$9,410	13%	$3,435	14%

Source: The College Board, "Trends in College Pricing 2015," Table 2A.

Table 4.2 Average tuition, fees, and room and board in 2015 dollars, 1975–76 to 2015–16, selected years.

Year	Private Nonprofit Four-Year	Five Year % Change	Public Four-Year	Five-Year % Change
1975–76	$16,213		$7,833	
1980–81	$16,213	0%	$7,362	–6%
1985–86	$19,708	22%	$8,543	16%
1990–91	$24,663	25%	$9,286	9%
1995–96	$27,202	10%	$10,552	14%
2000–01	$30,716	13%	$11,655	10%
2005–06	$35,106	14%	$14,797	27%
2010–11	$39,918	14%	$17,710	20%
2015–16	$43, 921	10%	$19,548	10%

Source: The College Board, "Trends in College Pricing 2015," Table 2A.

from students with large amounts of college debt, this has mostly led to increased discussions of the student debt problem in the media and in Washington. These conversations are important first steps toward reform; however, the focus of many national conversations on student debt has been on making sure students are informed about the amount of debt they are taking on and the associated interest rates. Making sure students are educated on the amount of debt they take out is critical, but this alone will not stop the increase in costs associated with higher education.

Universities are also partially measured on job outcomes for their graduates, an important consideration given the higher costs of education discussed above. However, universities also have a (sometimes competing) goal to produce well-rounded students who are prepared for lifelong learning. As students are only able to take a limited number of courses during their college career, universities have to balance preparing students for their eventual careers with courses in their major and requiring them to take liberal arts courses outside of their major. Many faculty members tend toward believing that the main goal of a student's education should be to produce a well-rounded learner, while many students and parents see the goal as better job outcomes for the student in the future.

In my opinion, much of this tension comes from students and parents who are funding their children's education. As discussed previously, college costs have increased, and many parents expect to see an increased return on their large investment in higher education. This, combined with recent economic downturns, has made job outcomes a primary focus for students and parents when evaluating colleges. Along with the higher costs of education, many students and parents have also come to expect all-encompassing job preparation from universities. While some of the burden is still necessarily on the student to gain work experience and make connections within their field, a higher burden is placed on faculty and other university employees to assist students with every aspect of their job preparation; for example, nearly all universities now have career placement offices that help students with their job searches as they approach graduation and with internships while in college. While this increased support from universities is, in my opinion, a positive aspect of the college experience for students, it does shift the focus more toward job preparedness and away from simply attaining a well-rounded learning experience.

The tension in this area can also be exacerbated by faculty from various academic departments. While the cost of an education continues to climb for students, funding from many state and federal sources has decreased, forcing universities to make tough decisions regarding where and how to cut funding. Faculty in more applied academic disciplines, such as health care or business, often cite their students' job placements and potential future contributions to the university as support for their budget needs. However, when funding decisions are made in this manner, faculty in liberal arts departments that may be less directly correlated with specific career fields are left at a disadvantage. This may be one factor contributing to the debate among faculty regarding the ultimate purpose of a student's college education.

In my experience as both a student and professor at East Carolina University, one way I have seen the university both manage costs and create a well-rounded educational experience for students is through the development of an honors college. At East Carolina University, approximately 100 students per year are admitted to the honors college, which carries a full four-year stipend to cover the costs of in-state tuition. Along with the reduced cost of attendance, students are also required to complete three colloquia courses in their first three years of study, a minimum of two honors seminars, at least two other honors courses, and a senior honors project. These additional requirements serve to both produce well-rounded graduates and to allow the students to learn more in-depth information about their majors by producing their own research.

As a faculty member, I have had the opportunity to advise senior honors projects, and I believe many universities could benefit from a similar program for their students. I also believe this type of project could be scalable, to a smaller extent, for a greater number of students. For example, for their senior honors projects, students within the business disciplines produce their own research, similar to a research project a faculty member would undertake, and present this research at academic conferences. Although a project to this extent may not be possible for a large number of students, this type of program could be of great benefit to both the faculty and the student. Making faculty aware of the potential benefits, such as research assistance and the development of fulfilling working relationships with undergraduate students, could garner more faculty interest in participating in these types of projects and allow more students to have this type of educational experience. Faculty do not receive course releases or stipends for supervising senior honors projects; however, they can provide valuable evidence of student engagement to be included with tenure and promotion materials. As a faculty member supervising senior honors projects, my time commitment has typically consisted of one to two hours every other week during the first semester of the student's project and slightly less time in the second semester.

My experience as an adviser of senior honors projects thus far has involved a series of one-on-one meetings with students, some of which could be accomplished in smaller groups (e.g., up to five students at a time). During the first several meetings, I give an overview of research in accounting; discuss my research interests and describe some of my current research projects; review my expectations for the student and give examples of my previous projects with students; and get an idea of the type of research project the student may be interested in. These initial meeting items could be discussed with several students at once, allowing more students to have exposure to academic research in their discipline without a significantly increased time commitment from faculty members. Afterward, some students may choose to pursue research projects either individually or in pairs, which would require an additional time commitment from faculty members. However, even if all of the students do not proceed to producing their own research projects, having this exposure to research in their chosen fields can still enhance the students' academic experience and understanding of the complexities in their fields of study. Currently, participation in a senior honors project is limited to honors college students (approximately 100 per year, spread throughout the university). Admittance to the honors college is determined before the students enter their freshman year, and students are required to maintain a 3.3 GPA to remain in the honors college.

Providing students with this type of opportunity can enhance their eventual job outcomes as well as their academic experiences. For example, delving deeply into particular areas in their fields gives the students an understanding and expertise that can be valuable to future employers. Faculty mentors can coach students on ways to highlight this experience and discuss it with potential employers. Students can list the experience on their résumé and highlight the number of hours spent on the project and a brief description of what they learned. Even in cases where the particular topic is not of interest to an employer, a discussion of this experience can show that the student is capable of taking initiative, learning something on their own, and going beyond the minimum requirements in an academic or employment setting. In my discussions with recruiters from the Big Four public accounting firms, they are impressed with the experience students receive and the initiative they show by completing a senior honors project, and I believe that this impacts recruitment decisions.

Another example of how this type of project can result in positive job outcomes for students is through the development of relationships with faculty members and informal mentoring. In my experience working with students on their senior honors projects, I have provided informal advice such as reviewing résumés, scholarship applications, and internship applications. I have also advised students on how to approach recruiters, questions to ask during job interviews, and other "soft skills" that are difficult to cover in a typical college course. Developing these relationships with faculty members outside of class can also increase students' confidence when they have a question regarding course material or their job search, and it can enhance faculty members' recommendation letters or references for students during the job search process. Studies have also shown that students' relationships with professors while in college can increase their workplace engagement after graduation.[2]

Having these types of professional mentor relationships and receiving both formal and informal career advice can be particularly important and valuable for high-achieving students from a lower socioeconomic background.[4] As many careers, including academia, have a strong "who you know" component, students who do not have connections through their parents or other adults in their life stand to gain even more than other students from having a mentor-type relationship with a faculty member. As a college degree is becoming more necessary for employment, students who would have joined the workforce a generation ago are now pursuing undergraduate degrees, and colleges will likely see a more diverse student population over time. This diversity will be beneficial to universities, but faculty members will also have to consider that with this more diverse student population, not all students will have access to a network of mentors prior to entering college.

Although providing this type of experience for students does result in an additional time commitment from faculty, many faculty enjoy these enhanced relationships with their students, and this can be an additional draw to increase faculty participation. Even for faculty who are not typically inclined to seek out additional opportunities to interact one-on-one with students, this experience can produce research assistance and additional publications. Assistance with data collection and writing first drafts of manuscripts is welcome for nearly any faculty member, and students who have a history of high achievement and are self-motivated (those who are most likely to pursue a research project) can provide this valuable assistance to faculty members. Through participating in mentorship of a senior honors project, I have found that this has a symbiotic effect on my research. These students are often very interested in research projects that I have going on and in hearing about my research stream, and discussing research with these students has helped me both articulate my research ideas and generate additional potential directions for new projects. Additionally, once these students have graduated, faculty can make use of these relationships to assist future students with job placements. Students who have mentor relationships with faculty members are more likely to stay in touch with them throughout their careers and can provide the faculty members with valuable links to the business community. Universities can encourage faculty participation and involvement in undergraduate research projects by providing an outlet for these students and their faculty mentors to present their research, such as a research competition or conference-like event.

A second and related issue affecting the public's trust in higher education is the increasing cost of higher education. Federal and state budgets are a major contributing factor to the cost of higher education for the student; for example, 47 states have reduced their per-student funding to public colleges and universities for the 2014–2015 academic year to amounts below what they funded in 2008.[5,6] From 2000 to 2013, the average state's contribution per student decreased by nearly $3,000 (in inflation-adjusted 2013 dollars), while federal funding per student grew by approximately $1,000 over this same time period.[6] This sharp decrease in state funding was only partially offset by increased federal funding; furthermore, of the total federal funding for universities, only 5 percent of this funding represents general-purpose appropriations, while well over 50 percent of state funding goes toward general-purpose appropriations.[6,7]

However, despite this decrease in funding, colleges and universities can also play a part in reducing costs for students. One way to do this is by increasing class sizes, thereby reducing the number of faculty necessary to educate the same number of students. Although this solution is commonly pursued by universities, there are downsides to increased class sizes. First, students will likely have a very different experience in a large class versus a small class. Large classes allow less opportunity for individual students to interact with and receive feedback from the faculty member. From a faculty perspective, increased class sizes result in a larger time commitment for grading assignments and responding to student questions. The student and faculty experiences both change quite a bit when class sizes are increased. However, many universities view this as a necessary evil to keep tuition costs down and student enrollment up.

One way universities can enjoy the cost savings of larger class sizes and lessen the negative impact on students is by being strategic about which courses they offer with larger versus smaller sections. For example, offering introductory-level courses or courses geared toward nonmajors can allow for cost savings without disrupting the more individualized attention and education students receive within their majors. Although this does mean that students are less likely to develop relationships with faculty members during their introductory courses, where they may be deciding on a major, this can be combated in part by specific efforts of faculty members to present typical career paths and give an overview of their field, providing resources to encourage interested students to explore the major and related career fields.

Linking an introductory-level course with an overview of the major and possible career paths can also reduce some of the criticism that colleges are focusing on academic development to the exclusion of job preparedness. Providing students with a well-rounded educational experience and preparing them for their future careers do not have to be mutually exclusive. Providing resources to students interested in a particular career path or major does not need to take a large amount of in-class time and can be accomplished through e-mailing or linking to Web pages with additional information. Many professional organizations provide introductory career information to students; for example, the American Institute of Certified Public Accountants hosts a Web page with information for students interested in careers within accounting called This Way to CPA (AICPA).[7] Faculty can leverage these types of resources to efficiently and effectively disseminate career information to students in an introductory-level course.

Although introductory-level courses lend themselves to larger class sizes, universities can still provide the small class size experience to students for select classes during their first few semesters on campus. Two ways to do this are by allowing students to take specific, smaller sections of introductory courses for their major, if they know in advance what they plan to major in. This gives students the advantage of having the opportunity to develop a relationship with a faculty member in their specific area of interest early on in their college career. However, this is not feasible for all students, as some have not decided on a major or change their major at some point. Students may not be aware of all the different options available to them, and therefore this type of course setup would only be useful to a portion of the student population.

Another way to give students the individualized attention of a small class early on in their college career is to require all students to take a seminar-style course in their first year on campus. These courses could be offered in a variety of subjects and provide students with the opportunity to delve into a particular topic of interest with a faculty member in a smaller class environment. This would allow students who are unsure of their major the chance to benefit from the smaller class environment for at least one course early in their college career as well. Universities could offer both major-specific courses and seminar-style courses as a way to target a diverse population of students—some who have determined their major, and others who have not. Specifically, ECU offers these seminars to their honors college students in a variety of disciplines. Once the initial seminar course has been developed, it could be retaught in future years at a slightly lower cost (e.g., no start-up costs of creating the seminars) to the broader student population. Beyond simply considering the costs of providing such courses, universities should also consider the long-term value of these types of educational experiences. Along with the potential for mentorship relationships to develop, students also have the opportunity to develop their analytical and critical thinking skills as well as both written and oral communication skills in a smaller seminar-style course. These skills are increasingly valuable to employers, and improved employment options can increase student wealth and provide them with additional resources that they can contribute back to the university after graduation.

While both of these ways of offering smaller class sizes would require additional faculty time, they can allow all students to benefit from smaller classes without the university having to completely do away with large classes. I believe that one of the key benefits of a college experience is the mentoring relationships developed with faculty members. While creating opportunities for these relationships to develop does require a time investment from faculty, these targeted ways of reaching a large student population can make it a feasible goal for universities. This investment in students while they are in college can pay off for both the students and the university in the future. Creating these connections with students can increase the likelihood that the students give back in some way to their university in the future. Alumni who have relationships with faculty members can give back financially and offer their time to future students. While the financial gifts have an obvious benefit for universities, the gift of successful alumni's time also allows students the opportunity to develop mentoring relationships with individuals in their chosen career path, which takes some of the burden off faculty members for providing students with valuable career information.

By investing in students and building relationships while they are enrolled in college, universities can create a pipeline of alumni willing to give back to their university and help future students, which will continue to build the reputation of the university and future student success. In the honors college specifically, we have been discussing whether to have alumni speak to current students via teleconferencing. This would allow the university to leverage the expertise and experience of so many of ECU's alumni who are spread out geographically and want to help but are not able to be physically present on campus. One potential benefit to alumni could be exposure to top students that they may want to hire, and maybe we could allow for a little sales pitch at the end of any alumni presentations.

Universities can leverage the experience and resources of their alumni in several ways. First, and most obvious to many in higher education, is through financial contributions to the university. While individual alumni can sometimes make significant financial donations, other alumni are only able to make smaller donations, but they may be able to leverage matching donations from their employers to increase their contribution to the university. Many employers now offer matching donation programs, and motivated alumni can suggest these programs to employers who do not yet have them in place. However, for alumni to take the initiative to request a matching donation program, they have to feel a connection to the university. Creating these connections while students are still in school is imperative, as is continuing these relationships once students have graduated.

Faculty can continue relationships with former students while also leveraging the experience and insights of these alumni by bringing them into the classroom, either physically or via Web-conferencing methods such as Skype. Alumni who have had a positive experience in school and maintained connections with faculty members are often eager to contribute to the education of current students. Faculty can have alumni provide feedback for students on applied projects, presentations, and mock interviews, among other things. Practice interviews are one way that students can gain valuable feedback that alumni who are professionals in the business world are often better equipped to provide than faculty members who may have been employed exclusively in academia for decades. Several accounting firms provide these practice interview opportunities for students, and in addition to helping the students, these accounting firms are able to connect with students that will one day be recruiting prospects early on in their college careers. This type of practice interview model can be scalable to a larger student population by recruiting additional big employers of the university's graduates and touting the benefits of connecting and screening students at an early stage. In addition to gaining practice interviewing and receiving feedback from potential employers, these types of events also give students the opportunity to connect with desirable potential future employers.

This type of event cannot be accomplished without some faculty involvement through recruiting employers, advertising the potential benefits to students, and spending time nurturing relationships with the alumni who participate. It is important for the university to create a reward system that recognizes and compensates faculty for these types of activities if they are important to university administration. An added benefit of getting alumni to come back to campus for student engagement events is that these alumni can see the tangible benefits of donations to the university, and this could cause them to consider increasing their financial contributions to the university. These increased financial contributions could be used, in part, to reward faculty for creating and maintaining these relationships with students.

A recurring theme in reforming higher education is the need for buy-in from department chairs, deans, and upper-level administration for new approaches toward reducing costs and increasing student engagement to work on a large scale. These individuals are facing many competing priorities and a diverse set of opinions from faculty members and are tasked with determining the most important priorities for the department, college, or university and creating reward structures for faculty that reflect these priorities. For many faculty members and university officials, however, student success is a key priority. Choosing to create reward structures that value faculty engagement with students can have the long-term payoffs of increased future donations from alumni and increased success and reputation gains for the university, which are also high among many university administrators' wish lists for their long-term impact on the university. Creating this type of environment will then attract like-minded faculty members and should serve as a self-perpetuating cycle where the university continues to attract top students and increase their reputation and alumni donations.

Notes

1. College Board, *Trends in College Pricing 2015*, published 2015. http://trends.collegeboard.org/sites/default/files/trends-college-pricing-web-final-508-2.pdf.

2. Julie Ray and Stephanie Kafka, "Life in College Matters for Life after College," Gallup, May 6, 2014. http://www.gallup.com/poll/168848/life-college-matters-life-college.aspx.

3. "About Us," Student Debt Crisis, accessed 2016. http://studentdebtcrisis.org/about.

4. Ann Coles and Tiffany Blacknall, *The Role of Mentoring in College Access and Success* (Washington, D.C.: Institute for Higher Education Policy, 2011). http://www.wsac.wa.gov/sites/default/files/2014.ptw.(31).pdf.

5. Michael Mitchell and Michael Leachman, "Years of Cuts Threaten to Put College out of Reach for More Students," Center on Budget and Policy Priorities, May 13, 2015. http://www.cbpp.org/research/state-budget-and-tax/years-of-cuts-threaten-to-put-college-out-of-reach-for-more-students.

6. "Federal and State Funding of Higher Education," The Pew Charitable Trusts, June 11, 2015. http://www.pewtrusts.org/en/research-and-analysis/issue-briefs/2015/06/federal-and-state-funding-of-higher-education.

7. "This Way to CPA," American Institute of Certified Public Accountants, accessed November 20, 2016. https://www.thiswaytocpa.com.

CHAPTER FIVE

Diversity in Higher Education

Kellie Sauls

In primary school, I was the only black student in my entire school. In my middle school, I was in the majority as an underrepresented minority student. In my high school, I was one of a handful of black students in my graduating class where the overwhelming majority of the student population was Hispanic (Chicano.) I believe these early educational environments are what caused me to be interested in diversity and specifically in education. I offer my experiences as a lens through which I view diversity in education.

If the goal of an educational institution is to educate, truly educate, its students, how does that institution best position itself to do that and create an environment for the best possible outcomes? How does an educational institution best determine that it's meeting its mission and producing those outcomes? Finally, how integral is diversity in enhancing those outcomes?

Census data reveals that the U.S. population is becoming increasingly diverse. If higher education institutions are producing the educated and capable professionals, artists, and public servants that they want to produce, then they are also producing graduates who can navigate the diversity landscape as they manage, create, express, cohabitate, and lead.

After spending the last 16 years working in higher education, I see that diversifying education is challenging. There are layers and complexities that cannot be adequately addressed in one chapter. Instead, I hope to highlight a few relevant items, identify those layers and complexities, and then attempt to spark innovative thought about how to address and make an impact in helping an educational institution meet its mission with diversity being a key element.

This chapter will not argue a social justice or moral obligation case for diversity in higher education, as I assume that everyone has already heard many of these arguments and drawn their own conclusions in this regard. I will however shift the framework through which we argue for diversity in regard to the student body in higher education and articulate approaches that may yield desired results. For the record, the definition of diversity includes race, ethnicity, family socioeconomic status, disability, gender, nationality, religion, and LGBTQ. However, for simplicity, I will address underrepresented minority populations, specifically African American, and focus my thoughts and ideas on students.

Given the types of higher education institutions that exist, my examples will primarily draw from public four-year degree-granting schools, and private institutions where stated. It is my hope that the readers of this chapter will find relevant argument overlap where it exists and generate additional thought, literature, and approaches where there is difference. Diversity is not a monolithic group, although the experience of marginalization can be.

The Problem

It is no surprise that predominantly white institutions (PWIs) are facing challenges in diversifying their student bodies. Specifically, colleges and universities are seeing declining enrollment of underrepresented minority students, primarily in the undergraduate ranks but also in the graduate school ranks.[1] This can be attributed to several factors, such as the Great Recession that started in 2007, the rise of for-profit four-year degree-granting institutions in 2004, and funding declines combined with students' reluctance of to incur loan debt.[2]

Like all recessions historically, the Great Recession of 2007 hit persons of color disproportionally hard. In 2009, at its peak, the overall unemployment rate was 10 percent according to the Bureau of Labor and Statistics; for African Americans, it was 16 percent, and it was 13 percent for Hispanics.[3] It stands to reason that the unemployment rate was higher and even doubled for African Americans and Hispanics in specific geographic areas. In these families, working-age children, which includes college-entering students, tend to be contributors to the economic well-being of the family unit. For these family members, this often means staying home, going to college part-time, or entering a local community college.

The rise of for-profit colleges greatly impacted underrepresented minority students in that 15 percent of all African American students attended a private for-profit college, which is larger than the 11 percent that attended a historically black college or university (HBCU).[4] As reported by the U.S. Senate Committee on Health, Education, Labor and Pensions (HELP), aggressive marketing and recruiting tactics, the appeal of flexibility in learning offered by these colleges, and the availability of Pell Grants resulted in a seven-fold increase in low-income students over a 10-year period.[5] Similar increases were seen with veterans as well. Unfortunately, the majority of these students left without a degree.

Where PWIs fell short, HBCUs often filled the gap. Once the only reliable source of higher education for African Americans, the HBCU has become one of many options for black (and other) applicants. Whether applicants were looking for a quality education with a culturally rich environment, an affirming culture, or a similar path as their ancestors, the HBCU has always welcomed black students and provided a significant nod to the black space in U.S. history. Forty years ago, black student attendance at HBCUs was 80 percent, but now it is 9 percent.[6] In addition, HBCUs are facing financial and fundraising issues that are forcing many to either close or consider closing their doors. In the past 40 years, 10 schools have closed, with the most recent in 2015, and more are expected to merge or close in the next 5 years. Ron Stodghill, an author and assistant professor at Johnson C. Smith University, predicts that by the year 2035, 35 HBCUs will remain open, only 33 percent of the 105 that once existed.[7]

Traditionally, tribal colleges and universities (TCUs) were established to meet the educational needs of Native Americans, specifically those in geographic locations that provided limited access to higher education, particularly American Indian reservations. Over time, tribal colleges began to meet the needs of many Native Americans seeking to further their education. Most of these colleges are two-year schools, with 11 of the 32 fully accredited institutions offering four-year degrees.[8] According to 2010 Census data, there are 5.2 million people who identify as American Indian and Alaska Native in some part or whole, with 2.9 million of those identifying as solely of that race. Of those, 22 percent live on reservations or on trust lands.[9] They still only represent less than 1 percent of all enrolled college students.[10]

The reluctance of Native students to leave their reservations, their families, and their communities is significant. When they do, they seek further education so that they can return and have an impact. This topic is a little more complex than that, but it has been simplified here to make the point that it is challenging to recruit Native American students to PWIs for a variety of reasons: The population is small. Tuition is cost prohibitive. The culture is so different. The support, or culturally sensitive approach to support, is not there. And the connection to the tribe is hindered. The

American Indian College Fund (AICF) reported that 82 percent of the Native Americans in their Full Circle Scholarship program attending TCUs completed their programs.[11] The last alumni survey conducted by AICF (in 2006) indicated that the majority were employed or pursued further education.[12] PWIs are struggling to understand why the Native American student numbers aren't there and what they can do to help that. Very few PWIs have figured it out.

The rising costs in higher education are also having an impact on diversity among colleges and universities, especially public ones. As public funds dwindle, colleges and universities rely more heavily on research grants and donated money. Institutions can raise money from their alumni, and they are also increasingly seeking support from corporate donors and partners.[13] Despite this financial pressure, four-year degree-granting institutions have seen an increase via dedicated diversity offices and staff, school-year diversity programming, and diversity-recruiting efforts over the last 20 years, but the needle has not moved as far as the representation of underrepresented minorities at PWIs. More specifically, at the top 100 research institutions, the percentage of black students has declined.[14]

Why This Is a Problem

Homogeneity in teams, departments, and organizations has existed for a long time in U.S. history and has in large part worked primarily due to the ignorance of what could have been possible had these entities been heterogeneous. Scott E. Page, a professor at the University of Michigan, highlights in his research not only the effectiveness of heterogeneous teams and groups, but how much more so they are than homogeneous ones.[15] If we give up, however, and let go of efforts to diversify education—in the student body, the faculty ranks, and the curriculum and pedagogy—then we stand to never reach the potential that could have been.

Prior to the agricultural revolution, the country was helped in large part due to free labor, that is, slavery. With mass production made possible by mechanization and the government's establishment of agricultural and industrial colleges, including HBCUs, the United States was able to sustain and grow its agribusiness. The Tuskegee Institute, Booker T. Washington, and George Washington Carver were part of establishing an extension within the land-grant colleges. Similarly, the industrial revolution was helped by the inclusion of women, immigrants, minorities, and working-class individuals of lower socioeconomic status (SES). This country was built upon its working class and its marginalized immigrants and citizens. Where would we be without them?

As the U.S. economy continues to shift from an industrial economy to a knowledge-based service economy, where disadvantaged groups in society historically get left behind, in which direction will the country go? The innovation and productivity increases that are so critical to increasing per-capita wealth and well-being require an education system that enhances skills for blue-collar and white-collar employees. Here are some of the challenges:

- By 2020, the U.S. economy will have a shortfall of 5 million college-educated workers.[16]
- The postsecondary educational attainment rate has changed very little over the past decade.[17]
- The United States ranks 10th among OECD peers in the rate of postsecondary education among young adults.[18]
- Low- and middle-income families are being priced out of college, resulting in declines in college attendance and completion rates.[19]
- Degree attainment with the younger population is not keeping up with the retirement of the older population.

As the population continues to grow and become increasingly more diverse, the need to educate also grows. Is the United States meeting the educational needs of its citizenship?

Increasing per-capita wealth and well-being relies to a certain extent on education living out a simple mission: to create citizens who can put what they have learned to work for, ultimately, the betterment of society—whether that is in business, government, technology, nonprofit, or arts industries. But it all begins with education. Homogeneity in education and increasing uneducated segments of society both play crucial roles in the potential demise of U.S. standing around the world.

Systemic Influences

The U.S. education system realizes it has a problem, but it does not know how to fix it. It is a pretty complex one, and, frankly, it will require more than solely the education system to alleviate it. There are several reasons that the problem persists. One reason is fear. Because the nation has done such a poor job of addressing its racially charged history, the consequences include continued Jim Crow–esque practices, continued school segregation, and significant diversity fatigue because we just aren't getting it right. Michelle Alexander, an associate professor of law at the Ohio State University, in her book *The New Jim Crow*, addresses how the mass incarceration of black Americans in the war on drugs is the continued marginalization of blacks in American society and spurred largely by the fear of black crime. As a result, blacks are denied voting rights, jury duty, and access to employment, education, and public benefits, creating a caste system of sorts.[20] School segregation is in large part due to housing. Our neighborhoods still remain segregated, a legacy of discriminatory housing practices as the result of fear of black homeowner influx. "White flight," a response to black homeownership in middle-class neighborhoods where white residents move out when black residents move in, continues to influence segregation.

On the one hand, people are afraid to be identified as racist, bigoted, biased, and, to a certain extent, blind. On the other hand, people vilify affirmative action, reparations, and race-conscious admissions. I have always believed that if America truly wanted a complete meritocratic admissions process, then the U.S. colleges and universities would look more like India and China than reflecting the communities in which they stand.

In the end, many Americans don't want true meritocratic admissions processes. They think they do, but they don't. They want the status quo, where it is believed a white American applicant always beats out a brown one. One example is the *Fisher v. University of Texas* case. Is Abby Fisher truly seeking a fair and meritocratic admissions process, or is she seeking a process that simply allows for her admission? If the former, I venture that she still would not gain admission to the university, and the population makeup of the school would look vastly different. If the latter, that leaves limited options than the one she is already pursuing.

I've often wondered why race is the easy target in these types of cases. Athletes, legacy applicants, children of donors, special attention applicants, and children of high-profile friends of colleges all receive considerable preferential admissions. I am not arguing for or against these practices here. I am simply underscoring the nonmeritocratic process that already exists and the parts of that considered acceptable and the parts not acceptable. It does not negate that those underrepresented minority applicants still have to meet the level of acceptance that other students do. In addition, the admissions process is also part art. For example, admissions committees are not looking to admit a homogeneous group of students. Nonacademic factors come into consideration as well. If applicants were admitted solely based on scores, this would not necessarily solve "the problem."

In her most recent book, *The Tyranny of Meritocracy*, Lani Guinier poses that "testocratic" merit is contributing to the lack of diversity in higher education. It assumes that test scores equate to students' value in the academic community and the society at large. It ignores all the things that support high test scores, such as well-funded schools, tutoring, thriving neighborhoods, and so on. She poses that a "democratic" merit process will help alleviate that because it looks at higher education as a public good and includes contributions to society.[21] This premise is at the core of what I have described and the solutions I will propose. Diversity is at the crux of the balance of art and science that is admissions.

Donor Influence

Something that has increased significantly over the past 30 years is the ever-growing influence of the higher education donor. The advancement and development profession has grown immensely as has its importance at higher education institutions. As public institutions have seen decreased support from state and federal governments, the reliance on college and university donors has grown. Certainly, there are altruistic reasons for giving to one's alma mater, one's child's school, and or the flagship state institution where one does business. I do not pretend to understand the motivations of all donors. I simply want to highlight a few things.

One percent of donors constitute major gift donors at institutions with goals of $1 billion or more.[22] Donors can give unrestricted funds freely and allow institutions to determine how best to allocate the funding that has been gifted. Donors can also give to certain funds, scholarships, campaigns, programs, and departments that are already in existence. They can also establish their own endowed entity, such as a scholarship, program, or chair, with or without restricted allocation. Donors can also initiate a fund or foundation to help alleviate restrictions already in existence. This is usually initiated and maintained via an alumni association of some sort.

As the *Stanford Daily* reported in 2013, the weight of money can be felt in admission.[23] There is, however, the notion of donor cultivation and understanding the level of engagement a donor expects beyond the gift transaction, such as serving in an advisory or governance capacity. I highlight this because those in the best position to give at a significant level are historically those with the resources to do so, which means that those who stand to gain most from these transactions are affluent individuals and their children, the majority of whom are white.

Race and Ethnicity Reporting

In 2007, the Department of Education changed the way higher education institutions report racial and ethnic data. Specifically, for the first time, one could self-identify both ethnic identity and racial identity. This change impacted how Hispanic and multiethnic and multiracial students were categorized and reported. Previously, students would simply check a box from a list highlighting races and ethnicities. For example, students could check "Hispanic" and "Black" if they were of both this ethnic and racial makeup. That data was reported as such. The new reporting poses a question before the list of boxes with racial categories that asks whether a student is of Hispanic or Latino ethnicity, and they must indicate "Yes" or "No." Every student completing the application must answer this question. If they answer "Yes," the institution only reports this ethnicity, with no indication of any racial makeup of these students. If the student answers "No," then the institutions can report the racial-identity responses. This captures any student who has any level of Hispanic heritage in his or her family background, no matter the usual self-identified race or ethnicity.[24]

This practice gives an inaccurate reflection of the racial identity of students at higher education institutions. For example, I have a friend who is of Panamanian descent. He is also a black man. He identifies as strongly with his Hispanic heritage as he does his black identity. Under the 2007 reporting guide, he would only be identified as Hispanic. I believe schools should be able to report not only ethnicity but also the racial identity (or identities) of those Hispanic students with an identified race. In addition, and already instituted, if a student has permanent residency or green card status, he or she can also indicate a race or ethnicity, including minority. This means that an immigrant with permanent residency or a green card can be identified as an underrepresented minority.

An argument can be made that even the correct accounting of the applicants who respond to these questions can produce a skewed impression of the representation of historically underrepresented minorities in higher education. As a result, I believe that this particular diversity in higher education is not represented in the reported data as accurately as it could be. For example, if someone from Zambia moved to the United States and obtained permanent residence status, he or she would be identified and reported as "Black/African American." This student's experience is not that of the historically underrepresented black population in the United States. It represents an immigrant experience that is a differently valued diversity.

Admissions Standards

Admissions offices have always been gatekeepers to higher education institutions. The admissions process has become increasingly complex and quantitative. As a result, some admissions offices have increased the weight given to the standardized exam. The effect is to disadvantage minority applicants as schools attempt to become increasingly selective.[25] What was originally intended to demonstrate one's level of exposure for learning has mistakenly been used as either an indicator of intelligence or an indicator of ability to learn. In contrast, the best indicator for college performance is actually an applicant's grade point average (GPA).[26] The standardized college entrance exam only indicates with any level of consistency the prospective student's family or parental affluence or socioeconomic status.[27] Recognizing this fact, some institutions, such as Smith College, Bryn Mawr, Wesleyan, and Wake Forest University, are already implementing standardized exam–free or standardized exam–optional criteria.

Some Current Efforts to Enhance Diversity

Universities and colleges are making efforts to increase diversity despite the challenges faced. This is particularly true for public institutions as they are under greater public and governmental scrutiny due to the public funds they receive. Their efforts to maintain race-conscious admissions processes have become difficult. Awarding scholarships or institutional grants only increases the challenge. To attract students of color, private organizations and foundations have established programs to meet the needs of this underrepresented population. Organizations such as the Gates Foundation and its Millennium Scholars program, Quest Bridge, the Posse Foundation, and the Ron Brown Scholar Program are helping to fill the gap for minority and low-income students. The organizations are helping students of color gain admission and access to higher education, but in regard to restoring trust, are the higher education institutions living out their purpose? Are higher education institutions just trying to meet numbers or are they adhering to the fine print in their mission statements as well?

Over the past 30-plus years, PWIs have established "feeder programs" in partnership with HBCUs. For many years, graduate schools have established memoranda of understanding (MOU) and formal programs to recruit students from HBCUs. Thirty-three percent of African Americans receiving PhDs in STEM fields earned their undergraduate degrees from an HBCU.[28] However, there are several issues with such feeder programs. Sixty percent of HBCUs offer graduate and professional degrees, which means there may be a tension in the effort to keep students against the pull of students to PWI programs. I have seen this phenomenon up close when attempting to recruit prospective professional school students from HBCUs with their own professional degree programs. It was often challenging to get decision makers at the HBCUs to allow a group representing the top graduate business programs in the nation to conduct information sessions and workshops. The second issue is that HBCUs tout their pipeline to graduate programs, but we have no knowledge of the retention rate. We know what PWIs are producing as far as total graduate degrees awarded, but we don't know how that compares to total students transitioned into the graduate programs. Is the pipeline working?

Some Recommendations

I have ideas, but they are different and will require determination to succeed from higher education institutions. I believe that if the ideas are implemented, they will not only enhance diversity but will also help majority students, education in general, and our society. I was once told by a diversity fellow at a higher education institution that any strong societal solution not only helps the targeted beneficiary but also many other nontargeted individuals, including the general population. He shared the example of sidewalk curb cuts having been established to assist the physically disabled, primarily veterans, to better navigate walking city streets. It then became an Americans with Disabilities Act mandate, but it benefited more than the disabled, such as parents with strollers, runners, children on bicycles, delivery persons with hand trucks, and so on.

Idea #1: What if we simply adhered to the mission of the organization, and made its application clear and transparent? If we defined the ideal environment that makes for meeting that mission and then established admissions and retention guidelines based on that environment? That way, everyone and anyone would have a clear understanding of the organization, how it defines itself, what it is ideally trying to do and align admissions (and hiring) and support services to meet that. If an institution includes diversity as a part of that mission in an ideal learning environment, this helps underscore decisions related to the same. If admissions, academic and student services officers could point back to the mission for decisions and if applicants/students could do the same, that would be a leap, a brave one.

Idea #2: What if we just got rid of the standardized exam as an application component altogether? We could use past curriculum, an academic assessment, and other qualitative elements to help determine academic alignment. The review of the past curriculum highlights student areas of interest, academic preparedness, and past performance. An academic assessment would highlight the school culture, pedagogy, and approach to student learning. It assesses the size of the school and the comparative demands of a particular curriculum as well as the support available and utilized. It also includes the relative SES of the student population, including the percentage of students eligible for free or reduced lunches.

These things not only provide important information about the student's background, but they also help determine the tools needed for success if admitted. The qualitative elements would include participation in activities outside of the classroom, including extracurriculars and community-based activities. In addition, information about the family culture and the social and interpersonal development of the applicant would be gathered. In other words, the most influential element of a student, the family, would be considered when developing the best academic plan upon admission: How does the student learn best? Is the student oriented toward the scientific approach to problem solving or the Socratic approach? Does the student respond better to a demanding atmosphere or a nurturing one? And how does the student engage and perform in groups versus alone? These things can highlight resilience and resourcefulness, or the lack thereof, and the leadership potential. They indicate an ability to learn from mistakes and thrive in an environment that is unfamiliar yet supportive. These things will not be used to keep a student out per se, but they could be used to help the student transition more successfully and to assign to an adviser (or two) as well as to engage in group activities early.

Idea #3: What if we gave every interested student access to a student training and enrichment program (STEP) that would take place over the summer? Such a program would have the flexibility to be specifically designed for each student to help him or her successfully transition to college and would increase the potential and actual success rate of every student. STEP is a preparation program that helps students fill any gaps socially, culturally, and academically. This will take a tremendous amount of resources, from staff and faculty to current students and alumni, as well as corporate partners.

Higher education institutions are partnering with companies and corporations in a way that yields little in terms of recruiting for both the institution and the companies. What exists now is money to support scholarships and programming, providing access to soft recruiting. In contrast, a STEP program, with a truly integrated partnership between the company and the college or university, incorporates the company at every key step of the student transition process.

Example: Joseph Evans, University STEP Program

Phase One: Joseph Evans accepts his offer of admission and submits his registration for the STEP program. Because an extensive profile has been created for Joe, he is automatically paired with an academic adviser and a partner company mentor, and he is connected with a peer mentor and the Office of Student Affairs. He is provided their names and contact information. His peer mentor reaches out to him right away, and they talk about what to expect during the STEP program.

Phase Two: Joe moves into his dorm at the start of the summer session and is greeted by his Student Affairs adviser. He is given a one-on-one orientation to the program. He is introduced to his roommate, and they are taken to lunch by the Student Affairs adviser. The next morning Joe is greeted by his academic Adviser to have a discussion and assessment session to determine his interests and potential career goals. Joe then goes to the STEP program's daylong orientation session.

Phase Three: Joe registers for classes and secures tutoring in those subjects identified as needing additional support resources. Joe continues to meet with each key member of his STEP success team (his mentors) throughout his first year of college. His peer mentor introduces him to the various organizations and programs on campus. Joe attends student organization–sponsored events, but he does not engage because he knows that it is in the plan for his second year of college, after he has established himself as a student.

Phase Four: Joe meets with his career services adviser and with his company partner mentor to help him plan and implement his summer internship search. Joe continues to be in contact with these two members of his STEP success team during the summer internship.

Years 2-4: Joe engages in similar processes, employing skills he develops over time. He relies less on the STEP program resources, but he uses them when they are most needed. He also engages in mentoring new STEP program students.

Idea #4: Educators need a clear understanding of the demands that exist in society for educated, skilled, and engaged professionals. Colleges and universities need to include as part of the university-wide state-of-affairs presentation, usually scheduled at the start of a new academic year, a revisit of the mission, strategic plan, and the specific ways the institution plans to meet the demands of its society. Follow-up discussions in small-group settings need to occur that address how programs will aim to meet those challenges. In the state of Virginia, the governor has traditionally sent out a challenge to all state employees each year to think innovatively and submit their best ideas to help address and solve some of the state's challenges and problems. College and university presidents could do the same to engage employees in problem solving by providing a challenge and incentive.

Communication is key to making it clear that university and college practices align with their missions. Being able to be transparent about decisions throughout the organization will be tantamount to anything else that the institution will do. As the institution looks to incorporate a transparent diversity-oriented practice, the communication of said practice provides opportunities for endorsement, engagement, and understanding. Business partnerships can help do the same. For example, business partners should articulate exactly how they are engaged, their anticipated outcomes, how the partnership works toward meeting the institution's mission, and what they hope to gain as the for-profit entity of the partnership. When it comes to diversity, given the issue highlighted earlier, the more transparent the better.

Idea #5: Colleges and universities should allocate a portion of every gift made to an endowment discretionary fund toward the university's diversity efforts and articulate that all of those funds will be accounted for and shared the same as all other gifted funds. This allows the college to demonstrate its commitment to diversity, ensures that there is a consistent line-item funding space for diversity, and sends a signal to alumni and friends of the college that diversity is a core element for which funds are raised and spent.

Idea #6: This diversity issue doesn't just pop up at the college level. It builds from the primary and even pre-K levels. The gap that develops starts at the pre-K level, where children of color are less likely to attend quality preschools that teach and expose children to critical socialization and skill development prior to entering primary school.[29] Each college and university across the nation should partner with local schools that suffer due to low SES and unequal access to resources. Higher education institutions shouldn't just exist in a community but should also be an integral part of that community, which means helping provide solutions to problems that are directly relevant to higher education challenges. If every college and university in the nation partnered with several elementary, middle, and high schools, I believe we would see a significant narrowing of the gap that exists in education delivery and attainment today, from primary level to higher education level. Community colleges are already doing this, as is the University of California through its K–12 partnerships and Michigan State University through its college of education partnerships. It could go one step further, with universities starting their own pre-K to 12 schools. Given the income stratification that can often exist in higher education, the schools would be guaranteed to have diverse representation with university employees' children alone.

Leveraging technology is simple. It is surprising how many school systems are not using technology to bring their classrooms into the 21st century. There are definitely low-income school districts that do not have the technology or access to it that hinders the ability to utilize technology in schools and classrooms. I would argue ways around that too. Some of the innovative and creative practices and programs listed below can be adapted for those schools that don't have the technology.

Some examples of programs that are designed to utilize technology to help in advancing education for the underserved include the following:

- DreamWakers: A new nonprofit that uses video conferencing to engage students in real-time career-related talks with working professionals.
- Self-paced programs (e.g., Charlottesville WALK program): High schools are utilizing self-paced online curriculum delivery platforms to help nontraditional student learners complete their high school program at their own pace.
- Dual Enrollment: High school students are taking online college courses while still in high school. They earn college credit, which in many cases earns them high school credit as well.
- Saturday School: Several schools are going to Saturday school programs where online learning and virtual delivery of courses is essential to skill development and knowledge attainment, especially if certain high school classes are not available.

These programs could be incorporated into a university's pre-K to 12 partnership to allow technology to enhance learning both in the classroom and outside of it.

Familial Engagement and Support

In first generation and underrepresented populations, there are often familial demands and strains placed on a child that are outside of the norm for college students from more affluent families. These students often apply to and attend college without the mentoring of someone experienced and knowledgeable in their family. In addition, if that student is a working student contributing to the household income, the awareness of the strain the family will experience when that student's income is no longer present can be stressful. The more the college or university can engage the family and educate the family about the student's process, transition, and expectations, the more that family will be able to encourage, support, and engage in that student's experience and success. If higher education institutions could take it a step further and invite parents and families to orientations, cover that cost, provide childcare, and so on, that would really help that family to engage. This will require a family services office or department at the college level to do this well. Dedicated staff to help address these types of unique yet important elements and challenges of first-generation college and underrepresented minority students' transition to college will go a long way toward enhancing the success of those students.

Required Light-Load Year-Round College and Employment Co-ops

Some college students need a little more time and a lighter load during the transition to college. These students (including first-generation college students and underrepresented minority students from low SES backgrounds) should be allowed to carry a 75 percent full-time student academic load in their first year and take one to two courses in the summer to make up for the light load during the traditional academic year. Federal aid and scholarships should allow for funding in the first year with this lighter academic load. In addition, employment co-op opportunities are great ways to help students develop professional skills, gain experience, and apply learning while still completing college. As highlighted above, some college students have financial family obligations, and a co-op employment opportunity helps solve two challenges: (1) a student can earn money that can be shared with his or her family, and (2) a company can recruit and retain talented students. This also pulls away from the stigma of students averaging longer than the traditional four years to earn their degrees.[30]

Leadership Requirement

The type of leader required to create a more transparent and diverse college or university is one with vision and a certain fearlessness, an effective and inspiring communicator, and someone who can clearly connect the dots for every possible audience and stakeholder. This leader may be rare, but I believe these types of individuals exist and are already in some way connected to higher education. This type of leader would establish a vision and get buy in and then make it happen with the help of those he or she leads.

These are sizeable tasks. However, leadership does not solely exist at one level of an organization, and it does not exist in a vacuum. Every institution and organization has leaders throughout and at every level. They just need the opportunity to help achieve a vision. This may be the hardest idea to implement of them all. Fearlessness in the diversity in education space is not the norm.

Conclusion

The United States has not always been kind to its marginalized populations, but it has always held a strong ideal toward which it strives. Given the history of diversity in this country over centuries, especially in regard to education, it is time for our education system to catch up with the sociological, technological, globalized, and mobilized nature of our society. Hopefully the ideas highlighted will spark conversation across the education sector and generate other more creative and innovative ideas. Our nation, our society, and our world need solutions for how we deliver education better, more equitably, and across the widest spectrum, accounting for every major difference, and still produce ethical, knowledgeable, and responsible citizen leaders. Given the defined mission of education, we have an obligation to do just that, and currently, we are failing. The time has come to be unapologetically deliberate about diversity in higher education, which means we need to know how we acknowledge it, nurture it, celebrate it, and use it to benefit our world. The time is now.

Notes

1. Susan Aud, Mary Ann Fox, and Angelina KewalRamani, *Status and Trends in the Education of Racial and Ethnic Groups* (Washington, D.C.: Institute of Education Sciences National Center for Education Statistics, 2010). http://nces.ed.gov/pubs2010/2010015.pdf.

2. United States Senate Committee on Health, Education, Labor, and Pensions, *For Profit Higher Education: The Failure to Safeguard the Federal Investment and Ensure Student Success* (Washington, D.C.: Government Printing Office, 2012). https://www.gpo.gov/fdsys/pkg/CPRT-112SPRT74931/pdf/CPRT-112SPRT74931.pdf;   James Cersonsky, "5 Ways Student Debt Resistance Is Taking Off," *Alternet*. October 25, 2013. http://www.alternet.org/education/5-ways-student-debt-resistance-taking.

3. United States Bureau of Labor Statistics, "The Recession of 2007–2009," *BLS Spotlight on Statistics*, February 2012. http://www.bls.gov/spotlight/2012/recession/pdf/recession_bls_spotlight.pdf.

4. Aud, Fox, and KewalRamani, *Status and Trends*.

5. United States Senate Committee on Health, Education, Labor, and Pensions, *For Profit Higher Education*.

6. Ron Stodghill, *Where Everybody Looks Like Me: At the Crossroads of America's Black Colleges and Culture* (New York: HarperCollins, 2015), 8–12, 49, 60.

7. Ibid.

8. "Tribal Colleges and Universities," United States Department of Education, White House Initiative on American Indian and Alaska Native Education, accessed 2015. http://sites.ed.gov/whiaiane/tribes-tcus/tribal-colleges-and-universities.

9. Tina Norris, Paula Vines, and Elizabeth M. Hoeffel, "The American Indian and Alaska Native Population: 2010," *2010 Census Briefs* (Washington, D.C.: United States Census Bureau, 2012). http://www.census.gov/history/pdf/c2010br-10.pdf.

10. Tribal College Research and Database Initiative, *Tribal Colleges: An Introduction* (Alexandria, VA: American Indian Higher Education Consortium, 1999). http://www.aihec.org/who-we-serve/docs/TCU_intro.pdf.

11. American Indian College Fund, "Fostering Success: Need and Resiliency among Tribal College Students," *Full Circle Study*, published 2012. http://www.collegefund.org/userfiles/file/FosteringSuccessBRF.pdf.

12. American Indian College Fund, *Championing Success: A Report on the Progress of Tribal College and University Alumni*, published 2006. http://www.collegefund.org/userfiles/file/FINALIHEP-rpt-TribalAlumni-4-10.pdf.

13. John S. McConnell, "Corporate Giving: Trends, Motivations and Strategies," Bentz, Whaley, Flessner, February 24, 2012. http://www.bwf.com/published-by-bwf/corporate-giving-trends-motivations-and-strategies.

14. Andrew McGill, "The Missing Black Students at Elite American Universities," *The Atlantic*, November 23, 2015. http://www.theatlantic.com/politics/archive/2015/11/black-college-student-body/417189.

15. Scott E. Page, *The Difference: How the Power of Diversity Creates Better Groups, Firms, Schools and Societies* (Princeton, NJ: Princeton University Press, 2007), 173.

16. David A. Bergeron and Carmel Martin, "College for All: Strengthening Our Economy through College for All," Center for American Progress, February 19, 2015. https://www.americanprogress.org/issues/higher-education/report/2015/02/19/105522/strengthening-our-economy-through-college-for-all.

17. Ibid.

18. Ibid.

19. Ibid.

20. Michelle Alexander, *The New Jim Crow: Mass Incarceration in the Age of Colorblindness* (New York: The New Press, 2012), 55–58.

21. Lani Guinier, *The Tyranny of Meritocracy: Democratizing Higher Education in America* (Boston: Beacon Press, 2015), 42.

22. Chuck Longfield, "Higher Education Fundraising Performance in 2013," *The Blackbaud Index for Higher Education*, published in 2014. https://www.blackbaud.com/files/resources/downloads/blackbaud-index-higher-education-report.pdf.

23. Justine Moore, "Connections to University Can Affect Admissions Decision," *Stanford Daily*. March 12, 2013. http://www.stanforddaily.com/2013/03/12/connections-to-university-can-affect-admissions-decision.

24. United States Department of Education, "Policy Questions on the Department of Education's 2007 Guidance on Collecting, Maintaining and Reporting Data by Race or Ethnicity," last modified October 15, 2008. http://www2.ed.gov/policy/rschstat/guid/raceethnicity/questions.html.

25. McGill, "The Missing Black Students."

26. Nicole Gorman, "Study Finds GPA, Not College Entrance Test, Best Predictor of Need for Remedial Classes," *Education World*, June 6, 2016. http://www.educationworld.com/a_news/study-finds-gpa-not-college-entrance-tests-best-predictor-need-remedial-classes-1761920910.

27. Guinier, *The Tyranny of Meritocracy*, 22.

28. Marybeth Gasman and Felicia Commodore, "HBCU vs PWI Debate: The Value and Rigor of a Black College Degree," *HBCU Lifestyle Black College Living*, May 30, 2014. http://hbculifestyle.com/hbcu-vs-pwi-debate.

29.   Katherine Magnuson and Jane Waldfogel, "Early Childhood Care and Education: Effects on Ethnic and Racial Gaps in School Readiness," *The Future of the Child* 15, no. 1 (2005): 169–196.

30.   United States Department of Education National Center for Education Statistics, *2008–09 Baccalaureate and Beyond Longitudinal Study* (Washington, D.C.: Institute of Education Science, 2011). http://nces.ed.gov/pubs2011/2011236.pdf.

CHAPTER SIX

Another Lost Generation Adrift: U.S. Military Veterans and Higher Education

Brian M. Welke

The Sun Also Rises, Ernest Hemingway's novel about a group of World War I expatriates on a journey in Spain, opens with a quote from Gertrude Stein remarking that the postwar generation is "lost." Hemingway shows that his generation of veterans were not exactly lost, but adrift in a sea of disconnectedness. Many veterans today are similarly adrift. They face an inability to connect to the very society that they volunteered to protect. I know because I was one of them.

This inability to connect to society is echoed in today's news coverage of the veteran suicide rate. Statistically, the veteran community's mortality rate is significantly lower while its suicide rate is significantly higher than comparable groups in the general population.[1] The most likely time for a veteran to commit suicide is within the first three years of separation from service.[2] Although veterans cannot be forced to get help, it can be made easier for them to find the firm ground they need. One of those ways to help veterans can be, must be, higher education.

For higher education to help veterans, we first need to understand what the disconnected feeling is and what it is not. It is not PTSD. Posttraumatic stress disorder (PTSD) is a psychological disorder brought on by trauma that needs to be diagnosed by a qualified medical professional.[3] Most veterans do not have PTSD. According to the Department of Veterans Affairs, the prevalence rate of PTSD among Iraq and Afghanistan veterans was only 13.8 percent in 2008.[4] In fact, the suicide rate among veterans who did not deploy is higher than those that did deploy to Iraq or Afghanistan.[5] These facts, and my own experience, lead me to believe that PTSD caused by combat, while certainly the most discussed issue pertaining to veterans, is not the main one most veterans will struggle with. They struggle with coming to terms with the fact that their way of life is suddenly over. The primary problem that the majority of veterans will face is the culture shock of reintegrating into civilian society.[6]

The Three Losses When Moving from Military to Civilian Life

Reintegration is really a problem of culture shock. Facing culture shock can be like being adrift in a sea of depression, loneliness, and an angst about everything but specifically nothing. Even though veterans may be surrounded by people, they feel alone. They are unable to connect with anything or anybody. The lost feeling comes from the difficulty in transitioning from a culture with a uniform to one without and the inability to find connections to the civilian life and society that veterans had had before they served. That inability, I would argue, is caused by three losses veterans experience when leaving service: loss of identity, loss of community, and loss of purpose.

The loss of identity is how veterans view themselves. There is a lot of pride and self-identification that goes into earning and then wearing a uniform. It becomes a part of who veterans are and how they view themselves: "I am a marine," "I am a soldier," "I am a sailor," "I am an airman." They are defined by a uniform. This self-identification is a part of them one day and gone the next. It is a quick transition when they hang up the uniform for the last time. When the utilities get folded into a footlocker, a door closes on that period of their lives. It is almost as if a coffin were slamming shut. Staff Sergeant Andrew Michael reinforced this when he remarked to me, "That last day when it ends, feels like a death. Something so close to you, a part of you, has died." It is now who they were, instead of who they are. This is a loss in how veterans view themselves, and it is a fundamental and rapid shift that many of them are not expecting.

Veterans also face a loss of community. They have had relationships so close that no matter how much time goes by, those affiliations with each other will always be strong. They have lived in such close proximity that they have forgotten what loneliness really is. Then upon separation, the very next day, they find themselves alone. They have lost the support structure that was around them so closely for so long.

Not only do veterans lose their community and a part of themselves, but they reenter a society with very different values than those from which they have just left. This division in cultures makes it exceedingly difficult to find anchor points. Veterans talk differently, they joke differently, and their communities are structured differently. Civilian society has become alien to them. Almost 20 years ago, *The Atlantic* documented this in compelling detail.[7] These feelings of separation that existed 20 years ago are still true today.

In modern American society, there are not many rules that govern the boundaries of social behavior. Veterans are coming from a society where the opposite is true. They are coming from a culture of discipline and submission to authority. Respect for authority is needed in the military, especially in combat. But the lack of structure in civilian society can be difficult to navigate for someone who has become used to taking orders. It is not that veterans are mindless lemmings, but it does take time to get used to the freedom that comes with being a civilian and not having a rigid command structure dictating most of the decisions that provide boundaries in which to live.

Veterans also come from a community where self-sacrifice and duty are not just slogans, they are a way of life. They come back to an individualistic society based around the self, the "me," when for the past number of years, it was the group, the "we," that came first—the unit, the squad, the platoon, the company. This is not meant to be a critique on society, just an observation that veterans are transitioning from one community to another that are different from each other. It is exceedingly difficult to connect with someone or with a group that has very different views about the place of the individual. While veterans are attempting to sort out the loss of identity they have experienced, they are also facing it alone in an individualistic society. Most veterans look forward to their EAS (end of active service) date, but once it arrives, it can be bewildering.

The third loss that contributes to the adrift feeling is the loss of purpose. Veterans are by definition driven. They are the ones who made it through the training and the selection process and kept striving for what came next, whether it was to earn the next rank, earn a position on a team, earn a certain qualification, or graduate from a specialized school. They finished what they set out to do. *Veteran* is the term used to show that their service is behind them, that they are no longer currently serving. By that very nature, their goal, their purpose, is a past chapter. They had accomplished what they set out to do, but many of them do not have a clear next step. They were so focused on what was directly before them that they did not think about what would come next, because, to be honest, many of them were not sure they would be alive to worry about the next step.

For so long, the path was clear. It was not easy, but it had borders and rules. They knew what was expected of them and what they had to do. They learned to follow orders. They learned to follow first, and then to lead. But once they received their separation papers, they left the narrowly defined path and entered an ocean of disorienting freedom.

There were no more markers, no more paths, just the freedom to choose their own direction, which is overwhelming when everything had been so easily laid before them just a few moments ago. This lack of structure, lack of direction, lack of not having a goal or purpose creates the feeling of being adrift in a frightening expanse, from horizon to horizon, with nothing to provide any direction, and all while being alone and struggling with who they are now.

Moving Effectively to Civilian Life through Higher Education

These three losses, identity, community, and purpose, are what veterans face by the simple fact that they are veterans. Higher education, whether undergraduate or graduate school, should be a central part of veterans' reintegration into civilian society. I know higher education can help veterans because it helped me. My experiences in undergraduate and then law school are what helped me along my path back into civilian life. The sense of identity, community, and purpose that veterans lost at the end of their service obligation are present on a college campus.[8]

Not only is education an excellent option for veterans to reintegrate into society, it has become a necessity in today's economy. Unlike the Greatest Generation, who returned home to a generally expanding economy, today's veterans have faced a stagnant one. Most veterans graduated from high school and then went directly into the military. They often cannot go right back to work in a career with higher prospects because almost all of those jobs that allow for upward mobility require some form of a degree. A college degree has become the equivalent of a high school diploma. The economic requirement of a bachelor's degree, however, may not be a bad thing for veterans because it allows them a step between military service and the "the real world" that eases their reintegration.[9] The traditional college experience can help veterans reestablish their sense of identity, community, and purpose.

College is touted as a great time for young adults to "find themselves." It is a time between adolescence and adulthood. It is a safe environment where they can discover what they are capable of intellectually after leaving the nest of home for the first time to be on their own. These are all things that a veteran could use to reestablish a sense of identity as well, an easing into the civilian version of oneself before facing the total freedom of life outside of a structured community. College is not the military in the sense that there are fewer rules of behavior and it is more egalitarian, but there is still a pecking order to the society that is clearly delineated. There are students, professors, and administrators. Although veterans can find this same structure in the corporate world, they first normally need a college degree to enter that world.

There are many self-identifying labels throughout higher education: business student, engineering student, Hawkeye, Hoosier. While these labels do not completely replace those of marine, soldier, sailor, or airman, they do form a footing upon which a veteran can reestablish and find a new sense of identity.

Not only is higher education a great time for reestablishing a sense of identity, it can be a great time for developing a sense of community. College, like the military, forces people into groups that they might not have selected for themselves. Students in the same program take classes together and see the same people at the bookstore or at tailgates and sporting events. These experiences are all similar to the military, where the community is restricted to a relatively small group of defined people with a united purpose.

Living in dorms, in university housing, or with roommates found on Craigslist means that, almost invariably, the veterans are going to be forced to be around their new peers. This familiarity and proximity can do wonders to help build new friendships as veterans go through the reintegration process. College builds friendships, and it also provides a safe environment where veterans can readjust their mannerisms to better fit into the civilian society they once protected. It is a sort of proving ground for social behavior that is cordoned off from the rest of society. College can give veterans much-needed time between separation and the real world in which to develop a new sense of belonging that was lost when they left the service.

Finally, higher education often imparts a sense of purpose into students' lives. College is where young students develop a passion for helping others, contributing to society, and mark out their career objectives. It sets up a career path and gives students goals to work toward. Veterans that have lost that direction and purpose at separation can gain it back in college.

College is also where veterans can develop the skills to achieve those new goals. It is meant to be a launching pad from high school to the workforce, but it can just as easily serve as a launching pad from military service to the workforce.

Making Higher Education Work for Veterans

Higher education is a unique opportunity to help veterans reintegrate to civilian life. The question thus becomes, how to do it. Universities can establish specific policies to help veterans ease into college life, provide a network of former service members to connect with on campus, and match upper classmen with new veteran students in the same major to foster mentorship. But the biggest impact can be made by individual professors and educators. I will share an example from my own experience that can be illustrative.

The professor that made me the most comfortable was also the one I probably disagreed with the most. It was in a political philosophy class with a retiring professor who first started teaching during Vietnam. The very first day after going through the syllabus, the professor asked whether there were students in the military and then followed by asking whether any had been deployed to Iraq or Afghanistan. I was the only one with my hand still in the air. He said, "Thank you for your candor," and then stated that he had asked the question so he would be sure of his audience and that anything he said was not meant to be offensive, even if it could be perceived that way. He also said that those who had served in a war zone were uniquely qualified to speak on matters of war and the use of force, which is an inescapable topic in political philosophy. He said we may disagree, but he would always do so with respect. We did disagree on a number of issues, but it was one of my most enlightening classes based largely on the fact that our differences were tempered with an underlying respect, awareness, and deference.

This was in George W. Bush's last year in office at the height of the unpopularity of the Iraq War. It would have been very easy for all of the angst in the media and society to dominate the discussion, but those negative feelings never entered the classroom. Our political and philosophical arguments took place without contentiousness. We disagreed without being disagreeable. It was a safe environment where my experience mattered and was respected.

This simple but powerful recognition of my past military experiences in an environment where it was relevant helped to reintegrate me, to welcome me back into civilian life. It helped bridge the gap in my identity by showing that my military and student identities were not at odds with each other but could exist symbiotically and reinforce one another. It helped reintegrate me into my community of students because it increased my class participation instead of allowing me to be just an observer. This simple recognition of my past experiences as something of value allowed my intellectual curiosity to grow instead of putting me on the defensive, which translated to a greater willingness to explore different fields of study.

Rebuilding the ROCC of Trust

The principles delineated by Aneil and Karen Mishra in their book *Becoming a Trustworthy Leader* describe the ROCC of Trust—Reliability, Openness/Honesty, Competence, and Compassion. These principles are well suited to veterans. They have experience evaluating and being leaders. What veterans need is a way to transition their military experiences into a civilian context. The lessons learned in the military can be honed by higher education to show what veterans learned of reliability, openness, competence, and compassion in their future careers. This can be accomplished though group projects in the classroom, campus clubs, extracurricular activities, sports, and even fraternities and sororities.

Most veterans already have the skill sets. They just need the opportunity to exhibit and practice them in a civilian way. It will probably mean taking on more of a collaborative approach as opposed to the more authoritative approach they are used to in the military, but exhibiting these skills in an educational setting can be good practice to get used to working with civilians. These opportunities will be an invaluable segue into leadership in a civilian setting.

A veteran can also contribute to classroom discussion in a way most students right out of high school cannot because veterans have experiences that most other students lack. Applying lessons learned through military experiences goes much further than simple recognition of those experiences. It is the respect and deference that goes further in helping a veteran than most other programs. That deference to experience, even if the veteran doesn't contribute very often, can speak volumes and help reintegrate the veteran into the student body and society at large.

Higher education should be one of the major paths that helps veterans reintegrate into society. It is a system already set up to foster and build a sense of identity, community, and purpose, which veterans often lack when they separate from military service. If universities and professors remember this, they can be integral components in society to prevent the current generation of veterans from becoming a lost generation.

Notes

1. Han K. Kang, Tim A. Bullman, Derek J. Smolenski, Nancy A. Skopp, Gregory A. Gahm, and Mark A. Reger, "Suicide Risk among 1.3 Million Veterans Who Were on Active Duty during the Iraq and Afghanistan Wars," *Annals of Epidemiology* 25, no. 2 (2015): 96–100.

2. Ibid.

3. "Understanding PTSD," U.S. Department of Veterans Affairs, accessed 2016. http://www.ptsd.va.gov/public/understanding_PTSD/understanding_PTSD.asp.

4. "Epidemiology of PTSD," U.S. Department of Veterans Affairs, accessed 2016. http://www.ptsd.va.gov/professional/PTSD-overview/epidemiological-facts-ptsd.asp.

5. Kang et al., "Suicide Risk."

6. The Department of Defense has developed the Transition Assistance Program to help address this issue. According to the American Legion, however, the higher education information provided by the program is voluntary and needs to be "reevaluated." http://www.legion.org/legislative/testimony/225815/review-transition-assistance-program-tap.

7. Thomas E. Ricks, "The Widening Gap between Military and Society," *The Atlantic* (July 1997). http://www.theatlantic.com/magazine/archive/1997/07/the-widening-gap-between-military-and-society/306158.

8. It is important to note that I think a physical presence on the campus is very important. Going to school online is a good choice for some, but for veterans facing the loss of community, full emersion into student life would likely be a better option.

9. With the Post-9/11 GI Bill, the financial incentives are also very strong for veterans to attend college.

CHAPTER SEVEN

Coaching Students for Success: Lead with Strengths

Karen E. Mishra

There is great debate as to the responsibility of a college. Is it to educate students? Or, is it to prepare students for a career beyond college? A recent survey of the World Innovation Summit for Education (WISE) attendees indicated that "it is chiefly universities' responsibility to prepare students for their first job" (69%); just 25 percent assign this responsibility to employers. But when asked to identify the leading challenges preventing universities from fully achieving this, these same attendees emphasize employers' responsibility more: 62 percent cite a lack of work or internship opportunities that prepare students for jobs, and 52 percent choose a lack of project-based learning. Ineffective career counseling is a distant third, at 38 percent.[1] In fact, a recent Gallup and Lumina Foundation study found that "96% of college chief academic officers believed they were turning out work-ready graduates, while just 11% of business leaders believed the same."[2] Obviously, there is a disconnect between academic and employer perspectives.

If career-readiness is perceived to be in the domain of the universities, helping students focus on strengths can be an effective starting point. Many universities are now utilizing StrengthsQuest by Gallup (the student version of StrengthsFinder 2.0) to help students understand, appreciate, and apply their strengths to challenges both on campus and to their future career goals. Strengths are defined as talents plus knowledge and experience.[3] "Talents are naturally recurring patterns of thought, feeling, or behavior that can be productively applied."[4] Strengths become talents with practice. One way to ensure that students get the most out of understanding their strengths is to mentor and coach them on their strengths. A recent survey by Gallup Higher Education found that only 22 percent of students had a mentor "who encouraged me to pursue my goals and dreams."[5] Gallup found that this mentor was critical for future professional well-being.[6] Research shows that students who are not using their strengths at work "report more negative attitudes and intentions to quit."[7]

Research has found that when employees use their strengths at work it leads to more engagement, less likelihood of quitting, and a stronger bond with colleagues.[8] That is a strong reason for universities to help students understand their strengths and apply them as soon as possible during college to make better-informed decisions about their future careers. Rath and Conchie have found that there are four traits followers want from their leaders: (1) trust, (2) compassion, (3) stability, and (4) hope.[9]

The positive psychology movement focuses on positive traits, such as strengths. Effective leadership starts with knowing your strengths and investing in others' strengths.[10] Building a strengths-based campus at the student, staff, and cabinet levels will drive engagement and well-being.[11] A strengths-based program can be part of a leadership-development program at the college level, one that is *not* being provided by employers but that will help students make better decisions about how to apply their own strengths to their future career paths.

Many colleges and universities are beginning to add strengths-based programs to their college curriculums. East Carolina University College of Business has added StrengthsFinder 2.0 to its four-course leadership program for undergraduate business majors. Kalamazoo Valley Community College uses StrengthsQuest in its college counseling center to guide and prepare all of its students for career readiness. Meredith College is using StrengthsQuest and StrengthsFinder 2.0 at both the undergraduate and graduate level to help students identify, appreciate, and apply their strengths.

Strengths-Based Coaching

Strengths-based coaching has been shown to be effective in the development of transformational leadership behaviors by helping employees apply those skills in the workplace.[12] The International Coach Federation (ICF) defines coaching as "partnering with clients in a thought-provoking and creative process that inspires them to maximize their personal and professional potential, which is particularly important in today's uncertain and complex environment."[13] Faculty and staff can be the leaders on campus who help students understand their strengths and how to "discover, develop and apply their strengths."[14] A recent *Harvard Business Review* report describes the role of a coach as someone who

- Develops high potential or facilitates transition: 48 percent
- Acts as a sounding board: 26 percent
- Addresses derailing behavior: 12 percent[15]

There are many ways that strengths-based coaching offers a value-added dimension to a student's education in that it allows the student to

- Achieve goals
- Experience higher levels of self-reflection and insight
- Lower levels of stress, anxiety, and depression
- Be more productive in their current jobs
- Find a better fit within their organizations
- Be more focused in their career development, as discussed below
- See themselves from a different perspective[16]

In addition, students may have found themselves criticized for their strengths in the past, such as "you are too impatient" (this student may be an activator) or "you are too nice" (this student may be a relator).[17] This has the effect of discouraging students from understanding their unique talents and skills as actual strengths instead of something just different from the person critiquing them. The advantage of a strengths-based adviser or mentor is that this person can help students see their strengths as being unique and helpful for their future success while recognizing the need to complement their strengths with those of others to avoid exposing weaknesses.

Strengths-based mentoring gives students an opportunity to not just gather useful job skills but to figure out how to use them along with their strengths to best prepare for the next step in their career. Colleges and universities can use strengths-based mentoring to assist students with career development and thinking through prospective career options.[18] In addition to understanding and applying strengths, there are other important skills a student learns through coaching, including

- Active listening
- Solving their own problems
- Preparing for difficult conversations
- Active inquiry[19]

One added bonus for students who go through strengths-based coaching is that they have learned to become a coach themselves for when they are managing people. Boyatzis, Smith, and Blaize found that managers who coach with compassion better sustain themselves by lowering their stress when they focus on providing compassion to others.[20] "Developing skill in the process of coaching others to improve their performance and achieve their potential in the workplace would seem to be one of the most important areas for manager and leaders of the 21st century."[21] Boyatzis et al. believe that this should be a part of management education as a way to go beyond teaching leadership to actually teaching leadership capability.[22]

How

As a recent graduate of Gallup's strengths-mentoring program, I have had the opportunity to learn how to help my students understand, appreciate, and apply their strengths through coaching. Each semester, I coach my students twice while they prepare a personal development plan. This plan asks them to reflect on their strengths and consider how they can apply their strengths to current challenges and opportunities. As Casey and Wuestman note, having a framework to coach is most helpful, which is why I use StrengthsFinder 2.0.[23] It is nonthreatening, positive, and an easy way to start an open conversation with students. Who does not love to talk about themselves?

To prepare for my first coaching sessions, I review the students' strengths so that I am prepared with the right questions to ask them about themselves, their strengths, and their future career goals. As James noted, the best formula for success and building trust with your students is preparation.[24] Demonstrating your competence and compassion is key to building trust.[25] This allows you to have the most impact.

Effective coaching is really about asking the right questions.[26] This comes with practice and by reading the student who is in front of you. As you get to know your students through their strengths and answers, you understand the best questions to ask to get to know them and to help them to know themselves better. As James suggests, "Knowing the right questions to ask builds trust."[27]

During our first coaching session together, I find it best to lead with open-ended questions, such as, "What is your dream job?" When I ask this, most students are usually stunned, as if this is irrelevant to our conversation and to their career plans. But I use this question to help them realize that their dream job is usually strongly linked to their strengths in a way that they might not have realized.

Next, I ask them how they plan to move from where they are now to where they want to be in their career. This is where most students are stumped. Their companies are not really helping them make this leap from here to there. This is where my previous work experience in human resources for General Motors helps, as I have seen and helped employees navigate the murky waters of the corporate ladder. I can suggest people to connect with for informational interviews, which companies might offer the opportunities that they are looking for, and developmental opportunities outside of work that will help them get the extra experience they need to move up the corporate ladder. It is all a matter of matching strengths to interest and opportunity.

As much as asking questions is helpful, listening to students is important as they navigate their way through their strengths.[28] Many students start the strengths process unsure about why they are going through this process or unclear about what they will gain by doing it, but they come out on the other end with an optimistic view of themselves and their future career. Many gain a new level of self-confidence once they realize that they are in charge of their future and that their strengths can get them where they want to go.

Results

After three years of coaching graduate students, I have ranked the top categories that explain how students feel about strengths coaching and what is has done for them in table 7.1.

One of the most important things I can do as a strengths coach is to help them identify their strengths as something unique and distinctive about them. Most of the time, students will look at their strengths and say, "Yes, so?" Their strengths are usually things that they know about themselves, but they figure that everyone can do the same things that they can

Table 7.1 StrengthsFinder coaching results.

StrengthsFinder and Coaching led to	Rank Order
A new career strategy	1
Renewed confidence	2
Aligning my strengths with my career path	3
Helping me to be more open to change in the future	4
Trusting in the value of my strengths	5
Being content with my current situation	6

do. It is not until I put the strengths of the class together on a spreadsheet and highlight which strengths are unique to them individually that they finally get the idea that a strength is theirs to cherish and have pride in, not to just grudgingly acknowledge. The difference between acceptance and embracing means the difference between a career and a calling. I have found that this gives students a new level of confidence in themselves— and thus why it so important.

Below are some quotes from graduate students and their thoughts about coaching:

> Among the new insights I learned about myself as a result of coaching is that I am where I need to be at this time, which was a pleasant revelation for me.—A.W.

> Through this process, I have found a much greater appreciation for the individualization of skills. I had a hard time understanding how my soft skills benefited a technical area like accounting. I understand better how what I am good at translates into my career path and how I can leverage those skills as I progress in my field. I have a lot to consider and some actions to take. The biggest thing I am taking away from this assignment is to stop focusing on the things I am not as strong at and stop trying to make myself fill those spaces. Trust in the value of my strengths and focus my efforts there. There is a need and a purpose for my combination of skills and nothing to apologize for or to fix.—C.P.

> Thank you for making time for individual coaching! I'm thankful that I signed up early for the sessions. The first coaching session built my confidence and provided some new options for exploration. The real aha is I never considered teaching—outside of Sunday school at church. As I've had time to think more about the possibility, I find it more appealing. Several of my colleagues from class have encouraged me to teach since I shared my personal development plan last week in class. The coaching session allowed me to see my strengths from your viewpoint and that was helpful and rewarding.—D.L.

> Coaching has helped me explore additional ways I can achieve my goals. I have looked at my strengths and how important they are to the advancement of my career. I was always aware that I had certain abilities but I was not aware that they were strengths, and that there is a method to align those with your career path.—R.L.

> I really appreciate the time spent providing our class with coaching sessions. I happen to already have a defined goal for my career path over the next five years, but found the advice she provided for searching, connecting,

and making opportunities with others in my industry of interest, very helpful. The exercise of analyzing our strengths was also incredibly positive in
affirming my career goals, in addition to providing helpful insight into the
areas which I excel in.—J.G.

In addition, once they see their strengths lined up along with their classmates, they see the power of using strengths in a team setting. When they
know their own strengths and those of their team members, they understand the motivation of their team members in a new way. Things people
do and say are not personal anymore; it is just how they are hardwired.
We now appreciate that person who is the glue for the team or who keeps
the team running on schedule. Often, students take StrengthsFinder 2.0 to
work with them to use there as well:

> Being made aware of the strengths, it has given me a newfound confidence
> in myself and my abilities. I plan to take these with me in the future, not
> only in searching for a new career, but also in my everyday life. I will use
> these strengths to help make myself a better person, friend, and colleague. It
> also will make me aware of other people's strengths and will give me a way
> to connect and communicate with them on another level.—S.G.

> From the very helpful coaching sessions, I gained further insights into how
> I might be able to tap into other people's strengths to help move my project
> forward.—J.C.

Knowing and appreciating one's strengths gives someone new areas for
career exploration, whether at a current employer or at a new one. Many
times, we feel stuck in jobs, underutilized or underappreciated, and we don't
know why. With a better understanding of our strengths, we see that if we
are not fully utilizing our strengths, we will not fully be happy and engaged.
This gives students permission to find new jobs, employers, and careers:

> The coaching that I have received has helped reshape my opinion of myself
> and the steps I will take to achieve my goals. The information given during
> the coaching sessions has restructured my strategy for changing my career
> from technical to business based. This class is essential within the MBA
> program because it has helped me and others identify areas of interest that
> we may have not been previously aware.—R.B.

> As I reflect back to this process of creating a personal development plan, I
> realize that the coaching sessions have been very helpful in gathering my
> thoughts and putting them into action. Just the act of saying what I wanted

out loud and sharing it with Dr. Mishra, my director, and Six Sigma Black Belts has helped me solidify my commitment to this career path. The coaching sessions helped me understand that I needed to have a solid plan in place and to consider what I needed to do to get there. They also helped me work through any doubts I had in accomplishing my goals.—A.O.

Throughout the semester my executive coaching sessions have helped me reinforce my strengths and helped me focus on defining my personal and professional goals. As a result of the coaching, I have learned more about myself, and what opportunities are out there for me. The coaching has really made me consider what direction I want to move in professionally after MBA school is complete. After the coaching sessions, I am confident that taking a new direction from my current employer is likely the best thing for me. It will allow me a chance to do something entirely different and help boost my professional skills. By creating a personal development plan, I'm well posed to achieve many great things.—J.H.

Finally, understanding and appreciating strengths have helped many students identify passions outside of work that they have left dormant or assumed were an outside activity, such as fund-raising or community activism. Once students embrace these interests and see how they are tied to their strengths, they are able to find ways to bring them into their workplaces to build a more engaging career:

"Choose a job you love, and you will never have to work a day in your life."—Confucius. I have learned quite a bit about myself through completing the SF 2.0 questionnaire and through career coaching. I have determined that upon graduation, I would like to pursue a career that has more of a focus on uplifting my community.—C.G.

Making Strengths Coaching Sustainable

This type of individualized coaching is very labor-intensive and may rely on one faculty or staff member who enjoys or has a strength in coaching. Depending on the number of students involved, this can be as time-consuming as teaching an additional course section each semester. One way to make this coaching model sustainable is to find a coaching partner. For instance, at William and Mary, over 100 retired and semiretired business executives provide coaching and mentoring for business students. Mohan Peter, one of the lead coaches at William and Mary, describes their MBA coaching: "Constant feedback is a mantra with us and it is gratifying to see our students learning to receive and give meaningful feedback. The students have consistently rated this as one of the best experiences in their MBA life and it is truly heartwarming when we as coaches hear back from our students about them coaching their reports and peers at work. That is the ultimate reward for our coaches."

To make coaching sustainable, one MBA in the southeast has partnered with a local ICF-certified coaching program, the Raleigh Coaching Academy. Each of the Raleigh Coaching Academy's students must provide 30 hours of pro bono coaching to fulfill their ICF certification. The partnership allows each MBA student to have 10 free hours of additional coaching once they have completed the MBA course where they had their initial strengths coaching. This is a win-win partnership that allows students to continue to receive coaching and RCA graduates to fulfill their coaching hours.

Many practitioner articles lament the fact that today's managers are not equipped with effective communication skills that can build trust with their employees. By providing coaching for future managers while they are in graduate school, they will have the tools necessary to learn to listen and communicate with empathy with their employees in the future. This also helps build trust between the school and the students, as students feel that they are receiving something more than just credit for their coursework. While they are students, they are gaining confidence in themselves and their strengths. In addition, they are receiving training that will help them build a more trusting relationship with their own employees in the future.

Notes

1. Lydia Said, "Global Education Experts Call for Closer School-Workplace Ties," Gallup, November 3, 2015. http://www.gallup.com/opinion/gallup/186458/global-education-experts-call-closer-school-workplaceties.aspx?g_source=CATEGORY_EDUCATION&g_medium=topic&g_campaign=tiles.

2. Lynn Schroeder, "Collaborate to Make Work Better," Chief Learning Officer, March 1, 2016. http://www.clomedia.com/articles/6751-collaborate-to-make-work-better.

3. Chuck Tomkovick and Scott Swanson, "Using StrengthsFinder to Identify Relationships between Marketing Graduate Strengths and Career Outcomes," *Marketing Education Review* 24, no. 3 (2014): 197–211.

4. "What Is the Difference between a Talent and a Strength?," Gallup, accessed 2016. http://strengths.gallup.com/help/general/125543/difference-talent-strength.aspx.

5. "Driving Long-term Success for Graduates Careers and Lives," Gallup, November 25, 2014. http://www.gallup.com/services/179768/gallup-higher-education-solutions.aspx.

6. Ibid.

7. Tomkovick and Swanson, "Using StrengthsFinder."

8. Ibid.

9. "What Followers Want from Leaders," Gallup, January 8, 2009. http://www.gallup.com/businessjournal/113542/what-followers-want-from-leaders.aspx.

10. Martin E. P. Seligman and Mihaly Csikszentmihalyi, "Special Issue on Happiness, Excellence, and Optimal Human Functioning," *American Psychologist* 55, no. 1 (2000): 5–183.

11. "Driving Long-term Success."

12. Doug MacKie, "The Effectiveness of Strength-based Executive Coaching in Enhancing Full Range Leadership Development: A Controlled Study," *Consulting Psychology Journal: Practice and Research* 66, no. 2 (2014): 118–137.

13. "Coaching FAQs," International Coach Federation, accessed 2016. http://coachfederation.org/need/landing.cfm?ItemNumber=978.

14. Larry Braskamp, *The StrengthsQuest Guidebook: Introducing Strengths-based Development and StrengthsQuest to Higher Education Leaders* (Princeton, NJ: The Gallup Organization, 2000), 1–6.

15. Diane Coutu and Carol Kaufmann, "HBR Research Report: What Can Coaches Do for You?," *Harvard Business Review* 87, no. 1 (2009): 1–7.

16. Kay M. Bower, "Leadership Coaching: Does It *Really* Provide Value?," *Journal of Practical Consulting* 4, no. 1 (2012): 1–5.

17. Laurie A. Schreiner and Edward "Chip" Anderson, "Strengths-based Advising: A New Lens for Higher Education," *NACADA Journal* 25, no. 2 (2005): 20–29.

18. Deborah Butler, Lisa Johnson, and Benjamin Forbes, "An Examination of a Skills-based Leadership Coaching Course in an MBA Program," *Journal of Education for Business* 83, no. 4 (2008): 227–232.

19. Ibid.

20. Richard E. Boyatzis, Melvin L. Smith, and Nancy Blaize, "Developing Sustainable Leaders through Coaching and Compassion," *Academy of Management Learning & Education* 5, no. 1 (2006): 8–24.

21. Ibid.

22. Ibid.

23. Joseph Casey and Denis Wuestman, "Lean Leadership: Coaching to Connect the Dots," *Strategic Finance* 97, no. 5 (2015): 23–25.

24. Angela James, "Earning Trust in the First Five Minutes: A Formula for Impact," *CliftonStrengths Coaching Blog*, December 4, 2014. http://coaching.gallup.com/2014/12/earning-trust-in-first-five-minutes.html.

25. Aneil K. Mishra and Karen E. Mishra, *Becoming a Trustworthy Leader: Psychology and Practice* (New York: Routledge, 2013).

26. Casey and Wuestman, "Lean Leadership."

27. James, "Earning Trust."

28. Casey and Wuestman, "Lean Leadership."

CHAPTER EIGHT

Developing Critical Skills: Lessons Learned from the Front Line

Laura Graham

In the movie *Taken*, Liam Neeson, as ex-CIA agent and beleaguered father Brian Mills, gives an iconic speech to the movie's antagonists who have kidnapped his daughter. Even if you haven't seen the movie, you probably know the opening lines: "I don't know who you are. I don't know what you want. If you're looking for ransom, I can tell you I don't have money, but what I do have are a very particular set of skills. Skills I have acquired over a very long career." Brian Mills and I have a few things in common. I may not be able to rescue a girl from traffickers or win Parent of the Year, Hardcore Division, but I too have a particular set of skills acquired over a long career. I teach college-level communications courses, and I spend my days teaching students critical skills to help them find their authentic, professional voices.

After more than 15 years in corporate and academic roles, my vantage point gives me a frontline view of the struggles our students face during school and when they start interviewing for internships and jobs. Students with good insights and interesting ideas can't adequately articulate them in written or oral presentations. Otherwise strong students repeatedly get passed over for jobs, or struggle getting into graduate school, or end up underemployed. Many of these students have the technical and functional skills they need to be successful in their fields, but they're missing "a particular set of skills," and that keeps them from reaching their goals.

For today's college students, then, the questions, become the following:

- What are those critical skills?
- Is there a gap between what they know and what they need?
- How can schools and universities teach these skills?
- How can students improve their skills even more on their own?

In this chapter, we'll look at each of the above questions so students, parents, administrators, and faculty have a clearer understanding of what skills students need and what we all can do to help develop those skills.

What Critical Skills Do Students Need?

To determine which skills are "critical," we need to answer a couple of questions first: Critical for what? Critical to whom? Other chapters in this book discuss performance measures for institutions of higher learning, and politicians and academicians currently engage in important conversations about results-oriented funding, employment rates and starting pay, and graduation rates.[1] The answer to these questions influence our goals as professors and set society's expectations for what outcomes students, employers, and the rest of us can expect and should demand.

Defining which skills are critical depends on whom the skills should benefit and where the skills will be applied. To use the current vernacular, who is the "customer"—the students and their families, the companies that will hire them, or society and the taxpayers who help fund the schools and pay for financial aid? If the student is the customer, then our decisions should be based on what the student's/customer's needs are. If the focus is the company who eventually hires the student, then we should develop courses and programs to prepare students to be good employees in the most important industries and positions. If our ultimate goal is providing taxpayers a return on their investments and an increase in contributing members of society, then we will produce citizen-scholars who work for the larger good.

What does each group think the critical skills are, and is there overlap or a common set of skills we can agree are critical to success in college and beyond, regardless of a particular perspective?

Students

Why do students choose to attend college in the first place? The Cooperative Institutional Research Program (CIPRA) at the Higher Education Research Institute at UCLA released its freshman survey in which today's college students list a number of reasons as "very important" when deciding to attend college:

- To be able to get a better job   85%
- To learn more about things that interest me   82
- To get training for a specific career   76
- To gain a general education and appreciation of ideas   72
- To be able to make more money   70
- To prepare myself for graduate or professional school   59[2]

According to another survey, conducted by the Association of American Colleges and Universities in 2015, students rank the following college learning outcomes as most important:

- Critical thinking and analytical reasoning skills   79%
- The ability to apply knowledge and skills to real-world settings   79
- The ability to effectively communicate orally   78
- The ability to work effectively with others in teams   77
- The ability to effectively communicate in writing   75[3]

Students want to get training and instruction to gain competency, get jobs or continue their education, and make money. They list developing communication, critical thinking, and teamwork skills as the most important learning outcomes—regardless of major.

Next, let's look at what employers and other business professionals want from the college graduates that they hire.

Employers

Employers are not coy about the skills they want in new hires. Across a wide variety of groups surveyed, common themes emerge. Employers need workers who can think, talk, write, and work in teams within their respective fields.[4]

Burning Glass Technologies, a job market research and analytics firm, conducted a survey of 25 million job ads in 2015. Their survey found that the top-three most critical skills employers are looking for are oral communication skills, organizational skills, and written communication skills.[5] Job search site Indeed.com reports that mentions of "critical thinking" in job search ads have doubled since 2009.[6] "We hear it over and over again," says Deborah Brame, director of student professional development at North Carolina Central University's School of Business. "Companies want strong communication skills."

In fact, the 2015 AACU survey asked employers to rate various learning outcomes, and their top-five choices were the following:

- Critical thinking and analytical reasoning skills   81%
- The ability to effectively communicate orally   85%
- The ability to work effectively with others in teams   83%
- The ability to effectively communicate in writing   82%
- Ethical judgment and decision making   81%[7]

As someone who has taught these skills to a wide range of students, from humanities, business, and technical majors to welding and automotive mechanics students, what's interesting to me is that these "soft skills" are seen as critical across industries and types of positions. Moreover, I'm a proponent of liberal arts education and giving students a "broad knowledge in a variety of areas of study," and employers agree.[8] According to the AACU 2013 survey, 80 percent of employers support such broad knowledge regardless of their major.[9]

On the other hand, no one is suggesting that the technical skills required for an industry are unimportant. In fact, three in five employers say it takes both field-specific knowledge and soft skills to be successful in the workplace.[10] However, just three years ago, nearly all the AACU employer respondents (95%) agreed that "a candidate's demonstrated capacity to think critically, communicate clearly, and solve complex problems is *more important* than their undergraduate major."[11]

In examining what recruiters want, Dr. James O'Rourke of the Fanning Center for Business Communication at Notre Dame found that the ability to interact successfully with others is the most desired trait; however, it can be the most difficult to find. Furthermore, technical skills are important for getting hired, but employers' needs change rapidly. "What got you in the door changes," says O'Rourke. "Tech skills are ephemeral, but soft skills are surprisingly durable."

Burning Glass's survey reports one in three skills requested in job ads are one of the soft skills. "Even in the most technical career areas (such as IT, Healthcare, and Engineering), more than a quarter of all skill requirements are for baseline skills."[12] According to James O'Rourke, the rise in interest in these soft skills can be traced back to the 1990s: "1990 was an inflection point, where the skill set for managers shifted." As management tasks were automated, the role of managers changed, requiring more focus on communication and critical thinking.

So, both students and employers agree that communication, teamwork, and critical thinking are important skills. Do taxpayers and society agree?

Taxpayers

Depending on which study you read, taxpayers subsidize an average of 53 percent of colleges' costs for instruction, student support, and administration. Room and board as well as athletics or student health fees aren't included in this figure.[13] That's a big investment. What do taxpayers get for that investment? According to the report "Education Pays: The Benefits of Higher Education for Individuals and Society,"

- All levels of government—federal, state, and local—receive increased tax revenues from college graduates.
- College graduates use fewer income support and other social programs in their lifetimes.
- Graduates are more active volunteers and voters.
- Graduation from college increases the chances that adults will move up in socioeconomic attainment.[14]

Let's think again about that "particular set of skills" from the opening of this chapter. In many ways, students, employers, and society all want to be or have the same thing: well-rounded graduates with discipline-specific knowledge and a particular set of skills that give them the confidence and the ability to add value as employees and citizens as well as to advocate for themselves and their ideas. These stakeholders agree on a short list of skills students need for success both in and out of college:

- Oral and written communication
- Critical thinking
- Working in teams

These skills cut across industries and specific positions and provide a pathway to reaching goals of students, future employers, and society.

But what, exactly, do students need to know how to do to be considered an effective speaker? How do we know that they can think? What does it mean to be a successful team player? What, exactly, should students be able to do?

Critical Skill #1: Oral and Written Communication

It's easy to think of communication skills being centered on large-scale presentations and 20-page reports with excellent grammar, but effective oral communication also has to include interpersonal and group communication.

According to Carla Ross, an associate professor of communications at Meredith College, "If you're going to be a leader in business, you need organizational communication skills, interpersonal skills—not just public speaking skills."

Effective written skills include being able to analyze an audience and situation in order to know what to write and to whom. Just as someone can be an excellent public speaker but rubbish working in a team, one can also turn in technically correct reports that are tone-deaf and unpersuasive due to poor audience analysis. "Good communication is flexible and adapts to the audience," says Ross. "Knowing your audience—that's huge."

Conrad and Newberry conducted an extensive review of 217 organizational and managerial leadership and business communication publications to identify and classify "the most frequently cited communication skills needed in business."[15] They developed a list of 24 skills and broke them into three major groupings: organizational communication, leadership communication, and interpersonal communication (see tables 8.1, 8.2, and 8.3).

What I like about this skills list is the focus on practical outcomes. These are skills we actually expect the students to be able to accomplish in whatever discipline-specific setting they find themselves. The outcomes listed here provide concrete ways in which to design and assess assignments to make sure I'm covering the most important skills.

Critical Skill #2: Critical Thinking

Critical thinking is difficult to define because there's no generally received definition of the skill. While mentions in job ads for "critical thinking skills" increase, employers still have difficulty in nailing down what they actually mean when they ask for those skills in their job candidates.[16]

One way to describe critical thinking is that it "encompasses the application of knowledge after careful and measured examination of all information and view points, to make decisions that are non-egocentric in nature."[17] The AACU, in its critical values rubric, defines it as "a habit of mind characterized by the comprehensive exploration of issues, ideas, artifacts, and events before accepting or formulating an opinion or conclusion." The Meredith College Think Strong program defines critical thinking as "a purposeful, self-directed process in which you take charge of knowledge, use reason to propel your scholarship and solve problems, and integrate these skills in your intellectual endeavors and actions."

Table 8.1 Organizational communication skills.

Skill Summary	Outcome
Initiating open discussion	The ability to create discussion and dialogue, explore opposition by individuals who advocate their positions, and convince others to adopt those positions through logic, argument, or debate
Resolving conflict	The ability to employ a range of processes aimed at alleviating or eliminating sources of conflict through processes including negotiation, mediation, and diplomacy
Creating information networks	The ability to design and institute formal or informal systems for managing the flow of information and providing person-to-person relationships through which information flows
Teaching important skills	The ability to provide skill remediation to employees in areas such as job performance, technical competency, interpersonal communication, and problem solving
Using information technology	The ability to employ equipment (usually computers) that enables managers and staff to access ongoing and relevant company information, including reports, planning data, and employee and customer feedback
Providing performance feedback	The ability to assess employee performance and provide performance feedback as a review of employees' performance
Negotiating	The ability to produce an agreement on courses of action, to bargain for individual or collective advantage, or to craft outcomes to satisfy various interests
Writing business correspondence	The ability to produce written communication used in business, including letters, memos, bulletins, and reports
Making convincing presentations	The ability to provide informal or formal talks delivered to decision-making groups to convey information or make a point

Source: D. Conrad and R. Newberry, "Identification and Instruction of Important Business Communication Skills for Graduate Business Education," *Journal of Education for Business* 87, no. 2 (2012): 112–120. doi:10.1080/08832323.2011.576280.

Table 8.2   Interpersonal communication skills.

Skill Summary	Outcome
Active listening	The ability to employ an interpersonal and interactive process to actively focus on, interpret, and respond verbally and nonverbally to messages
Building rapport	The ability to create a harmonious relationship, bond, or kinship based on mutual respect, friendship, camaraderie, or emotional ties, making someone feel comfortable and accepted
Demonstrating emotional self-control	The ability to display balanced models through retaining, mastering, and dominating one's reactions provoked by pleasant or unpleasant emotion
Building trust	The ability to construct the reciprocal faith in others' intentions and behavior through a shared belief that you can depend on each other to achieve a common purpose
Relating to people of diverse backgrounds	The ability to recognize and respect differences in people and communicate appropriately in verbal and nonverbal exchanges
Demonstrating respect	The ability to show esteem for or a sense of the worth or excellence of a person, a personal quality or ability, or something considered as a manifestation of a personal quality or ability
Building relationships	The ability to establish a relatively long-term association between two or more people based on liking, trust, and respect, creating regular business interactions, interdependence, or some other type of social commitment

Source: D. Conrad and R. Newberry, "Identification and Instruction of Important Business Communication Skills for Graduate Business Education," *Journal of Education for Business* 87, no. 2 (2012): 112–120. doi:10.1080/08832323.2011.576280.

Regardless of what specific definition is used, critical thinking includes the following characteristics:

- Self-reflection—the ability to recognize and examine your own biases and privilege and to realize how they affect decision making
- Independence—the ability to stand your ground and form your own opinions and solutions without being unduly influenced by others

Table 8.3 Leadership communication skills.

Skill Summary	Outcome
Arousing enthusiasm	The ability to inspire a whole-hearted devotion to an ideal cause, study or pursuit, or merely being visibly excited about what one's doing.
Being a change catalyst	The ability to initiate change through providing information to employees that will convince them of why a change in necessary and will compel them to embrace it.
Creating group synergy	The ability to compel organizational members to interact and produce a joint effect that is greater than the sum of the members acting alone.
Building team bonds	The ability to establish team cohesiveness, which is the extent to which members stick together and remain united in the pursuit of a common goal.
Expressing encouragement	The ability to provide support and confidence, raising or increasing an individual's self-esteem and confidence to make choices and decisions.
Providing motivation	The ability to move a person or group toward desired goals by increasing his or her willingness to exert effort and energy to achieve the goals.
Being persuasive	The ability to guide people toward the adoption of an idea, attitude, or action by rational and logical means relying on appeals rather than coercion.
Building optimism	The ability to create a disposition or tendency to look on the more favorable side of events or conditions and to expect that most favorable outcome despite obstacles and setbacks.

Source: D. Conrad and R. Newberry, "Identification and Instruction of Important Business Communication Skills for Graduate Business Education," *Journal of Education for Business* 87, no. 2 (2012): 112–120. doi:10.1080/08832323.2011.576280.

- Creativity—the ability to innovate, creating new ideas, solutions, and areas of inquiry
- Curiosity—the ability to take an interest in the world and other people along with the desire to learn something new
- Analysis—the ability to gather and examine information and insights from a variety of sources to determine validity and usefulness
- Decisiveness—the ability to make a decision based on the best analysis available, even in the absence of complete information

In other words, we want students to be able to look at information from multiple sources, taking into consideration others' viewpoints while blocking their own egos and biases, in order to make good decisions and ask good questions.

Critical Skill #3: Working in Teams

The term *teamwork* implies working together in a group with common goals and interacting over time to achieve a common objective. Successful teams are characterized by compromise and respect as well as clearly understood and functional roles and a commitment to accountability and open communication.[18] In general, millennial students are used to working in teams and tend to be good at it.[19]

Many students I've taught, however, dislike working on group projects, largely because of bad past experiences. They're certain they can do the work better and faster on their own. Another reason students dislike group work is the difficulty of coordinating disparate schedules to arrange meetings. While these are real challenges requiring extra effort to overcome, and they cause almost as much headache for the instructor as the students, we keep insisting on assigning group projects and assignments. Why?

First, working in teams is an important skill for success (see above), and second, when done well, group work helps students be more engaged and to develop stronger interpersonal skills in both seated and online classes.[20] In fact, Ku found that students satisfied with their teams were more satisfied overall with their online class experience.[21] Graham reports that the inclusion of "learning communities," which can include study groups and other team-based learning interventions, increases the persistence of STEM students to graduation.[22]

Effective teamwork requires specific interpersonal skills, such as the ability to give and receive constructive feedback. The lists of communication skills from tables 8.1, 8.2, and 8.3 include several skills and outcomes that deal directly with group communication. In fact, each of the interpersonal communication skills, such as active listening and building rapport, is applicable for team settings, along with several of the leadership communication skills.

Learning to work effectively in geographically diverse teams is becoming more important, too. I include a group project in my online class sections *because* of its logistical challenges, not in spite of them. It's important to give my students the experience of working in a virtual team because as the market has become more and more global, many work teams today are not colocated. In a 2012 survey conducted by the Society for Human Resource

Management, 46 percent of respondents indicated their organizations use virtual teams to boost productivity, utilize global talent, and minimize costs.[23]

Now that we've identified and defined the skills we want, let's take a look at the distance between what students need and what they have when it comes to these critical skills.

Is There a Gap in Millennial Students' Critical Skills?

Students just starting college must think they need additional instruction in the critical soft skills we've been discussing or they wouldn't have reported them as major learning objectives.[24] Indeed, some students understand they have significant work to do in specific areas. For example, 21 percent of freshmen surveyed either had taken or expected to need remedial writing instruction in college.[25]

Because I teach written and oral communications as well as interviewing and job search skills, I see a broad range of student issues. Of course, there are the high achievers who already have these critical skills, but the majority of my students have issues with one or more communication, teamwork, or critical thinking skills. I find their writing skills—everything from basic grammar and mechanics to using effective support and persuasion—especially troubling. For example, many of my students regularly use the wrong words because they write the way the words sound when spoken, not how they should be written: "should of" versus "should have" is a common error.

They also often confuse opinion for evidence, as though their belief that something is true is the same as if it were actually true. I remember an extensive conversation with a student who just could not process the fact that the statement in his paper that professors who use PowerPoint slides were less popular than those that did not required actual evidence to back it up. "I believe" and "everyone knows" still feature prominently in some students' work. What I'm working on right now, however, is teaching them to be able to take the audience's perspective so they can decide what evidence, topics, and reasoning will be most successful in informing or persuading.

College administrators and instructors see a need for increased interpersonal skills as well. Brittany Hochstaetter, the administrative department head at Wake Tech Community College, works with students every day: "They need to learn to advocate for themselves, to read nonverbal feedback and learn to negotiate—especially face-to-face."

Some students have to be reminded about basic skills and even exhibit poor communication in daily interactions. "I remember one student," says Deborah Brame, "who sent me an e-mail that said, 'I have a question.' That was it—no salutation, no introduction, and no actual question."

Carla Ross agrees. "Common courtesy isn't so common, unfortunately," says Ross. "I had students who could not understand why texting while someone is talking is rude."

The real concern is how these skill deficiencies affect the students when it's time to interview for jobs and internships. Unfortunately, Brame sees the same problems in the interview process: "Students have trouble during interviews making connections between what's on their résumé and what the interviewer is asking. They answer questions with just a few words, don't use good eye contact, and recruiters say they feel like they're pulling information out of the students."

Mind the Gap

We might not expect new students to be masters of these skills yet, but what is more concerning is that employers are still reporting skill deficiencies once students graduate. There is certainly a gap between how prepared *students* think they are and how prepared *employers* think new graduates are.

A 2006 survey by the Conference Board found that lack of basic writing skills as well as applied written communication skills was a serious issue with college graduates:

> Nearly half the employer respondents (46 percent) report that two-year college graduates are "deficient" in basic Writing in English; over a quarter (26 percent) rate four-year college graduates "deficient" in basic Writing in English. And when asked about applied skills, almost half of the employer respondents report "deficiencies" in Written Communications among two-year college graduates (47 percent), while over a quarter (27 percent) report this as a "deficiency" among four-year college graduates.[26]

Unfortunately, more recent research also points to a similar lack of interpersonal and oral communication and critical thinking skills among college students and recent graduates.[27]

Research does show that millennial students are used to working in teams.[28] In fact, employers rated recent graduates highest in "working with others in teams."[29] Unfortunately, even in these skill sets, employers don't give recent graduates very high marks.

The below chart (figure 8.1), based on findings in the 2015 AACU survey, indicates the serious gap between student and employer perceptions. Students rate themselves as much more skilled than employers do.[30]

Why are college graduates still missing these critical skills? No doubt there are a variety of factors, but researchers often point to the use of

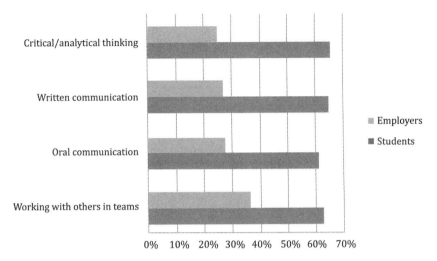

Figure 8.1   Relative importance of several critical skills.

technology, parental influence, and lack of preparation in schools and universities.[31]

Some research shows that millennial students—digital natives who have spent their lives connected—have different brains than Gen Xer digital immigrants like my generation. According to Gary Small, the director of UCLA's Memory and Aging Research Center at the Semel Institute for Neuroscience and Human Behavior, constant and early exposure to technology has rewired millennial brains to be better at some tasks, such as multitasking. And regardless of whether brains are in the process of being rewired to be better at multitasking, "better" is relative, as there is a large body of research that indicates multitasking harms student test scores, GPA, and general academic performance.[32] Another downside is that the time spent connected and plugged in to technology has hurt millennials' people skills. Fortunately, Small also points out that brains are flexible, malleable, and able to be retrained.[33]

In my classes, I see a lack of critical thinking skills that manifests itself in an inability to analyze and evaluate content or draw conclusions from specific instance to general principle. Students struggle to implement planning and reflection into their process before skipping right to implementation. There's a lack of patience in handling data as well; when they are given an assignment, they want to google the topic and pick the first three results rather than digging deeper.

Research finds this lack of "information literacy" in students in other countries and in other schools than mine.[34] Researching this topic for this chapter, however, has shown me that I sometimes confuse my students' technical literacy with informational literacy and that I need to do a better job in my classes of teaching the effective use of information and information literacy as a separate skill.

Carla Ross taught a "netiquette" class in the Meredith College PRISM program, a precursor to the current "Think Strong" critical thinking training program. She spent significant time teaching students to make connections between the pieces of information they found online as well as learning to evaluate it. "I taught them to question information before putting it in the knowledge base. Who said that? Where did it come from? Why can't we just take information from *Wikipedia*?" says Ross.

Today's students have a strong grasp on technology, but they need to learn to use technology as a tool to aid communication, teamwork, and problem solving, not as an end in itself.

> If Millennials are going to become valued knowledge workers, they must learn not only what information to gather, but also how to verify and understand it in context. In order to analyze, synthesize, and represent that information in a way that is relevant to the problem at hand, they will need to know more than how to scan; they need to learn to read deeply and between the lines.[35]

In addition to the use of technology, other factors contribute to students' lack of communication and basic work-readiness skills. Some point to the role parents play in hampering students' skill development.[36] On one hand, there are parents who lack communication and professional skills themselves, so their children lack a model to emulate. Majumder found a correlation between parenting style and academic achievement in higher education, with the uninvolved style producing lower academic achievement.[37] Carla Ross also sees a decline in what skills students develop before college. "They're not getting these things at home," she says. "After 30 years of teaching, it's a breakdown on all levels."

On the other end of the spectrum, there are overinvolved parents who may hinder their children's development by running interference for them and not allowing them to hone these critical skills.[38] Empathy—the ability to put oneself in another's position—is necessary for effective audience analysis, persuasion, and interpersonal communication, but "helicopter parenting" promotes a sense of narcissism and entitlement.[39] Dina Maloney, from EPIC Coaching and Consulting, concurs: "Parents are enabling their kids; they think they're helping, but they're not. Students could save themselves, but they don't get the opportunity."

Whether it's due to the use of technology or modern parenting, clearly, there's a skills gap with today's students. Unfortunately, that gap isn't being closed during the school years either.[40]

Amy Griswold, who teaches at Texas Woman's University, sees a disparity among students from different educational systems: "Sometimes it depends on the states they come from. For example, students from Texas schools have better skills than students I taught from North Carolina schools." Griswold points out that many high school English departments no longer focus on grammar: "They read and talk about books, but there's not much focus on writing." This lack of focus may have been due to a lack of grammar assessment required in the now-discontinued No Child Left Behind standards and tests.[41]

Unfortunately, there can be a disconnect between what colleges and universities (and the governing bodies that oversee them) say they want and what they are willing to require and support. It's a classic example of "rewarding A while hoping for B."[42] If you don't require communications classes or provide support for additional services, you can't expect student skills to improve. For example, in 2014, community colleges in North Carolina produced a new Comprehensive Articulation Agreement so that community college graduates would know what classes would transfer to four-year universities in the UNC system.[43] If classes won't transfer, then students have to retake those classes or take another class to make up for the hours in their BA/BS degree program. According to the CAA,

> The Associate in Arts (AA) and Associate in Science (AS) degree programs include general education requirements that represent the fundamental foundation for success and include study in the areas of English composition, communications, humanities and fine arts, natural sciences and mathematics, and social and behavioral sciences. Within these discipline areas, community colleges must include opportunities for the achievement of competence in reading, writing, oral communication, fundamental mathematical skills, and basic computer use.

Unfortunately, despite this ostensible commitment to general oral communications, the focus seems to be only on presentations. According to Brittany Hochstaetter, "Only public speaking is a UGETC (universally transferrable course) despite the need for interpersonal skills."

To get students workforce ready, today's colleges and universities need to develop specific programs and strategies to teach, develop, and practice critical soft skills, and many schools have done just that. Next, we'll look at what some schools are doing to help their students.

How Can Colleges and Universities Help Students Develop These Critical Skills?

Despite the above issues, in general, administrators and faculty are realizing the need for intensive communication, critical thinking, and teamwork skills training, and many schools are developing programs to address these needs. However, it's vital that we make sure these efforts actually produce the changes we want. After all, most schools have been offering public speaking and freshman composition classes for decades, but their graduates still get low marks in the workplace for oral and written communication skills.

Education for Use

Conrad and Newberry suggest that one explanation for the gap between the practical outcomes employers expect and the graduates' actual skills is the way these critical skills are taught in school.[44] The discrepancy may be the result of instructors' "emphasis on theories and models versus practitioners' emphasis on skills and abilities that produce practical outcomes."

This chapter is not the place for an exhaustive discussion of the theory versus practice debate in higher education. Theoretical research is an important part of the academy and helps those of us who take a more applied approach describe what is happening in a given situation and sometimes to predict possible outcomes. For example, in marketing communications classes, research on cognitive biases helps explain advertising strategies.

Over the last few years, however, my teaching style and practice has changed. Previously, I spent a lot more class time on theories and principles, believing that students could then extrapolate from the principles and apply them in myriad situations, especially when I had students in many different courses of study. We would complete homework and in-class exercises and speeches, but I also gave written exams to test their recall of theories and seminal research. Today, I no longer give written exams. Although I still teach the theories and research that underpin the practical exercises and outcomes, all major assignments require students to apply the principles, techniques, and tools we cover in class to demonstrate their skills.

In addition, I draw more explicit connections between what we study in class and how students can use those skills in other college classes and in their future careers. For example, recently in class, after independently studying the principles of effective report writing via a reading assignment and online simulation, the students worked in small groups in a directed analysis of a sample report. After discussing the strengths and weaknesses of the item and how it could have been improved, we discussed how they could use these same techniques and examples to improve future assignments in our class as well as reports, papers, and analyses they would complete in other classes. Since making these changes, I have had many more students tell me how they've been using our classwork to help them in interviews, essays, and discussions in other classes.

Obviously, this focus on praxis—using a set of theories or principles in application or "doing"—isn't a new concept. In 1944, Eduard Lindemann concluded that the purpose of adult education is "education for use."[45] However, in teaching soft skills, perhaps we need a more application-driven approach.

What follows isn't an exhaustive catalog of programs and strategies, but is rather an overview of the kinds of ways higher education is addressing the need for critical skills, using specific programs and institutions as examples.

Communication across Disciplines

Some colleges and universities have developed oral and written communication programs that decentralize the teaching of communication skills. For example, rather than teaching writing solely in English departments, many schools are focusing on discipline-specific writing and teaching students to write for specific applications for the profession to which they aspire. These schools have developed programs to prioritize writing across the curriculum.

Each program is different, but most require students to take basic composition courses in which the focus is on learning how to write across disciplines. Students then must take other discipline-specific courses designated as "writing intensive" and which follow specific guidelines for writing assignments and how they're conducted and graded. The 2015 *U.S. News and World Report* college rankings surveyed personnel at 1,500 schools to find the schools with the best reputations for these programs, and the following schools were mentioned most:[46]

Bard College, NY	Harvard University, MA
Brown University, RI	Kenyon College, OH
Carleton College, MN	Massachusetts Institute of Technology, MA
Clemson University, SC	Princeton University, NJ
Colorado State University, CO	Stanford University, CA
Cornell University, NY	University of California–Davis, CA
Duke University, NC	Washington State University, WA
Elon University, NC	Williams College, MA
George Mason University, VA	Yale University, CT

Other schools are changing English composition courses to function less like feeder classes for English majors and to be more focused on discipline-specific writing. Amy Griswold points out how the freshman composition course and program at the Texas Woman's University has changed:

> It used to be a prep course for English majors—studying character, theme, etc. Now it's a preparation for writing in other disciplines. One assignment is a paper about how to write a paper in another class—a lab report, art paper, historical essay. It's more applied.

Duke University—one of the schools in the *U.S. News* ranking—offers a specialized program as part of the Thompson Writing Program. The Duke Reader Project pairs undergraduate and graduate students in qualifying courses with alumni or Duke employees who have relevant professional experience. The students receive feedback from these alumni on how they can improve their projects and how those projects would be viewed in a professional setting.[47]

Many schools offer similar speaking intensive programs and courses. The goal is to give students instruction and practice in interpersonal, group, or public communication in various settings and across disciplines. Speaking intensive classes usually require faculty to provide instruction in group communication, for example, before making an assignment, and then provide evaluation and feedback on their communication skills as well as on the content-specific deliverable of the project.

To be successful, however, these programs must be implemented well. Most programs offer faculty training and support designed to make sure students receive appropriate instruction and feedback in either written or oral communications. But the course outcomes are often only as good as the professors and instructors who teach them. And sometimes these programs are implemented such that there is incentive for securing the "intensive" designation to increase enrollment or fulfill a school-wide requirement, but there must also be a subsequent assessment of whether or not program goals are met.

I'm also wary of unintended consequences: that diffusing instruction across the curriculum will dilute it. Much like state legislatures who cut education spending once a state lottery is approved, administrators should not use the addition of writing or speaking intensive designations in discipline-specific courses as a reason to cut program requirements for specific communications or writing courses. Students need more practice and skills training, not less, and eliminating a requirement for students to take public speaking or interpersonal communication, for example, in exchange for another discipline-specific course with oral communication instruction as a small part of it is a bad bargain if the goal is to increase student skills.

The University of Pennsylvania offers the Communication Within the Curriculum program (CWiC) "that supports student speaking as a means of both communicating and learning."[48] The program offers a variety of workshops and training for students and faculty and a Speaking Center where students can work with a mentor or coach to improve their presentations. This program includes CWiC-affiliated courses across disciplines, much like speaking intensive courses in other schools, but they require students to meet with a CWiC adviser to practice at least one presentation. CWiC also offers critical speaking seminars each semester in which instruction and practice are combined with discipline-specific content. These seminars require more practice with a CWiC adviser, and half the course grade is based on two class presentations.

When administration or governing bodies change priorities, some departments must advocate for themselves to other departments within their institutions. For instance, before a recent redesign in program requirements and the new articulation agreement was produced, all students at Wake Technical Community College in Raleigh, North Carolina, were required to take a communications course, usually Introduction to Communications or Public Speaking. Once the new mandate was handed down, those requirements were left up to individual programs.

Brittany Hochstaetter from Wake Tech contacted other departments to discover what specific types of communications their students would need on the job, and she and her instructors redesigned several courses to more closely align with those programs' learning outcomes. "I basically ran Public Relations for the Communications Department, and viewed the other departments as customers," says Hochstaetter. "And it's working." Most programs that had required one or more communications classes still do.

While some schools have decentralized teaching communication across the curriculum, others advocate a more centralized approach. James O'Rourke, of Notre Dame, points out some advantages to a more centralized approach. First, it relieves pressure on faculty in other disciplines, and second, it makes course scheduling and the workload distribution and the division of labor more effective. At the Fanning Center for Business Communication in the Mendoza School of Business, students can take 1.5 or 2.0 credit courses in a modular, seven-week format. Courses may include Business Speaking, Business Writing, Persuasion, Technical and Business Presentations, and Intercultural Communication.

In addition, the Fanning Center can tailor what they offer based on what employers and students need. For example, the MBA program has many students for whom English is a second language. "About one-third of our MBA students are non-native English speakers," says O'Rourke. "We developed class sections specifically for those students."

Some schools take a "both/and" approach to teaching communication or other critical skills: offering centralized instruction from a particular department or center while also using the intensive approach across the curriculum. Notre Dame is in the process of incorporating additional writing requirements in the curriculum. One writing class will be delivered by the Fanning Center, and a second, discipline-specific course will be delivered by the college.

Many colleges and universities offer writing and speaking centers where students can be tutored by faculty, peers, or graduate students. In these centers, students bring an assignment for feedback and coaching. Centers offer a safe place for students to practice presentations or to get suggestions for revisions to written work. When possible, I offer extra credit on assignments that my students take to the writing or speaking center on campus. It's worth it to me to provide the incentive since students who receive coaching turn in better written work and give better presentations, and this process mirrors the way students will need to search out and acquire resources and additional development tools in the workplace.

For centers to be effective, the tutors may need training in the expectations that different disciplines have for their assignments. For example, our Writing Center at NCCU requested a School of Business faculty member to give a workshop for their tutors on how business communication and the assignments we give in the School of Business differ from other types of academic or professional communication and assignments. It was a good exercise for me to specifically think through that question, and I've incorporated my workshop information into the first meeting of my class for each new semester.

Some schools are recognizing a need for these skills in graduate students as well and have developed professional development programs for their master's and PhD candidates. The Pratt School of Engineering at Duke University offers the PhD Plus program in which students take seminars and workshops on career development topics, including communication and coaching, team development, and negotiation, as well as other topic areas. Dr. Zbigniew Kabala, an associate professor of civil and environmental engineering, says the program came out of a realization that PhD programs weren't teaching all the skills necessary for their students' success:

"We basically stuck PhD students in a dark corner in the library for three years, then when they emerged with their dissertations, we expected them to give a presentation in front of 30 people."

Teaching Critical Thinking

Teaching critical thinking skills to students can be done on the macro or micro level through specific programs explicitly related to critical thinking or through intentional instruction as part of discipline-specific courses. There is disagreement in the literature about whether critical thinking can be learned as a separate set of skills that can then be used in multiple settings or whether it requires specific content, but diffused throughout the curriculum.[49] Abrami et al. concluded that students improve their critical thinking skills best when they are in instructor-led dialogue about real-world problems.[50]

Meredith College offers the Think Strong program to teach critical thinking. In the program, first-year students attend seminars on topics such as "Reflections of Body Image in the Media" or "The Future of Technology" in which students "are challenged to excel, inspired to think deeply, and thoughtfully make connections between what is learned in the classroom and the world around them through experiential learning."[51] In future semesters, students are taught to apply those skills in upper-level courses and participate in guest lectures. Assessment tools are part of the program, and faculty have access to critical thinking and creative thinking rubrics from the AACU as well as proprietary rubrics for assessing learning outcomes.

Niu et al. conducted a meta-analysis of 31 research projects and found a small but statistically significant rise in students' CT skills when universities offered single instructional interventions lasting longer than 12 weeks, but not when designed as holistic programs throughout the degree program.[52]

Flores et al. conclude there is "a need to be more intentional in developing critical thinkers," and they make five recommendations for higher education:

- Redefine success in education to include the development of critical thinking as one measure
- Develop a culture of critical thinking rather than more programs for critical thinking
- Train instructors to teach critical thinking and develop the infrastructure to support them

- Allocate significant sources and demonstrate a "top-down" commitment
- Collaborate with employers to develop clear goals to measure success in teaching critical thinking[53]

That last point—collaborating with employers—highlights one way to think about critical thinking. On some level, what we want is for students to begin to think like the professionals in their disciplines. College and university classes may teach using case studies or begin to focus on discipline-specific writing. We encourage students to complete internships or in-class projects with "live" clients to give them experience in working and thinking like the professionals they will become.

Students, parents, and employers expect schools and universities to teach critical skills, and rightly so. But while schools and universities are using a variety of innovative and specific ways to teach critical soft skills, students bear some responsibility for making sure they get the skills they need. Schools can offer the most wonderful, well-designed programs possible, but if students don't take advantage of them, the skills gap won't close.

Now let's look at how students can improve their skills on their own.

How Can Students Improve Their Skills on Their Own

As you see in the previous section, today's college students have many opportunities within their academic programs to build and improve their critical soft skills. For that improvement to happen, however, students must make an intentional commitment to learning and practicing these skills outside of classes. When they get into the workplace, students will be expected to find and complete additional professional-development opportunities. Whether this expectation is mandated (in professions requiring a certain number of hours in continuing education) or simply part of the world of work, students need to cultivate the lifelong learner mind-set.

Sometimes, it just requires enough curiosity to try something new. While employers may not specifically call out intellectual curiosity as a desired skill, I personally believe this is one of the most important traits for long-term success. And there's research to support that belief. Von Stumm found that intellectual curiosity, or a "hungry mind," was just as powerful a predictor of academic success as intelligence.[54] Similarly, a 2012 survey of studies published between 1997 and 2010 found that, other than intelligence and school performance, the best predictors of student success were conscientiousness and intellectual curiosity.[55]

Given that curiosity and desire to improve, what should students do while in school so they aren't one of the unprepared graduates employers decry?

An Education, Not Just a Degree

Beyond major or degree program requirements, students need to choose courses that will help them improve their soft skills. Hochstaetter sees a need for students to choose courses that may not be on their program of study if necessary. "They need skills in negotiating and interviewing," she says, "but if it's not on their advising sheet, they won't take it."

In addition, students should look for classes with smaller enrollments whenever possible. Small classes provide for more individual attention from instructors and allow more rapport building and discussion with classmates. The more in-depth discussions you have in classes, the more practice you get in group dynamics, interpersonal communication, and persuasion.

Students also need to be willing to step out of their comfort zones and stretch themselves. From my experience, students who are not comfortable with their written or oral communication skills are the students who should be taking those courses the most.

I remember one student in an Intro to Communications class who had severe stage fright. He wasn't just nervous; he had debilitating anxiety. Over the course of the semester, he worked very hard, but he still nearly froze every time he spoke. I was seriously concerned he wouldn't make it through his final speech. I nearly wept when he finished that presentation. His eyes were closed for at least half of it, but he finished. I nearly shouted, "Hallelujah," though, when he told me he was signing up for Public Speaking the next semester. He knew employers would expect him to speak in public and that he had to improve or he'd miss opportunities for promotion.

It's easy to encourage students to take extra courses; however, there is a real push in many schools to keep people on a very specific path. The stereotype of the college student taking two or three semesters to find himself or herself is long gone in this age of performance-based funding and focus on four-, five-, and six-year graduation rates. And yet, employers still want liberal arts–trained employees.[56] We need to keep providing space for students to grow their skills via other courses while still keeping forward momentum in their academic programs.

Join the Club

Deborah Brame suggests students take advantage of networking events and campus clubs to practice their skills outside of class: "Students need to take every opportunity they have to be in the presence of someone who is where they want to be." But I know from experience that we have trouble getting students to come to networking events, even ones put on by great companies who are looking for interns and employees. Many students feel uncomfortable because they don't have the skills, but they won't get the skills if they don't practice by coming to events.

An example of one solution is a recent event sponsored by Coastal Carolina Credit Union. CCCU put on a breakfast event for our students in which they gave tips and techniques for networking. Then, they conducted a separate exercise where students practiced networking with each other. It was an excellent event, and we scheduled it during a particular class time to make sure students attended. Other students were invited, and many of them did attend. But when we hold similar events and just invite students rather than make it a part of their classes, we have very low turnout. This lack of engagement highlights the main point of this discussion: students have to take responsibility for their education and take proactive steps to improve their critical skills. Brame points out that some students don't attend events because they aren't aware they are available. Students need to find how their career services department and program or school usually communicates with students and then make sure they faithfully check those sources. Many schools are using text and social media to communicate with students.

In addition to official school programs, many colleges offer a Toastmasters Club or other student-led initiative that allows for oral communication practice and evaluation. The Pratt School of Engineering at Duke offers the PRATTically Speaking Toastmasters chapter for engineering students. A Duke University professor is also a member of the Toastmasters chapter that meets on NCCU's campus. This club is unique in North Carolina in that it is the only club that combines student and professional members. The professor is a big proponent of Toastmasters as a way to supplement student skills: "There's not enough opportunity to present in classes. Students have amazing potential, but they don't have the opportunities."

Student clubs provide another avenue for developing and practicing critical skills. Most disciplines have student chapters of professional organizations, such as the American Marketing Association or National Association of Black Accountants (NABA), which provide students with leadership opportunities and exposure to professionals in their fields.

Several of my students recently attended a NABA conference where they met professionals from all across the country and were offered internships on the spot during networking events.

There's No Substitute for Experience

Brian Mills, from the movie *Taken* and this chapter's introduction, points out that his particular set of skills were acquired over a long career, and, frankly, there's an argument to be made that in expecting recent graduates to have fully developed communication and critical thinking skills, we're requiring a level of development usually reserved for professionals with multiple years of experience.[57] Employers even admit that they require more of their entry-level employees now than they did in the past.[58] My students often feel like they're in a catch-22: they need experience to get jobs, but they can't get jobs without experience.

There are ways, however, to get experience while still in college, but students have to be proactive in seeking out these opportunities and be prepared for interviewing and navigating a professional environment to take advantage. Some schools, such as Meredith College, require an internship of all students. This requirement puts extra pressure on students and the college to find and manage quality internships. No school wants their students to be unpaid coffee gofers. Rather, they want their students to come away from the experience with real-world experience.

Internships provide excellent opportunities for students to practice communication, critical thinking, and teamwork skills in a professional environment. Co-ops and job shadowing experiences can offer valuable insight into a profession and career as well as provide valuable contacts for future employment. According to the NACE Job Outlook, 56.5 percent of students who participated in an internship received a job offer before graduation, compared to 36.5 percent of students who received a job offer without participating in an internship. For those students who participated in a paid internship at a private company, the offer rate goes up to 72.2 percent.[59]

Show, Don't Tell

In addition to helping develop critical soft skills, participation in the above activities gives you valuable examples to demonstrate your skills to employers. It's not enough to list "Effective Communicator" on a résumé. Employers don't want buzzwords; they want proof that a candidate actually is a good communicator and can think critically and work well with others by using those skills in an applied setting.

Employers still value internship and apprenticeship programs the most, but they do value other applied learning or project-based learning experiences.[60] Experiential learning can also include capstone projects, honors theses, research projects, major class projects, or student consulting projects as well as simulations or campus leadership roles. Community service projects provide another opportunity for experience if students will seek out opportunities in their disciplines.

I encourage my students to find volunteer opportunities with organizations that need help in marketing or event planning or who need a new Web site or social media strategy. The students receive valuable skills and experience, while the organization receives much-needed quality support. For example, a quick search in NCCU's community service partner database reveals the following organizations that could provide great experience:

- Veteran's Helping Veterans of America, Inc.—event coordination, bookkeeping, social media coordination
- Be the Match Marrow Registry—event planning, public speaking
- Indigo Consortium (supports female veterans)—marketing, administrative duties
- NBN Sports (nonprofit youth sports and mentoring)digital marketing, event planning

So, when graduates are in an interview and the recruiter asks, "How do you work in teams?" or "Give me an example of your problem-solving skills" or "Why should I hire you?" they have ready examples of specific projects with measurable outcomes. But again, the onus rests on students to take advantage of the programs and opportunities schools provide. Students need to build a coherent plan for developing and practicing oral and written communication skills, effective teamwork, and critical thinking.

Conclusion

The purpose of this chapter was to give students, parents, and those interested in the value of higher education a look at what critical skills today's students and graduates need to have to be successful in college and in the world of work. Today's students need the following skills, regardless of discipline or degree program:

- Oral and written communication
- Critical thinking
- Working effectively in teams

Unfortunately, there is a large gap between the skills students need and graduates think they have and employers' perceptions of their skills. Schools and universities are providing instruction and programs to help close those gaps, and they can do more. But students also can take responsibility for and control of their education to make sure they graduate with the skills they need as well as practical experiences to demonstrate those skills to employers.

In the end, there's no magic solution, but it takes a true partnership among faculty, administrators, employers, and community partners who are committed to growing these skills and students who are actively pursuing an education, not just a degree. In my classes, I'm drawing more explicit lines between what my students say they want and what specific skills they will need to reach their goals.

After all, Bryan Mills didn't earn his "particular set of skills" by wishing really hard and believing in himself. And he didn't wait to develop those skills until he was in the fight of his life. Today's students can and should prepare themselves while in school to be articulate, critical-thinking team players when they graduate.

For my business communications class, I've taken the below quote, from that great philosopher Terry Pratchett, as my North Star:

> *If you trust in yourself . . . and believe in your dreams . . . and follow your star . . . you'll still get beaten by people who spent their time working hard and learning things.*—Terry Pratchett, *The Wee Free Men*[61]

Notes

1. P. Fain, "Performance Funding in Massachusetts," Inside Higher Ed, June 17, 2015. https://www.insidehighered.com/quicktakes/2015/06/17/performance -funding-massachusetts; M. Shear, "With Website to Research Colleges, Obama Abandons Ranking System," *New York Times*, September 12, 2015. http://www .nytimes.com/2015/09/13/us/with-website-to-research-colleges-obama-abandons -ranking-system.html?smprod=nytcore-ipad.

2. CIPRA, "The American Freshman: National Norms Fall 2015," Lumina Foundation, accessed May 7, 2016. https://www.luminafoundation.org/resources/the -american-freshman-2015.

3. Hart Research Associates, "Falling Short? College Learning and Career Success," Association of American Colleges & Universities, accessed May 7, 2016. http://www.aacu.org/leap/public-opinion-research/2015-survey-results.

4. Hart Research Associates, "Falling Short?"; "The Human Factor: The Hard Time Employers Have Finding," Burning Glass Technologies, accessed May 7, 2016. http://burning-glass.com/wp-content/uploads/Human_Factor_Baseline_Skills

_FINAL.pdf; "What Do Candidates Expect from You during Their Job Search?,"
CareerBuilder, accessed March 2, 2016. http://www.careerbuildercommunications
.com/candidatebehavior.

5. "The Human Factor."

6. M. Korn, "Bosses Seek 'Critical Thinking,' but What Is That?," *Wall Street Journal*, October 21, 2014. http://www.wsj.com/articles/bosses-seek-critical
-thinking-but-what-is-that-1413923730.

7. Hart Research Associates, "Falling Short?"

8. Hart Research Associates, "It Takes More Than a Major: Employer Priorities for College Learning and Student Success," Association of American Colleges & Universities, accessed December 7, 2015. https://www.aacu.org/publications-research
/periodicals/it-takes-more-major-employer-priorities-college-learning-and.

9. Hart Research Associates, "Employers More Interested in Critical Thinking and Problem Solving Than College Major," Association of American Colleges & Universities, April 10, 2013. https://www.aacu.org/press/press-releases/employers
-more-interested-critical-thinking-and-problem-solving-college-major.

10. Hart Research Associates, "Falling Short?"

11. Hart Research Associates, "Employers More Interested in Critical Thinking."

12. "The Human Factor."

13. N. Johnson, "College Costs and Prices: Some Key Facts for Policymakers," Lumina Foundation, April 3, 204. https://www.luminafoundation.org/resources
/college-costs--and-prices.

14. Sandy Baum, Jennifer Ma, and Kathleen Payea, *Education Pays: The Benefits of Higher Education for Individuals and Society* (published online: College Board, n.d.).

15. D. Conrad and R. Newberry, "Identification and Instruction of Important Business Communication Skills for Graduate Business Education," *Journal of Education for Business* 87, no. 2 (2012): 112–120. doi:10.1080/08832323.2011.576280.

16. Korn, "Bosses Seek 'Critical Thinking.'"

17. K. L. Flores, G. S. Matkin, M. E. Burbach, C. E. Quinn, and H. Harding, "Deficient Critical Thinking Skills among College Graduates: Implications for Leadership," *Educational Philosophy and Theory* 44, no. 2 (2012): 212–230. doi:10.1111/j.1469-5812.2010.00672.x.

18. R. B. Adler and G. R. Rodman, *Understanding Human Communication,* 11th ed. (New York: Oxford University Press, 2012).

19. E. P. Werthe and L. Werthe, "Effective Training for Millennial Students," *Adult Learning* 22, no. 3 (2011): 12–19. doi:10.1177/104515951102200302.

20. W. Ofstad and L. J. Brunner, "Team-based Learning in Pharmacy Education," *American Journal of Pharmaceutical Education* 77, no. 4 (2013): 70. doi:10.5688/ajpe77470; H. Ku, H. W. Tseng, and C. Akarasriworn, "Collaboration Factors, Teamwork Satisfaction, and Student Attitudes toward Online Collaborative Learning," *Computers in Human Behavior* 29, no. 3 (2013): 922–929. doi:10.1016/j.chb.2012.12.019.

21. Ku et al., "Collaboration Factors."

22. Mark Graham, Jennifer Frederick, Angela Byars-Winston, Anne-Barrie Hunter, and Jo Handlesman, "Increasing Persistence of College Students in STEM," *Science* 341 (September 27, 2013). http://www.fgcu.edu/STEM/files/Increasing _Persistence_of_College_Students_in_STEM.pdf.

23. Theresa Minton-Eversole, "Virtual Teams Used Most by Global Organizations, Survey Says," Society for Human Resource Management, July 19, 2012. https:// www.shrm.org/hrdisciplines/orgempdev/articles/pages/virtualteamsusedmost byglobalorganizations,surveysays.aspx.

24. Hart Research Associates, "Falling Short?"

25. Ibid.

26. The Conference Board, *"Are They Really Ready to Work?: Employers' Perspectives on the Basic Knowledge and Applied Skills of New Entrants to the 21st Century US Workforce"* (published online: The Conference Board, 2006). http://www.p21.org /storage/documents/FINAL_REPORT_PDF09-29-06.pdf.

27. Douglas Belkin, "Test Finds College Graduates Lack Skills for White-collar Jobs," *Wall Street Journal*, January 16, 2015. http://www.wsj.com/articles/test-finds -many-students-ill-prepared-to-enter-work-force-1421432744?KEYWORDS =college+graduates; V. C. Milliron, "Exploring Millennial Student Values and Societal Trends: Accounting Course Selection Preferences," *Issues in Accounting Education* 23, no. 3 (2008): 405–419. doi:10.2308/iace.2008.23.3.405. Flores et al., "Deficient Critical Thinking Skills"; J. L. Hartman and J. McCambridge, "Optimizing Millennials' Communication Styles," *Business Communication Quarterly* 74, no. 1 (2011): 22–44. doi:10.1177/1080569910395564.

28. Werthe and Werthe, "Effective Training."

29. Hart Research Associates, "Falling Short?"

30. Ibid.

31. Andrea Hershatter and Molly Epstein, "Millennials and the World of Work: An Organization and Management Perspective," *Journal of Business and Psychology* 25, no. 2 (2010): 211–223. doi:10.1007/s10869-010-9160-y; Jessica Brack and K. Kelly, "Maximizing Millennials in the Workplace," *Executive Development Blog*, November 6, 2014. http://execdev.kenan-flagler.unc.edu/blog /maximizing-millennials-in-the-workplace; Judy Lin, "Research Shows That Internet Is Rewiring Our Brains," UCLA Newsroom, October 15, 2008. http://newsroom .ucla.edu/stories/081015_gary-small-ibrain; Jon Marcus, "Colleges Step in to Fill Students' Social-skills Gaps," Hechinger Report, January 3, 2013. http://hechingerreport .org/colleges-step-in-to-fill-students-social-skills-gaps; C. Segrin, A. Woszidlo, M. Givertz, and N. Montgomery, "Parent and Child Traits Associated with Overparenting," *Journal of Social and Clinical Psychology* 32, no. 6 (2013): 569–595. doi:10.1521/jscp.2013.32.6.569.

32. R. Junco and S. Cotton, "No A 4 U: The Relationship between Multitasking and Academic Performance," *Computers & Education* 59 (2012): 505–514.

33. Lin, "Research Shows."

34. Jorden K. Smith, Lisa M. Given, Heidi Julien, Dana Ouellette, and Kathleen DeLong, "Information Literacy Proficiency: Assessing the Gap in High

School Students' Readiness for Undergraduate Academic Work," *Library & Information Science Research* 35, no. 2 (2013): 88–96. http://dx.doi.org/10.1016/j .lisr.2012.12.001; W. Badke, "Why Information Literacy Is Invisible," in ed. J. Hagen-McIntosh, *Information and Data Literacy: The Role of the Library* (Oakville: Apple Academic Press, 2016), 129–141. (Original work published in 2010.)

35. Hershatter and Epstein, "Millennials and the World of Work."

36. Marcus, "Colleges Step."

37. M. Majumder, "The Impact of Parenting Style on Children's Educational Outcomes," *Journal of Family and Economic Issues* 37, no. 1 (2016): 89–98.

38. Hara Estroff Marano, "Helicopter Parenting—It's Worse Than You Think," *Psychology Today*, January 31, 2014. https://www.psychologytoday.com/blog/nation -wimps/201401/helicopter-parenting-its-worse-you-think.

39. Segrin et al., "Parent and Child Traits."

40. K. Holland, "Why Johnny Can't Write, and Why Employers Are Mad," NBC News, November 11, 2013. http://www.nbcnews.com/business/careers/why -johnny-cant-write-why-employers-are-mad-f2D11577444.

41. Liana Heitin, "Will the Common Core Step Up Schools' Focus on Grammar?," Education Week, February 23, 2016. http://www.edweek.org/ew/articles /2016/02/24/will-the-common-core-step-up-schools.html.

42. Steven Kerr, "An Academic classic on the Folly of Rewarding A, while Hoping for B," *Academy of Management Perspectives* 9, no. 1 (1995): 7–14. doi:10.5465/ame.1995.9503133466.

43. "A Comprehensive Articulation Agreement between the University of North Carolina and the North Carolina Community College System," accessed March 12, 2016, http://www.northcarolina.edu/sites/default/files/comprehensive _articulation_agreement_oct_2015.pdf.

44. D. Conrad and R. Newberry, "Identification and Instruction of Important Business Communication Skills for Graduate Business Education," *Journal of Education for Business* 87, no. 2 (2012): 112–120. doi:10.1080/08832323.2011.576280.

45. M. K. Smith, "What Is Praxis?," *The Encyclopaedia of Informal Education*, accessed March 11, 2016. http://www.infed.org/biblio/b-praxis.htm.

46. "Writing in the Disciplines," *U.S. News & World Report*, accessed March 5, 2016. http://colleges.usnews.rankingsandreviews.com/best-colleges/rankings /writing-programs.

47. Cary Moskovitz, "The Duke Reader Project: Engaging the University Community in Undergraduate Writing Instruction," *Liberal Education* 97, no. 3/4 (2011): 48–53.

48. "The Communication Within the Curriculum Program (CWiC)," Penn Arts & Sciences, University of Pennsylvania, accessed March 1, 2016. http://www .sas.upenn.edu/ugrad/hdbk/cwic.html.

49. Emily R. Lai, *Critical Thinking: A Literature Review: Research Reports* (published online: Pearson, 2011). http://images.pearsonassessments.com/images /tmrs/CriticalThinkingReviewFINAL.pdf.

50. Philip C. Abrami, Robert M. Bernard, Eugene Borokhovski, David I. Waddington, C. Anne Wade, and Tonje Persson, "Strategies for Teaching Students to Think Critically: A Meta-analysis," *Review of Educational Research* 85, no. 2 (2015): 275–314.

51. Meredith College, "Think Strong: Focus on Critical Thinking," Meredith College, accessed January 7, 2016. http://www.meredith.edu/academics/think -strong.

52. Lian Niu, Linda S. Behar-Horenstein, and Cyndi W. Garvan, "Do Instructional Interventions Influence College Students' Critical Thinking Skills?: A Meta-analysis," *Educational Research Review* 9 (2013): 114–128. doi:10.1016/j.edurev .2012.12.002.

53. Flores et al., "Deficient Critical Thinking Skills."

54. S. von Stumm, B. Hell, and T. Chamorro-Premuzic, "The Hungry Mind: Intellectual Curiosity Is the Third Pillar of Academic Performance," *Perspectives on Psychological Science* 6, no. 6 (2011): 574–588.

55. Ian Leslie, *Curious: The Desire to Know and Why Your Future Depends on It* (New York: Basic Books, 2014).

56. Hart Research Associates, "Falling Short?"

57. Korn, "Bosses Seek 'Critical Thinking.'"

58. Hart Research Associates, "It Takes More Than a Major."

59. "Class of 2016 Student Survey Report," National Association of Colleges and Employers, accessed March 5, 2016. http://www.naceweb.org/surveys/student .aspx.

60. Hart Research Associates, "Falling Short?"

61. T. Pratchett, *The Wee Free Men* (New York: HarperTempest, 2003).

CHAPTER NINE

Combating the Crisis of Completion

Austin L. Hollimon

The importance of a college degree in our society is growing exponentially. In 1976, when Gallup first asked its pool of surveyors whether a college degree was important, only 36 percent said yes. In 2013, 76 percent of Americans surveyed said earning a college degree was "very important."[1] Even with increasing agreement about a college degree's value, we still face a crisis of completion in our colleges and universities. Across the United States, only 77 percent of the high school seniors we send to college will return for their second year, and only 59 percent will earn a bachelor's degree within six years.[2]

The number of students leaving college is alarming in both its scope and degree, but most notable is who is dropping out of college. More than any other predictive factor, parent income determines who finishes and who drops out of college.[3]

Among students whose parents belong to the bottom socioeconomic quartile, only 9 percent of students who enroll in college will earn a bachelor's degree within six years.[4] This is shocking by itself, but what gives even greater pause is how achievement for the economically disadvantaged differs so greatly from the top economic quartile. Over 77 percent of students from the top income bracket will earn a bachelor's degree within the same six-year time frame.[5] These alarming numbers reverse the widely held belief that "an education is the key to social mobility." Rather, this data hints that perhaps socioeconomic status is a precursor to college completion. In short, being born to affluence is responsible for finding affluence.

With only 1 in 10 of our most economically vulnerable students finishing a college degree, we have a serious question to answer: Have we as a society truly made progress toward the American dream when our educational attainment is governed, in practice, by the Matthew Effect (He that has more shall be given, and he that has not, all will be taken away)?[6]

Poor students and vulnerable populations are facing a crisis of completion. Today more than at any other time, those who are concerned about higher education, along with our leaders and civil servants, are challenging and must continue to challenge universities to increase graduation and retention rates for the financially vulnerable and other at-risk populations.

These education leaders are increasing accountability in our colleges and, today, more than 32 states distribute funds to universities based on institutional performance, which includes measuring retention and graduation rates as a barometer of success. Another five states will be embracing these new funding models in 2016–2017.[7] These funding changes give incentives for institutions to investigate why at-risk populations are struggling to complete college and to take steps to reverse these trends.

Our graduation gap is so large that a student from the top economic quartile earning an 800 on the SAT has a greater chance of graduating than a student with *twice that score* from the bottom economic quartile.[8]

This data challenges the "theory of inherent inferiority" that pervaded higher education circles for generations. The theory holds that students who drop out are just "not cut out" (translation: not smart enough) for college or are lacking the work ethic and personal responsibility required to succeed. I personally am wary of the theory of inherent inferiority because I have seen people try to bestow skills upon me that I do not have simply because I earned my degree from Princeton University. I appreciate the privilege, but I would be misguided to forget my friends and family members who never earned degrees and yet possess equal or greater intellectual prowess and work ethic as myself. I know for a fact that I did not earn that degree on account of any inherent superiority.

I am aware that, as a nation, we no longer say we ascribe to the "inherent superiority" complex. Rather, many people share the sentiments President Obama expressed when he said, "Every American should have the right to go as far as their talents and hard work will take them. That is what college is all about. That is what America is all about."[9] So, if we believe that, why are so many of our poorest Americans seemingly shut out from earning their college degrees, and what can be done about it?

To answer these questions, we founded a company, CommitU, that is dedicated to researching and ultimately solving the problem. The solutions are many, but how we ultimately chose to focus our efforts stems from a particularly unique place.

Top-Down Solutions: Education's Systemic Overestimation of Its Own Efficacy

We started with an understanding, a deeply personal understanding, that going to college is like traveling to a foreign land for many poor students. The university experience requires a unique set of skills to navigate successfully. Going to college doesn't come with an instruction manual. But when we founded CommitU, we asked ourselves, "Why not?"

Typically, when we think of "education reform," we think of changing the systems around student achievement—a top-down solution. There is a large and growing industry dedicated to serving institutions with innovations in the measurement and tracking of student-degree progression. An entire army of large companies, from Blackboard to Starfish, are investing millions of dollars in improving outcomes for at-risk populations. Most of these companies are developing software programs that help universities identify indicators of students in "academic jeopardy." Whether it's simply missing class, turning in an assignment late, or categorizing failing grades, technology is being innovated and implemented to support universities and their students with real-time data.

Many of these programs started by asking what the university needed to help increase retention rates. At CommitU, we listened carefully and conducted dozens of interviews with universities to learn their problems. However, we also found it important to study the challenges *students* said they faced by creating a bottom-up approach to helping students navigate their new collegiate world. We particularly focused on students from at-risk populations, including first-generation college, low-income, racial minority, and rural students, who each must overcome additional hurdles. While we interviewed dozens of students and graduates of universities, I could not forget my own struggles and the obstacles I had to overcome back in college.

The Lessons We Failed to Learn the First Time

I was just a young black man from a Title I school in Decatur, Georgia, when I arrived, frightened, to Princeton University in July of 2008. I understood college as a place to go to be prepared for a career, yet I couldn't major in anything I wanted to pursue. The only purpose for this education seemed to be to get a job on Wall Street—of which I wanted no part. I wandered somewhat aimlessly through my freshman year, and even failed a class in economics. I lacked a purpose for enduring the pain.

Like many students, I was also lacking a sense of belonging in frigid New Jersey. It was a shock to the system being the only black student in my seminars, where I was occasionally asked to give the "black perspective." My Title I high school experience was light years from Princeton in a thousand different ways. My new Princeton classmates had traveled and lived around the globe, and sometimes my world in East Atlanta seemed like it was an eternity from Central Jersey. I felt so alone, both academically and culturally. I felt isolated because my lifestyle was so different, isolated because my high school experience was so different, and, at times, even isolated because I couldn't figure out how race fit into my collegiate experience. I thought, for a long time, that I was unique.

When I failed that economics class, which I had studied so hard for, I was truly devastated. It was clear to me that, despite all of my efforts, I must be inferior. How else could I explain the success of the other students, who seemed to have barely spent more than an hour studying for that final, outperforming me by so much? At the end of my freshman year, any belief I had once had in my academic ability was wavering.

As it turns out, lacking a sense of purpose, belonging, and belief is one of the most common experiences that college students from at-risk populations endure, and for each of these challenges, there are real remedies that exist.

In time, I found my own purpose by applying passion to running track while I was in school, and I forged a network of administrators, teachers, and friends to help me navigate Princeton. With that network of support, I was able to build confidence, and working with my professors helped me to eventually graduate from Princeton with honors and awards to bear on the way out! Even still, I never forgot the helplessness I felt my freshman year. It is from that struggle that the idea to empower students through CommitU was born.

The Three Dimensions of a Complete Student

Purpose, belonging, and belief are essential ingredients in the success of anyone doing anything. At CommitU, we found that so many of our vulnerable students are missing these three key ingredients. When these young people have doubts in these areas, leaving college becomes the most viable option. So, when we launched our company, our goal was to design flexibly implemented programming to help ward off these feelings of insecurity before they manifest as academic problems or a need to drop out. Our mission is to support universities with the tools to inspire students to use their education to pursue their unique purpose, foster and cultivate their own belonging, and maintain a belief in themselves even when they encounter tough times.

We were inspired by one of Dr. Martin Luther King's less famous but deeply inspiring sermons, "The Three Dimensions of a Complete Life." Dr. King eloquently inspired each of his parishioners to remain "in the pursuit purpose, belonging and belief." So, we developed an intervention to be implemented in just two to six hours during orientation and remediation periods. We begin engaging students in the process by asking one simple question: "If you could pick anything in the world to become an expert in (dance, music, drama, chess, astrophysics, etc.), what would you commit to?" This short and unique question allows us to open the doors of engagement for the student so that we can slip in lessons related to building networks, creating a personal identity (and reason) for being in school, and applying a growth mind-set to overcome the inevitable challenges.

CommitU in Action

Our objective is not to force students to pick a major with this commitment question, but our work requires the student to be at the center of creating their own mind-set. A personalized intervention where the student is at the center is the most effective. We also discovered from our research and investigation into psychology that interventions that are subtle in their objectives, use stealthy approaches, and do not control or stigmatize the student are most effective.[10]

Initially, as we looked to partner with universities, we struggled with *where* and *how* an intervention of this variety would fit. After interviewing our customers at universities, we found that most schools have one particular area that they have not optimized to address retention. Specifically, it's their orientation programming. So, we have taken pains to assist schools in implementing orientation programming that provides at-risk students with the tools to effectively navigate college and increases retention rates.

The Privilege of Purpose

A verse in Proverbs declares, "Where there is no vision, the people perish." Too many of our students show up to their universities without a vision, having never been challenged to imagine the purpose of their education. In this 21st-century world, when our students have so many answers at their fingertips, we must challenge them to ask of themselves the greatest question scholars and philosophers have been asking for millennia: "Why am I here?"

For students of privilege, answering the "why" question is not as essential. Their life experiences, filled with engineers, educators, doctors, and attorneys, foster an inherent sense of direction and belonging. An article in the *New York Times* explains the differences that privileged and disadvantaged students face:

> Every college freshman—rich or poor, white or minority, first-generation or legacy—experiences academic setbacks and awkward moments when they feel they don't belong. But white students and wealthy students and students with college-graduate parents tend not to take those moments too seriously or too personally. Sure, they still feel bad when they fail a test or get in a fight with a roommate or are turned down for a date. But in general, they don't interpret those setbacks as a sign that they don't belong in college or that they're not going to succeed there.[11]

Psychological Interventions

Psychologists David Yeager and Gregory Walton, who have assisted in developing a tremendously effective retention program for the University of Texas, acknowledge the need for designing retention solutions with the student in mind:

> Understanding what school feels like for [the student] can lead to nonobvious but powerful interventions. A common problem is that students have beliefs and worries in school that prevent them from taking full advantage of learning opportunities.[12]

Ability and Belonging

According to Walton and Yeager, students in transition periods struggle with two things: *ability* and *belonging*. Students from all backgrounds have to overcome these challenges, but the related fears, anxieties, and doubts impact groups who consider themselves "under the microscope" more deeply. These students, such as women in engineering programs, first-generation college students, and African Americans in the Ivy League, often interpret poor feedback as a sign that they perhaps do not belong.[13]

When it comes to ability, students from these disadvantaged groups can be influenced by what psychologist Carol Dweck calls "theories of intelligence."[14] When trouble comes, the fixed mind-set says, "You're just not good at this, and there is no way to get better." Although the students are capable of improving academically, this thought process precludes them from taking the necessary steps because they feel that their efforts are futile. Unfortunately, the insecurity that breeds this mind-set is deeply entrenched in many of our students from low-income backgrounds.[15] So, armed with the knowledge that this is what too many of our students are experiencing when they enter into college, we are motivated to design a method to empower them with what Carol Dweck terms the "growth" mind-set.

How the University of Texas Improved Mind-Sets and Increased Retention

With an understanding of how disadvantaged students experience college, we then have to ask, how can we reshape the experience for these at-risk students? An intervention piloted with more than 8,000 incoming freshmen who made up the University of Texas at Austin (UT) class of 2016 serves as an example. UT used software to identify students who had risk factors that affect the likelihood of their completing college (first-generation college students, a low socioeconomic background, graduating from a low-performing high school, etc.). The program split students into two groups: "belonging" and "disadvantaged." Members of both groups read either a generic article about the weather at UT or a mind-sets article that shared the stories of students who initially felt they didn't belong on campus but eventually came to find themselves. The students completed a reflection on the article, and no follow-up occurred. The results of the intervention were astounding.

The University of Texas has a benchmark of completing 12 credit hours during the first semester, which distinguishes those students who are on pace to graduate from those who are behind. Among students from "disadvantaged" backgrounds, 80 percent usually make the 12-credit threshold compared to 90 percent of students from "belonging" backgrounds.

After this intervention, there was no significant difference in the number of credit hours earned by students from the "belonging" groups, whether they read the generic article or the mind-sets article. However, following this simple intervention, 86 percent of students from the "disadvantaged" group who read the mind-sets article completed 12 credit hours compared to a completion rate of 82 percent among those students who read the generic article. A four-percentage point gap is a huge improvement, especially considering that these students also stayed in college at higher rates beyond the first semester. This is the power of even a subtle mind-set intervention and an important indicator of the importance and power of subtly exposing students to the "growth" mind-set.

We also know from research completed by large education companies, such as Blackboard, that the most effective programs to improve retention begin working with students during their freshman year.

CommitU: Solving the Crisis of Completion

Armed with the knowledge that freshman programming is among the most effective, CommitU has developed interventions to support universities with onboarding and orientation programming that helps at-risk populations succeed. At CommitU, we have identified the space and the methodology and are now in the early stages of supporting universities in the development of uniquely individualized approaches to helping students find purpose, belonging, and belief.

Conclusion

Even as we work to measure our success in retention rates, the true impact on CommitU programming is threefold.

First, our goal is to inspire students to recognize that they are in fact pursuing a college degree to make their dreams come true. While they will eventually choose an academic discipline, this college journey is a personal trek that helps make *their unique* dreams come true.

Second, we believe that students who do not come from privileged networks (and even those who do) can and should be taught how to create those networks with people connected to their passion. We know that the connected student is the successful student. Building relationships with administrators, professors, and peers is an essential part of this.

Finally, our mission is to help students establish a belief that they belong and that they can achieve. As David Yeager explained about this particular intervention, "We don't prevent you from experiencing those bad things. Instead, we try to change the meaning of them, so that they don't mean to you that things are never going to get better."

CommitU does not have a monopoly on any of these ideas or beliefs. We share them here because we realize that *all* universities can be more effective in helping students by attacking deficiencies in purpose, belonging, and belief.

We are a young company focused on one part of the crisis of completion. We will continue to help universities develop well-researched orientation and remedial programming to help students realize their potential. We are thrilled to be a part of the army working to solve the crisis of completion, and we will continue supporting schools and students for as long as there is work to be done.

Notes

1. Jeff Jones and Lydia Saad, "Gallup Poll Social Series," December 5–8, 2013.

2. "The Condition of Education," National Center for Educational Statistics, updated May 2016.

3. Susan Dynarski, "For the Poor, the Graduation Gap Is Even Wider Than the Enrollment Gap, *New York Times*, June 2, 2015. http://www.nytimes.com/2015/06/02/upshot/for-the-poor-the-graduation-gap-is-even-wider-than-the-enrollment-gap.html. Specifically, the data is from the "Advantage of Wealth in College" table in the article from the Department of Education's *Educational Longitudinal Study*.

4. The Pell Institute for the Study of Opportunity in Higher Education and the University of Pennsylvania Alliance for Higher Education and Democracy, *Indicators of Higher Education Equity in the US: 45 Year Trend Report*," 2015 revised edition. http://www.pellinstitute.org/downloads/publications-Indicators_of_Higher_Education_Equity_in_the_US_45_Year_Trend_Report.pdf.

5. Melissa Korn, "Big Gap in College Graduation Rates for Rich and Poor, Study Finds," *Wall Street Journal*, February 3, 2015. http://www.wsj.com/articles/big-gap-in-college-graduation-rates-for-rich-and-poor-study-finds-1422997677.

6. Russ Alan Prince, "How the Rich Get Very Rich: Leveraging the Matthew Effect," *Forbes*, April 8, 2015. http://www.forbes.com/sites/russalanprince/2015/04/08/how-the-rich-get-very-rich-leveraging-the-matthew-effect.

7. "Performance-based Funding for Higher Education," National Conference of State Legislatures, July 31, 2015. http://www.ncsl.org/research/education/performance-funding.aspx.

8. Richard D. Kahlenberg, *Rewarding Strivers: Helping Low-income Students Succeed in College* (New York: Century Foundation, 2010).

9. Barack Obama, in a speech at the Georgia Institute of Technology, Atlanta, GA, March 10, 2015.

10. David Yeager, Gregory Walton, and Geoffrey L. Cohen, "Addressing Achievement Gaps with Psychological Interventions," *Kappan Magazine* 94, no. 5 (2013): 63–65.

11. Paul Trough, "Who Gets to Graduate," *New York Times Magazine*, May 15, 2014. http://www.nytimes.com/2014/05/18/magazine/who-gets-to-graduate.html.

12. Yeager, Walton, and Cohen, "Addressing Achievement Gaps."

13. Trough, "Who Gets to Graduate."

14. Carol S. Dweck and J. Bempechat, "Children's Theories of Intelligence," in S. Paris, G. Olson, and H. Stevenson, eds., *Learning and Motivation in the Classroom* (Hillsdale, NJ: Lawrence Erlbaum Associates, 1983), 239–256.

15. Gregory M. Walton and Geoffrey L. Cohen, "A Brief Social-belonging Intervention Improves Academic and Health Outcomes of Minority Students," *Science* 331, no. 6023 (2011): 1447–1451.

CHAPTER TEN

Preparing Varsity Athletes for the World of Work

Vin McCaffrey

Since the advent of collegiate sports, the student-athlete experience has equipped college students with the discipline and skills necessary for professional achievement beyond school. In many cases, an involvement in collegiate sports has served as an accurate predictor for future personal success. In fact, many of the most influential figures of the last 50 years can list collegiate athletics as part of their pedigree:

- Dwight Eisenhower was a college football player at the U.S. Military Academy.
- John F. Kennedy played several sports as an undergraduate at Harvard University.
- Richard Nixon played college football at Whittier College.
- Gerald Ford played college football at the University of Michigan.
- Ronald Reagan played football and swam at Eureka College.
- George H.W. Bush played college baseball at Yale University.

As a matter of fact, 9 of the last 11 U.S. presidents were collegiate student-athletes. College-athlete alumni are highly represented among business executives as well. In 2014, 55 percent of women that held C-suite executive positions had competed in athletics during college.[1] Examples of successful college-athlete alumni are too numerous to ignore the correlation between the student-athlete experience and professional achievement.

I launched Game Plan in 2008, motivated by the belief that the skills and discipline an individual develops through the student-athlete experience are not only readily transferable to the workforce but very much in demand. A lot has happened since 2008, and I've met many individuals who share my interest in student achievement beyond college. One such individual was Dr. Aneil Mishra. When Aneil shared with me his vision of restoring trust in higher education, it resonated. I believe that the student-athlete experience is one of the greatest services an institution of higher education can provide. My goal is that by sharing insights into the unique collegiate student-athlete experience, I can demonstrate why it has such an amazing track record for producing success in the classroom, on the field and court, and, perhaps most importantly, in the real world.

To understand the student-athlete experience, it is important to understand the role of the student-athlete in the broader context of college athletics as a whole. College athletics were introduced with the intention of providing a well-rounded experience for participating students while expanding the university's brand identity beyond just an institution of higher education. Present-day college athletics have clearly evolved from their humble beginnings in the 19th century, when college sports programs included boat clubs, rowing, and rugby. Today, nearly every institution of higher education in the world is engaged in college sports.

In the United States, present-day college athletics have evolved to include three primary governing bodies: the National Collegiate Athletics Association (NCAA), the National Association of Intercollegiate Athletics (NAIA), and the National Junior College Athletics Association (JuCo). Altogether, there are nearly 1,800 athletics departments in the United States, with well over 500,000 student-athletes competing annually. Among the three associations, the NCAA and its members capture the majority of the spotlight—particularly at their highest competitive level, Division I. In 2015, Division I athletics comprised 351 athletics departments nationally, spanning multiple conferences, with over 14 sports being played in both women's and men's programs.

A university's athletics department can represent one of its most substantial revenue streams. Hence, each year universities across the country make sizeable investments in their athletics departments with the hope that they will reap a large economic reward. In 2015, *USA Today*'s annual database of finances for athletics departments reported over $8 billion in budgets across the 231 Division I athletics departments that reported their finances.[2] To put this into perspective, each athletics department on average has 500 participating student-athletes. That means Division I athletics departments spend on average $70,000 per athlete; the highest-ranking schools spend over $100,000 per athlete.[3]

The reality is that these budgets are neither distributed evenly across universities nor their individual athletic programs. As an example, in Game Plan's home state of North Carolina, we have college athletics departments operating with budgets ranging from an excess of $80 million annually to less than $7 million annually. Both of these athletics departments compete at the Division I level, but it is clear not all departments are made equally.

I mention the massive size of athletics department budgets not to debate how equitably they are distributed, but to demonstrate the clear economic implications associated with the impact an athletics department has on its university, its local market, and, in some instances, a national level. Take for example the University of Alabama (UA), which employs over 12,000 individuals in Alabama. In 2014, UA's seven home football games generated over $180 million in ticket sales. Moreover, according to UA's Center for Business and Economic Research, for every $1 in state funds appropriated to the university, it generates $17.[4] This demonstrates that a university's athletics department can be a serious engine for economic growth.

At the heart of every college athletics department are its student-athletes. The hour-to-hour schedule that the student-athlete manages is frequently referred to as the "student-athlete experience." This is the experience that Game Plan is focused on. We believe that the discipline and time management skills developed while enduring such highly allocated schedules strengthen a student-athlete's work ethic. So, what does the average day look like for a student-athlete? I have included a three-day sample of an in-season schedule of a Game Plan customer in table 10.1.

This is not an isolated example of a student-athlete schedule. Such a rigorous schedule can be physically exhausting, mentally fatiguing, and emotionally draining. However, it may also lay the groundwork for powerful student-athlete development. Such a taxing schedule is integral to the development of the core skills that employers find so compelling in student-athletes as they enter the workforce. As a young 18- to 22-year-old, student-athletes are learning to manage demands on their time, meet deadlines, and remain agile when moving from one project to the next.

The magnitude of athletics department's budgets and revenues demonstrate just how significant the economic value associated with a successful college athletics program can be. To realize this economic value, universities must devote large amounts of resources to their athletics departments. These sports are expensive to run. Coaching salaries, facilities, and scholarships do not come cheap. The result of these investments is that the student-athlete experience incorporates multiple stakeholders,

Table 10.1   Typical three-day schedule for a game plan customer.

	Monday	Tuesday	Wednesday
8:00 a.m.	Class	Team breakfast	Class
9:00 a.m.			
10:00 a.m.		Proctored study table	
11:00 a.m.			
12:00 p.m.	Free time		Free time
1:00 p.m.	Practice	Team lunch	Lunch / Meeting with coach
2:00 p.m.	Free time	Free time	Class / Study time
3:00 p.m.	Bus ride to away game	Pre-game shoot around	Trainer / Pre-practice
4:00 p.m.			Practice
5:00 p.m.		Return to hotel / Free time / Check-out	
6:00 p.m.			
		Travel to gym	
7:00 p.m.	Check in and free time	Game tip off / Game ends	Free time/Dinner
8:00 p.m.			
9:00 p.m.	Team dinner		Proctored study table
10:00 p.m.	Proctored study table	Shower and prep for departure	
11:00 p.m.	Back to room / Free time	Bus ride	
	Lights out		
12:00 a.m.			
1:00 a.m.		Arrive home / Back to dorm	

including students, coaches, administrators, and alumni. As we will see, these stakeholders have a vested interest in measuring an athletics department's success—using countless performance indicators—all in an effort to create collective accountability. It's this collective accountability that drives a student-athlete's success on the field and as a student. Game Plan believes this accountability also aids in preparing student-athletes for the rigors and challenges of the real world.

What Inspires a College Athlete?

Many college athletes began playing their sport of choice before the age of 10. An athlete's sport gives him or her purpose and a sense of control, and the student-athlete experience is his or her primary motivator. However, the reality is that the vast majority of college-athletes reach their apex in college and do not advance past that level. What's more, a professional outlet does not exist for most collegiate-level sports beyond the collegiate level. For those select few sports that do offer professional opportunities, the unlikelihood that a student-athlete will actually progress to that level is well documented. The NCAA reports that a mere 1.6 percent, 1.1 percent, and 0.9 percent of its football, men's basketball, and women's basketball athletes will advance to the professional level, respectively.[5]

Regardless of a student-athlete's prospect of a professional athletic career, there is still significant pressure to perform even while at the college level. Coaches, staff, and administrators create high expectations to instill accountability in student-athletes. A student-athlete's in-sport performance is closely measured and managed by coaches who, in their own right, are strongly incentivized to achieve success. A coach's success is not only measured by wins and losses, but also by the academic performances of his or her athletes. These performance indicators are used in determining a coach's pay and any allocation of funding to the athletics department from a governing body, such as the NCAA. Obviously then, it is in the coach's interest of self-preservation to ensure his or her players are achieving at the highest levels athletically and academically.

The governing bodies of college athletics have long been measuring the academic success of programs, coaches, and student-athletes by their graduation rates. The graduation rate of student-athletes is a simple measurement that can be measured consistently across institutions and is generally considered an objective in line with the missions of the university and the athletics department. Establishing graduation rates as an objective has been quite effective, to say the least. In 2015, the graduation rate for

Table 10.2   NCAA APR noncompliance penalties.

Third Level
May include coaching suspensions, financial aid reductions (including loss of scholarships), and restricted NCAA membership (including championships)
Second Level
Adds additional practice and competition reductions, either in the traditional or nonchampionship season, to the first-level penalties
First Level
Teams limited to 16 hours of practice per week over five days, with the lost 4 hours to be replaced with academic activities

Division I athletes climbed to 86 percent, a two-percentage point increase over the previous year.[6]

As governing bodies such as the NCAA established academic benchmarks for college athletic programs to meet, they brought forth regulations and penalties associated with not meeting these requirements. One such benchmark is the Academic Progress Rate (APR) created by the NCAA for Division I athletic programs. An athletic program's APR collectively measures student-athlete's GPAs, retention rates, and graduation rates in each individual program.[7] The NCAA uses these figures as inputs to a formula that produces an APR score that measures the success of a coach and each individual athletic program. If the program fails to meet the established criteria, it faces penalties that include loss of scholarships and postseason play along with other punitive damages (see table 10.2).

The vast majority of NCAA athletics departments meet or exceed the APR requirements, despite the fact that their student-athlete's time is so highly allocated between school and sport.[8] In 2015, only 21 of the 351 athletics departments with a minimum of 14 programs received postseason bans, and only 28 faced less serious penalties. So how is it that student-athletes can achieve academically despite their ultrademanding schedules—schedules that make you stressed and tired just by reading them? It is the athletics department's unwavering commitment to the student-athlete's success.

As I founded Game Plan, I began to notice a common theme while speaking to administrators in athletics department and coaches alike: an athletics department's commitment to success is not switched on and off easily, and their commitment to academic success is often as untiring as their commitment to their student-athletes' athletic excellence.

The Learfield NACDA Director's Cup: A Case Study

In 1993, the National Association of Collegiate Directors of Athletics (NACDA) formed an award named the Learfield Director's Cup to signify the overall athletic achievement of a Division I athletics department, accounting for success of each of its teams. In 1995, a similar award was announced for Division III programs. To determine a winner, the NACDA scores the cumulative success of an athletics department based on each individual sports program's championship ranking along with the size of the championship bracket.

At the Division I level, Stanford University has won the award 21 times. For Division III programs, Williams College has won the award 18 of its 20 years. During that time, Williams and Stanford have also been ranked among the most elite academic institutions in the United States. In 2015, Stanford was ranked fourth overall academically, and Williams College ranked first among liberal arts colleges.[9] It's clear that a college's athletic success often goes hand in hand with its academic success, and the most successful athletics departments create a culture that recognizes academic and athletic achievements as not mutually exclusive. In fact, as we will see, the true leaders of college athletics are breaking barriers and expanding their vision to include not only academic achievement but career and world-readiness as well.

Commitment and Collective Accountability

The burden of achieving academic success is not left to rest on the shoulders of a young 18- to 22-year-old student-athlete. As we have seen, athletics departments also have a vested interest in the success of their student-athletes. Their commitment is demonstrated by the large amount of resources they invest in infrastructure designed to support the academic success of their student-athletes. Since governing bodies such as the NCAA have established first and foremost the goal of student-athlete graduation, athletics departments have made graduation rates a number-one priority. To help the student-athlete achieve this goal, athletics departments have invested in support organizations for student-athlete academic achievement and development. These organizations are designed to provide the student-athlete with academic advising, tutoring, and personal and professional development.

An athletics department's student-athlete support organization will have one if not several individuals with a dedicated focus on student-athletes, depending on the amount of resources it has at its disposal. These individuals will oversee academic advising, assist the student-athlete in selecting his or her major, provide tutoring, and even manage the study table. The University of Oregon's investment in their John E. Jaqua Academic Center for Student-Athletes is a great example of dedication to student-athlete academic success. This 40,000-square-foot facility boasts an auditorium with 114 leather seats, 35 tutor rooms, 25 academic and life-skills advising offices, a conference room, a computer lab, a graphics lab, a library, study carrels, a lounge with a wide flat-screen TV and plush sofas, and a full kitchenette and cafe, all outfitted with state-of-the-art equipment.[10] The University of Oregon is not an isolated example either. There are countless examples across major college athletics, including Michigan State University, the University of Georgia, and the University of Michigan.

A student-athlete's commitment to the achievement of his or her goals stands in stark contrast to that of a nonstudent-athlete because, in this case, it's not a voluntary matter. The athletic department's overarching commitment to the success of the student-athlete, athletically and academically, at times, does not accommodate the student's discretion. They know that other stakeholders will hold them accountable for their academic success. It is this collective accountability—coupled with the incentives and penalties outlined earlier—that strongly compels the athletic department and their student-athletes to achieve academic success. This culture of collective accountability and commitment surrounding the student-athlete experience is ultimately the catalyst for student-athlete development.

In founding Game Plan, we became advocates for the student-athlete experience and actively promoted its value to employers. As it turns out, this evangelism was much easier than we expected it to be. In fact, in many cases, the value of the student-athlete experience and how it prepares student-athletes for life beyond college was already well understood. The reality was that student-athlete alumni had laid the groundwork for our mission with their exceptional discipline and work ethic. Many employers already knew that student-athletes make great employees and could even share anecdotal experiences that indicated their work ethic.

It was then that I discovered the true value that Game Plan was providing to athletics departments: Game Plan complements and expands an athletics department's capabilities, which amplifies the value student-athletes derive from the student-athlete experience. In short, we have found that the more comprehensively Game Plan is able to engage a student-athlete via our platform, the more valuable our extended brand is to employers. Athletics departments were already graduating their student-athletes and meeting the academic requirements put forth by governing bodies such as the NCAA. The question Game Plan wanted to answer was, what comes next?

Life beyond Sports

The value we provide to athletics departments was clear: Game Plan will assist you in preparing the student-athlete for life beyond sports. This puts athletics departments at an advantage and allows them to

- *Attract talent and recruiting.* By focusing on preparing student-athletes for life beyond college, coaches have an improved proposition for recruiting talent: "Students will graduate, and we will prepare them for their careers."
- *Increase revenue.* The worthwhile cause of preparing student-athletes for life beyond college prompts donors, student-athlete alumni, and sponsors to invest in the athletics department brand that can tout student-athlete success beyond graduation.

The challenge Game Plan now faced was twofold:

1. We needed to expand the scope and measurement of student-athlete success to include not only academic performance but also success in life after sports. Athletics departments have expended significant amounts of resources to create programs designed to improve student-athlete academic success. Expanding the scope of these programs to include a student-athlete's career beyond school meant change for many. This transition is particularly difficult as governing bodies such as the NCAA do not currently account for (and therefore do not make economic or punitive decisions based on) a student-athlete's life beyond sports.
2. We needed to redefine the student-athlete journey using a comprehensive model that includes several phases of development. Career preparation encompasses far more than a simple résumé workshop. Game Plan needed to demonstrate how each phase of student-athlete development complements the success of each subsequent phase and, ultimately, how these phases culminate in preparing a student-athlete for success in his or her life after sports. If Game Plan could redefine the student-athlete journey in the eyes of athletics departments, our value as an organization would be made clear.

The competitive nature of collegiate athletics compels athletics departments to aggressively recruit prospective athletes. Even though governing bodies do not currently account for student-athlete success in life beyond sports, athletic departments have increasingly found it useful to assure prospective and current athletes of their investment in student-athlete success beyond sports. As an example, it was announced in 2015 that Gene Smith, the athletic director of the Ohio State University, had a new bonus structure in place based on the number of graduating senior student-athletes who successfully found employment.

Game Plan's role became clear once athletics departments began to mobilize resources to improve the likelihood of career success for its student-athletes. We view our role to be both a trusted adviser to the journey that can provide best practices associated with the student-athlete's preparation for life after sports as well as a resource to assist the athletics department in the application of those practices.

What is implied with the example at Ohio State is that student-athletes weren't finding jobs even though the academic performances of student-athletes were meeting NCAA standards. Since its launch, Game Plan has been focused on this important missing piece. More importantly, we've been focused on quantifying the journey a student-athlete evolves through and, ultimately, how he or she achieves the outcome of full-time employment and world-readiness.

So, if world-readiness is the ultimate goal, what phases must a student-athlete go through to successfully achieve this state? When we launched Game Plan, we were surprised to learn that a comprehensive framework for the student-athlete development process did not exist. Over the years, Game Plan has worked to codify the student-athlete development process and develop a comprehensive framework—we call it the *student-athlete journey*. This framework enables athletic departments to more accurately monitor a student-athlete's development and then apply resources accordingly based on which phase he or she is struggling with. We suggest that the student-athlete journey moves through four phases of development to achieve world-readiness. They are foundation setting, academic performance, career development, and world-readiness.

Foundation Setting

The *foundation setting phase* of development focuses on the transition from high school to college. This transition is difficult for any student, but it can be especially challenging for a student balancing academics and sports. The key activities associated with the transition are twofold. First, measuring a student-athlete's conscientiousness, introversion or extroversion, and other dominant aspects of his or her personality and, second, a self-awareness process that helps the student-athlete understand his or her goals, the resources made available to him or her, and the large time commitment that will be required. Surveying a student-athlete's personality early on will allow an athletics department to predict any academic obstacles he or she may encounter as a student and then proactively prescribe additional tutoring, study-tables, or academic advisement.

Academic Performance

The *academic performance phase* stresses a student-athlete's ongoing academic success. One key activity a student-athlete completes during this phase is determining which available areas of study (majors) complement his or her personality, interests, and aptitude. Game Plan has found that if a student-athlete is interested in subject matter, he or she will be more engaged and satisfied with academic coursework. Game Plan has administered our interest inventory assessment to over 20,000 student-athletes to aid them in selecting their major.

In addition to matching a student-athlete's interests to their major, Game Plan believes that teaching fundamental skills such as how to properly take notes in class, read a textbook, and communicate with professors during office hours are integral to academic success. A student-athlete's overall GPA along with his or her GPA within his or her major serve as key measurements of success during the academic performance phase.

Career Development

The *career development phase* represents the student-athlete's transition into the workforce. This phase focuses first on gauging a student-athlete's career interests (based on the results of the interest inventory assessment he or she completed during the academic performance phase) and then preparing him or her for success while interviewing for positions and evaluating job offers. After a student-athlete has selected a profession or industry, he or she can begin to build a professional network of potential employers. The next step is to develop a résumé and perform mock interviews so that he or she will be better positioned to acquire an internship or, ideally, a full-time position. The success of this phase of development will be measured by the quality of a student-athlete's résumé and mock interview performance along with how promptly he or she was able to acquire an internship or a full-time position.

World-Readiness

The *world-readiness phase* of development represents the student-athlete's transition away from his or her sport and on to the next phase of his or her life. At some point, every student-athlete must effectively and healthily make this transition. It is a significant challenge that every student-athlete wrestles with to some degree. In the end, the goal is for the student-athlete to understand his or her athletic identity and appreciate it as an asset as he or she transitions to the next phase in life.

As the student-athlete makes this transition, it is important that he or she also achieves a basic level of financial literacy. This includes learning the basics of budgeting and saving so that he or she can develop the financial habits necessary for future success.

Comprehensive Student-Athlete Development: A Blueprint for Success

Athletics departments are held accountable for athletic and academic success by their governing bodies. They invest huge amounts of resources to improve the win-loss records of their programs as well as the GPA, retention rates, and graduation rates of their student-athletes. As college-athlete recruitment becomes increasingly competitive, athletics departments must continue to expand their definition of student-athlete development to include success in life after sports.

Leaders in college athletics, such as Gene Smith at Ohio State, have begun to recognize that comprehensive student-athlete development and athletic achievement go hand in hand. These leaders have created a culture of collective accountability by expanding the scope of student-athlete development to include success in life beyond sports. Game Plan's framework takes this one step further by redefining the student-athlete journey and establishing a replicable blueprint for this journey. Our framework allows athletics departments to specifically pinpoint which phase a student-athlete is struggling through—allowing the student-athlete to be proactive in assuring his or her academic and professional success. By accepting this new definition and adopting our framework, athletics departments will be able to comply with the increasingly strict regulations of their governing bodies and achieve a competitive advantage when recruiting talented student-athletes.

Notes

1. Barbara Kotschwar, "Women, Sports, and Development: Does It Pay to Let Girls Play?," Peterson Institute for International Economics, no. PB14-8, March 2014. https://piie.com/sites/default/files/publications/pb/pb14-8.pdf.

2. Steve Berkowitz et al., "NCAA Finances: 2014–2015 Finances," *USA Today*, accessed June 2016. http://sports.usatoday.com/ncaa/finances.

3. "Trends in Spending and Institutional Funding," Athletic & Academic Spending Database for NCAA Division I, Knight Commission on Intercollegiate Athletics, accessed 2014. http://spendingdatabase.knightcommission.org/fbs.

4. Samuel Addy and Ahmad Ijaz, "2013–2014 Economic Impacts of the University of Alabama," Culverhouse College of Commerce, Center for Business and Economic Research, University of Alabama, June 2015. http://cber.cba.ua.edu/rbriefs/UA_Impact_2013_2014.pdf.

5. "Estimated Probability of Competing in Professional Athletics," NCAA, updated April 25, 2016. http://www.ncaa.org/about/resources/research/estimated-probability-competing-professional-athletics.

6. Michelle Brutlag-Hosick, "Graduation Success Rate Continues to Climb," NCAA, November 4, 2015. http://www.ncaa.org/about/resources/media-center/news/graduation-success-rate-continues-climb.

7. "Academic Progress Rate Explained," NCAA, accessed May 2015. http://www.ncaa.org/about/resources/research/academic-progress-rate-explained.

8. Ibid.

9. "Williams College," *U.S. News & World Report*, accessed 2016. http://colleges.usnews.rankingsandreviews.com/best-colleges/williams-college-2229; "National Universities Rankings," *U.S. News & World Report*, accessed 2016. http://colleges.usnews.rankingsandreviews.com/best-colleges/rankings/national-universities/data.

10. Howard P. Chudacoff, "Let's Not Pay College Athletes," *Wall Street Journal*, March 28, 2016. http://www.wsj.com/articles/lets-not-pay-college-athletes-1459206949.

CHAPTER ELEVEN

Alumni Nation

Karen E. Mishra and Aneil K. Mishra

One item that may not be high on students' and families' lists when choosing a school is the alumni network. This is because as an entering student, an alumni network may not be the most important salient aspect to consider. Indeed, according to a survey conducted in late 2014 and published in 2015 by the New America Foundation, the top factors students cite when choosing a college are (1) the majors and programs that are offered, (2) the availability of financial aid, (3), how much it costs, (4) where it is located, and (5) how many graduates find full-time employment in the field within six months.[1] At one of the schools where we have taught, students even told us that they selected this school precisely because it had a winning basketball team. These students happened to be lucky on two more counts: one, this school has a highly ranked business school, and two, it is ranked among the top 50 most powerful alumni networks.[2] These two items will help those students in their careers more than they anticipated. One study found that "providing a high quality educational experience is critical to garnering future support from future alumni."[3]

Schools are increasingly focused on cultivating a strong and loyal alumni base because of the financial, network, and other benefits. As the most powerful alumni networks attest, loyal alumni have higher rates of giving and support the school in other ways, as well, such as hiring recent graduates and returning to campus to provide ongoing mentoring and support.[4] This financial support, in particular, is becoming more and more important for public schools, especially, as state funding diminishes and must be replaced with private giving. Indeed, public higher education costs have increased due to a 79 percent decrease in state funding over the past decade.[5] Colleges and universities have had to be creative in making up that gap. Alumni giving is the first place where colleges and universities look, but without a loyal alumni base, giving will not follow. In addition, for private schools to close the tuition gap between themselves and public schools, alumni giving can make a big difference.

Factors Affecting Alumni Loyalty

First, however, schools must figure out how to create a loyal alumni base, and building trust with them is essential. According to a 2015 survey of 1,100 alumni, 22 percent of alumni are currently giving financially to their alma maters, with another 37 percent having donated in the past and may consider donating again.[6] This same survey argued that trust was a key factor in whether alumni choose to give; three of the four dimensions of the ROCC of Trust—discussed in chapter 1—were illustrated in the survey results. Ninety percent of donors believe their alma mater spends donated funds wisely (Competence) versus 67 percent of nondonors believing this. Eighty-four percent of donors believe that their alma mater values their opinion versus 52 percent of nondonors (Openness). And 80 percent say they benefit from association with their alma mater (Compassion) as contrasted with only 48 percent of nondonors.[7] The one dimension of trust that alumni do not mention is whether their alma mater is reliable.

One study found that alumni who volunteer the most to the institution are not the most academically successful students but rather the students who had been most engaged.[8] Therefore, schools must start by engaging their own students to create a loyal alumni base. Indeed, another study found that colleges and universities can increase alumni giving by improving student satisfaction with student affairs.[9] Students affairs on most campuses includes all of the nonacademic departments on a university campus that make up the extracurricular life of a student, such as housing, dining, health and wellness, fraternities and sororities, and information technology. All of these support the life of a student while he or she is living at college. Academics still matter, and another way that institutions can strengthen their alumni base is by building high-quality academic programs.[10] In addition, by pairing a quality education with well-rounded extracurricular activities, engaged students become engaged alumni.[11] When students feel ownership of their education and their school while they are on campus, they are more likely to remain highly engaged as alumni.

Another study examining alumni support found that those who identify with the role of alumna or alumnus are more likely to support their institution in recognized ways, such as attending events, volunteering, joining the alumni association, and making a financial contribution.[12] The key then is to help alumni feel connected to that role through the school, their fellow classmates, friends, and family. The more an alumna or alumnus feels connected to the role, the more frequently she or he will participate in alumni activities and the closer connection she or he will have to the alma mater.

Alumni Connections Are Not Initially Paved with Gold

Schools often think that financial giving is the first and most important way that alumni can give back to their school. But, especially for recent alumni who are still paying off student loans, there are other ways to get them involved in the life of the school and make a connection to that alumni role without making them feel like they have to make a financial gift. One way to begin fostering strong connections with alumni is simply to invite them back to campus. During classes or at career clubs, students enjoy hearing from alumni about their jobs, how they found them, and other career advice. This helps the alumni feel connected through having shared time and expertise.

We both regularly invite our former students back to campus, regardless of how long they have been working, and they have served as great sources of advice for our current students when it comes to job searches; conducting informational interviews to help our students learn about various companies, careers, and industries; and providing valuable information on salaries, likely interview questions, and other important career intelligence. As these alumni progress in their careers, they have even hired our current students for both internships and full-time jobs. Indeed, as we built our own Trust Network of alumni across the several universities at which we have been professors, and at some point, alumni began hiring one another without even involving the hub, that is, us, in the interviewing or hiring process.[13] The network had indeed become fully interactive without our direct involvement.

Paying Back and Paying Forward: Alumni as Mentors and Coaches for Students

Many schools have formalized the process of alumni sharing their time and expertise. The Mason School of Business at the College of William & Mary was one of the first to invite retired executives, including William & Mary alumni, to have permanent positions on campus coaching students and teams. These *executive partners*, as they are called, even have their own office spaces on campus. As a lead coach, Dr. Mohan Peter, an MD, told us,

> We are fortunate in having well over a hundred retired or semiretired executives who have settled in the Williamsburg area and are available to us as resources for coaching our students. Coaching is distinct from mentoring. We therefore train our coaches in the art and science of coaching through ongoing activities that enhance their coaching skills. This is an ongoing process and possibly the most critical part of the program.

The William & Mary coaching program is quite extensive, with students able to meet with their coaches many times during their business program. In addition, students and coaches create personal connections, as well. "The coaches also host the student teams for dinner at the coaches' homes for an evening of get to know the students." This program is designed to bring out the best in students while maximizing the talent, knowledge, and resources of the executive coaches. As Dr. Peter stated, "Our pool of coaches makes it possible for almost any student to connect with coaches who have worked in that field. This is invaluable for the student to get a detailed understanding of the ins and outs of a field that they may want to pursue a career in." This is easily a model that other schools could use to bring in retired alumni who want to give back by more than just writing a check.

Princeton University is embarking on a new effort to include more alumni in its career advising, as well. In an interview with Pulin Sanghvi, the executive director of Career Services, he described how students are driving a change in career mentoring and advising: "I think this generation is much more focused on learning how to do different things and then building 'spikiness,' or unique professional attributes that become the ingredients and the recipes that they'll bring forward into the world." They are looking to utilize the vast Princeton network (which is number 12 on Best College Values' list of the 50 most powerful alumni networks) already in place to help students connect their education to their passion.[14] As Career Services Director Evangeline Kubu noted, "Our new model incorporates alumni into every aspect of the work that we're doing with students."

Sanghvi further defined the role of alumni: "We help each of our students define unique visions for their career and their lives. We then connect them in personalized multidimensional ways to the resources, people, organizations, and opportunities that will help make their unique visions a reality. Our primary goal is to seed a lot of really great first conversations and then trust that the longer lasting, deeper mentorship relationships will form more organically."

Lifelong Learning, Career Development, and Personal Growth for Alumni

With a U.S. economy that is still in recovery and unemployment rates among recent college graduates still above levels from before the Great Recession, alumni are expecting more and more from their universities, whether in the form of career development or executive education.[15] Sixty-three percent of alumni "indicate that their alma mater has played an important role in their employment—either in the past, currently or both," and "68% of alumni say they have benefited professionally from connections to their alma mater."[16] If schools want their alumni to identify strongly as such, they must be prepared for those alumni to turn to them first when they need career help.

One school that changed the name of their alumni relations program is the University of Richmond. Seeing an opportunity to reach out to alumni and extend those alumni networks into career transitions, the University of Richmond changed the name of alumni relations to Alumni and Career Services. According to Kristin Woods, the assistant vice president for alumni and career services,

> Fostering lifelong relationships between the University of Richmond and its alumni continues to be an important goal. Doing so through these types of programs and services benefits everyone. And, we know that the more people feel engaged, the more likely they are to give back, be it by hiring another Spider, referring a prospective student to us, or making a financial gift.[17]

The University of Michigan Ross School of Business has also made a significant effort by offering all of its alumni tuition-free access to their open-enrollment executive education programs, which typically cost $10,000 per week.[18] Ross alumni may also sponsor up to two other colleagues, friends, or family members, who can attend these programs at a 50 percent discount. This Alumni Advantage program also offers other University of Michigan alumni who are not Ross alumni a 50 percent discount on these programs as well.

Trust Is the Critical Ingredient in Alumni Networks

Trust is both a necessary antecedent to and consequence of effective alumni networks. To the extent that fellow alumni trust one another more than they trust nonalumni, it may facilitate the sharing of information and encourage them to help one another in ways that they would not otherwise do:

> Sharing an alma mater can provide a base level of trust for entrepreneurs to start a conversation with someone who might become a business partner, an investor, or a key employee. Many small companies could not succeed without those connections. When you're first starting out in any endeavor, trust is incredibly pivotal. Just having that relationship makes everything smoother.[19]

However, in the absence of building trust-based relationships with alumni, universities may miss out on important help when their students need it most. One of the reasons that we created our Trust Network is that some of our former students were working at prestigious firms such as McKinsey Consulting and did not trust the career development staff at our universities to provide them with high-quality candidates for on-campus job interviews. They turned to us instead to vet candidates based on our personal knowledge of students. In addition, at that time, there were no career services provided to alumni at the business schools at which we taught, meaning that job opportunities for more experienced candidates were not being shared with our schools by our alumni. We professors, on the other hand, having kept in touch with many former students, did know of alumni who would be suitable candidates for these more senior positions. We could then connect alumni with students and alumni with one another, job providers to job seekers.

From these initial inquiries by our alumni for high-quality job candidates grew a regular e-mail job-posting service, then a job portal, and now a LinkedIn group, Facebook page, and other social networking efforts to help our alumni from several different colleges and universities help one another. However, the social capital has accrued to our own created network of alumni from various institutions, rather than their respective colleges and universities, because those other institutions still haven't made proper efforts to engage with their alumni.

One of the ways that we encourage our students during strengths coaching is to reach out to members of our alumni Trust Network to conduct informational interviews. This allows them a low-stress way to learn about a new job or a new industry without actually quitting their job and possibly making a mistake based on their personal interests and fit. We have never had alumni say no when we've asked if they would talk to or mentor one of our current students, even if those alumni attended a school where we formerly taught.

Indeed, alumni have the opportunity to bridge differences in social class and provide opportunities to first-generation and underprivileged college students in ways that formal curricula and government programs cannot match. Robert Putnam, in *Our Kids: The American Dream in Crisis*, discusses the advantages that affluent kids have relative to their underprivileged counterparts:

> When adjusting to college, choosing college majors, and making career plans, kids from more affluent, educated homes engage a wider array of informal advisors—family members, faculty, and outsiders—whereas kids from poor families typically consult one or two members of their immediate family, few if any of whom have any college experience at all. In short, the social networks of more affluent, educated families amplify their other assets in helping to assure that their kids have richer opportunities.
>
> Affluent families provide their kids with connections that poor families can't. But connections are important not merely for getting into top schools and top jobs. At least as important as the pipeline from a prized internship to a corner office job are the ways in which social capital can protect privileged kids from the ordinary risks of adolescence.[20]

However, successful college and university alumni are in a unique position to apply their human capital, that is, their academic and professional experience and success, along with their social capital, their professional networks, to transforming the experiences of underprivileged students in ways that have been happening for affluent students for decades. What is necessary is a call to action—and a commitment of financial, material, and human resources—by college and university leaders to help broaden and deepen relationships between alumni and students with disadvantaged backgrounds. This would strengthen the claim that higher education can make upon taxpayer support at a time when colleges and universities, especially those with large endowments, are increasingly under attack for their nonprofit status.[21]

Both students and alumni alike will have more trust in their schools if they feel like they are part of a college or university where the relationship starts but has no end. Students and alumni want to feel appreciated and respected. They want to know that they are more than just their bank accounts. Once alumni feel that they can make a meaningful contribution to the life of their school, they will act in more supportive ways and the money will follow. This will rebuild trust in colleges and universities and also provide for the long-term needs of those schools.

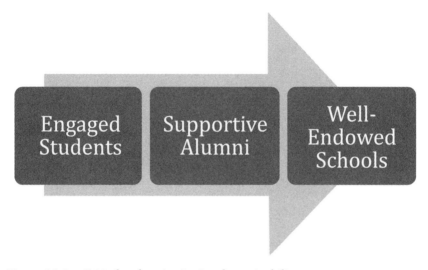

Figure 11.1   Critical path to institutional sustainability.

Notes

1. Rachel Fichman, "College Decisions Survey: Deciding to Go to College," New America Foundation, May 28, 2015. http://www.edcentral.org/collegedecisions.

2. "The 50 Most Powerful Alumni Networks," Best College Values, accessed 2016. http://www.bestcollegevalues.org/top-alumni-networks.

3. D. J. Weerts and J. M. Ronca, "Characteristics of Alumni Donors Who Volunteer at Their Alma Mater," *Research in Higher Education* 49, no. 3 (2008): 274–292.

4. J. T. Mcdearmon, "Hail to Thee, Our Alma Mater: Alumni Role Identity and the Relationship to Institutional Support Behaviors," *Research in Higher Education* 54, no. 3 (2013): 283–302.

5. Kellie Woodhouse, "Who's to Blame for Rising Tuition?," Inside Higher Ed, May 5, 2015. https://www.insidehighered.com/news/2015/05/05/report-says -administrative-bloat-construction-booms-not-largely-responsible-tuition.

6. "2015 Alumni Engagement and Giving Survey," Corporate Insight, slide 12, accessed 2016. http://pages.corporateinsight.com/2015-alumni-survey.

7. Ibid., slide 17.

8. Weerts and Ronca, "Characteristics of Alumni Donors."

9. A. L. Stephenson and D. B. Yerger, "Optimizing Engagement: Brand Identification and Alumni Donation Behaviors," *International Journal of Educational Management* 28, no. 6 (2014): 765.

10. Weerts and Ronca, "Characteristics of Alumni Donors."

11. N. E. Rau and T. D. Erwin, "Using Student Engagement to Predict Alumni Donors: An Analytical Model," *Journal of Nonprofit Education and Leadership* 5, no. 2 (2015).

12. Mcdearmon, "Hail to Thee."

13. Weerts and Ronca, "Characteristics of Alumni Donors."

14. "The 50 Most Powerful Alumni Networks."

15. Alyssa Davis, Will Kimball, and Elise Gould, "The Class of 2015: Despite an Improving Economy, Young Grads Still Face an Uphill Climb," Economic Policy Institute, briefing paper #401, May 27, 2015. http://www.epi.org/publication/the-class-of-2015.

16. "2015 Alumni Engagement and Giving Survey," Slide 9.

17. "Business Briefs," National Association of College and University Business Officers, accessed 2016. http://www.nacubo.org/Business_Officer_Magazine/Magazine_Archives/September_2011/Business_Briefs.html.

18. "University of Michigan's Ross School of Business Redefines Alumni Status to a Lifetime Partnership," Michigan Ross, October 12, 2015. http://michiganross.umich.edu/news/university-michigan-s-ross-school-business-redefines-alumni-status-lifetime-partnership.

19. Tozzi, 2008.

20. Robert D. Putnam. *Our Kids: The American Dream in Crisis* (New York: Simon & Schuster. Kindle Edition), 210.

21. Larry Kaplan, "Congress Presses Large Colleges and Universities on Their Endowments," Nonprofit Quarterly, February 17, 2016. https://nonprofitquarterly.org/2016/02/17/congress-asks-questions-about-large-college-and-university-endowments/?utm_source=hs_email&utm_medium=email&utm_content=26337024&_hsenc=p2ANqtz-9WTjR1Fg3rMA3gbzGafXYjyaKMFIpi_ASM_RdyasP-J0QnDHIWQbVov7VKaGNYmwvBqzCKVZLkmhcpgeBdjv9KaEoaHn_SKv7PKGXmECdWBXczVNs&_hsmi=26337024.

CHAPTER TWELVE

Online Education: Higher Education Savior or Selling Our Souls to the Devil?

Christine M. Wallace

In *Faust*, a learned scholar with great knowledge and intellectual ability strikes a deal with the devil to have "everything." In one scene, Faust allows Mephistopheles to wear his academic cap and gown and impersonate him to advise a student seeking advice on his education.[1] In many ways, those of us who have been prophets of online education have been portrayed as devils impersonating scholars with our promised benefits of *online* for our institutions, our students, and higher education as a whole. Nothing could be further from the truth.

Often online education has been purported as some new-fangled approach to learning that has no basis in the research and has not been tried and true. Take the time to review the history of online education, originally called "distance" education, and it is easy to see that the origins of online have been around for at least 300 years. Some of the earliest notions of distance education date back to 1728, when a "new way" to teach shorthand was marketed using a correspondence course.[2] By the late 1800s the University of Wisconsin had begun the first official distance education programs in the country.[3] This methodology has evolved since correspondence courses and the original machine learning, which was developed by Carnegie Mellon and IBM with the Andrew Project.[4] Today, online education is a model and a methodology with experts, research, processes, and best practices.

While there have been some questionable players hawking less-than-employable degrees and using sales and marketing approaches that are reminiscent of snake oil or traveling medicine shows, in the world of online there have also been high-quality programs that have developed alongside these less-than-reputable players. Think Embry-Riddle's Online Campus, Penn State's World Campus, or UMass Online. These example institutions have comprehensive and professional systems for online education that are connected to their home universities but have structures and systems that are separate. This is a successful model. Unfortunately, it often requires separate accreditations. For most institutions dipping their toes into online education, it is vital that the traditional faculty still own academic programs and make the primary decisions so that accreditation extends to online programs.

Faculty involvement with online programs and delivery is imperative. It is high-quality experts teaching that make the difference between a quality course or program that is average and one that is mediocre. The truth is that teaching is still at the core of learning, but how we teach has changed. While faculty are vital to high-quality online programs and courses, many of our more experienced faculty members were likely never trained in pedagogy or andragogy, unless this is their area of expertise in education. Fewer still are experts in instructional design.

The result of allowing faculty untrained in these areas to develop one-off courses on their own is a noncentralized and less-than-best-practice approach that rarely serves the student taking the course or the institution as a whole. These courses are largely developed for the convenience of the professor and do not provide a holistic and comprehensive approach. In several examples where students have failed abysmally, the courses were developed requiring so many software applications and registrations to use materials that students not only got mired in the process but spent so much time learning several software applications that they missed the primary objectives of the course. Furthermore, the registration process to use the software was slightly complicated and did not integrate directly into the course. In another course, there were so many different assignments due on different days every week that students could not create a rhythm or understand when assignments were due. Assignments were not created to integrate into the LMS calendar. In addition, detailed rubrics were not used, and an easily understandable point distribution for assignments not employed. Students could not make judgments about the importance of assignments. This leads to spending to too much time on minor items and too little time on important assignments. The course was considered a failure by both the instructor and the department; however, it was not the course, but its design, that had failed.

Everything that works in a classroom does not work online, and vice versa. There are a series of best practices that begin in development and extend to teaching, mentoring, and grading students that are specific to online education. As a result, a collaborative partnership between online professionals and expert faculty provides the best possible opportunity to develop high-quality online programs and courses—a win-win-win for students, faculty and the institution.

Failure to develop this type of working relationship results in a string of one-off courses that make it difficult for students to succeed as a whole. In addition, if adding online to a university menu is, in part, to increase revenue, this type of development will add little or nothing to an institution's bottom line. One-off online courses allow the institution's current student body to stay in their pajamas and take a class from their dorm rooms. If your students who are already on campus are the only students taking your online courses, your revenue has only shifted from the face-to-face (F2F) classroom budget line to online. In short, this does not add one extra dollar of revenue to the budget. While this might seem like a great idea for some students, it robs traditional faculty and students of the F2F interaction that their parents had hoped for and are paying for in college.

The traditional undergraduate campus experience is a still an important type of higher education experience. Young adults have many lessons to learn on campus. The average 17- to 22-year-old is still trying to understand who they are and what their talents may be. There is no substitution for a great faculty person who recognizes the talent of a young person in the classroom and cultivates that talent on a daily basis. Many of us would not be where we are today without those mentors. More so, there is no substitution for the kind of social interactions and opportunities a traditional campus experience can provide. One can take part in protests, participate in hobbies, make lifelong friends, find mentors, deal with conflict, fall in love, and discover that life is much more than a Facebook page or a text message.

But for the adult learner, those that either missed or were excluded from the opportunity to have that traditional experience, something else is necessary. Graduate students currently working or living far more complicated lives than their parents need a different approach. Few can afford to quit the job that pays the bills or leave family that may need their time and attention to give an institution of higher learning their full-time attention. In both of these cases, online education may be the answer. "May" is the operative term. Not everyone learns well in an environment where an instructor is not pacing the learning in the front of the classroom. The "sage on the stage" model works best for some individuals. The idea of a "guide on the side" is irritating for others who think the goal of education is input-output: the instructor gives me the information I need to know in a lecture, and I regurgitate it back on an exam or paper. While there may still be some situations where this works best, research has shown that a different approach is usually necessary for long-term learning and integration into daily life to occur.[5]

On the other hand, every traditional classroom, whether graduate or undergraduate, would benefit from an online companion. At the very least, the online component could provide a syllabus, due dates, and a way to hand in assignments and save trees. At the other end of the scale is the F2F classroom that provides stimulating online forums prior to coming together in the F2F classroom to jump-start the discussion. Also, preliminary examples of experiments and results as well as safety videos that can be completed online allow more time to work on higher-level thinking in the classroom. If the evolution for online continues to move in this direction, soon there will not be terms like *online*, *hybrid*, and *F2F*; there will only be learning and the blurred lines between methodologies.

To be successful online, a student must be a self-starter and motivated to take responsibility for his or her own learning. They need to understand that instructors are mentors and guides with expert knowledge that can assist them in the integration of new ideas and concepts and the creation of their own. These concepts are at the very core of Malcolm Knowles's ideas of adult learners and vital for all adult learners, but more so for the online learner.[6] For all adult students, this is an important concept, but for those students that choose the online approach, it is more important. At the same time, it is important that the programs be at a level, quality, and standard that supports adult learning. How does this happen?

Development of Quality Online Programs

The development of high-quality online programs and courses begins with institutional leadership. Without the support of the president and provost or chief academic officer, quality online programs cannot be developed. Further, the board of trustees must also be on board because the development of online programs must be paired with a marketing approach that is significantly specified and differentiated from anything currently used to market a campus-based program or activity.

One example of how a board of trustees can make a difference is the online success of Southern New Hampshire University. The president's vision has been embraced by the board, and it has led to a business model that continues to astound and support not only online venues but those on campus. Another example is the launch of Kettering University's Global Campus, which was conceived by President McMahan and gained strong and continued support from the board.

The failed University of Illinois Global Campus is at the other end of the spectrum. While President B. Joseph White lauded the Global Campus as the "fourth campus" of the University of Illinois in his inaugural address, in less than five years, it was stamped as a failure when the faculty objected to its practices. The board of trustees closed it down before it had a chance to fully evolve. That failure started a decline that ultimately led to President White leaving the university.

Market Research

The development of any program for online must begin with significant market research. The need to show that any program leads to "gainful employment" is a requirement today.[7] Gone are the days of "we will build it, they will come" or thinking that a niche program does not have to produce enough income to cover the costs. This is not something traditional academia has considered in the past. There are many programs and courses that are on the books at some universities that simply do not have significant numbers to run or run with only a few students, thereby not covering the costs of running the program or course.

While it still makes sense to have programs that match directly with the mission of the university (for example, a religious studies program for a religiously affiliated school or a women's studies program for a university with these roots), for the most part, institutions of higher learning must become choosier in deciding how to spend their limited resources in the future. That future is now.

Any program being considered for online development must have a thorough market research analysis. This needs to include examining other institutions with the same or similar program; expected accreditations; Integrated Postsecondary Education Data System (IPEDS), which provides information, in part, regarding specific degrees awarded each year from each institution; perspective employer analysis; Department of Labor statistics; census data; and a determination of where and if there is a market for the new program. Another general MBA is probably not worth the time and effort unless you are a significantly respected business college or university with leading-edge faculty. The market is flooded with online MBAs. However, a differentiated MBA with a lean toward a specific segment of the market may be worthwhile.

Once the research is compiled, a critical analysis must be completed to determine whether there is a return on the investment (ROI) and when that return will materialize. The average payback is about three years, but an institution may require something shorter or be willing to wait longer for those benefits to manifest. While the idea of ROI is something most academics and academic institutions have not considered in the past, it has always been at the core of online programs. Online programs have been required to justify their existence more than most traditional programs. Online programs look at all the costs associated with the development of a program, including cost of instructional designers, subject matter experts (SMEs), creation of media, software required, and intellectual property costs.

Additionally, there must be a cost associated for general overhead (does the online team work in a building on campus with the lights on and computers on their desks?). This is something one can think of as what it costs to deliver one credit hour of learning to a student and then use that number to cover general overhead. There are also costs associated with online overhead, which include the Learning Management System (LMS) and other software required for exams, texts, and so on. Each institution must make its own decision about what to include in the overall cost of development. That determination can make the calculation complex or very simple. An institution can decide what costs they will include in their overhead and which they will not.

Once the costs have been determined, it is a fairly simple math equation to determine how many students must be paying for the courses before it is profitable. While perhaps a new and somewhat controversial idea, this same type of equation can aid not only online programs but traditional programs as they make decisions about which programs require resources and which should be discontinued. Also, if the whole institution agrees to the details of this equation, all programs are evaluated apples to apples and without emotion. While this is only part of the determination regarding programs and resources, it is a valuable aspect of the decision making.

Program Development

Next, a program of study (POS) must be developed for every program considered. A program of study is defined as a set of courses, specializations, concentrations, or certificates with credit-hour assignments required to complete the degree. A solid POS must also include overarching program outcomes. The best way to do this is not in a vacuum but by using a collaborative process called a *Program Summit*.

A Program Summit is a one- to two-day meeting of minds to develop all the items listed above. It requires about 40 hours of preparation for the team leading the summit as well as preparation for all the attendees. An example attendee list includes

- Members of the department that own the program
- The online development team
- Outside subject matter experts not part of the institution (these may or may not be academics)
- The marketing team responsible for the program
- An employer board

An *employer board* is a group of individuals who are prospective employers of graduates of this program. It is best to have them attend the meeting live or via Web conference, but only to attend for a portion of the meeting prior to discussions about the program details. This board can be individuals from different companies or organizations to provide insight into the types of skills they seek in employees in their industry. This is a great test to keep from moving too far away from the goal of actually helping graduates find jobs when they have successfully finished their degrees.

As part of the preparation for the summit, all market research, potential goals of the program, and even a potential budget should be discussed. The online team or the department where the program will reside should build a few potential programs of study based on the research.

After a well-facilitated meeting, a new program of study is drafted with the names of subject matter experts (SMEs) potentially available to aid in the individual course development as well as course names and general descriptions. Over the next several months, this program should be thoroughly vetted by the department that will own the program for approval and then through the official university academic approval process. This ensures faculty ownership and participation in the development process—something that is vital to accreditors.

Course Development

This is probably the most important aspect of the online process and the most complex. The best process for course development is a collaborative one, where the online development team, which includes a person responsible for all program development and an instructional designer who work with at least one subject matter expert per course. Ideally, another academic from the department with a comprehensive view of the entire academic program to be developed will also be part of this team. In a *Course Summit*—not to be confused with a Program Summit—the learning outcomes for the course, the assignments that meet those outcomes, and all the items for the discussion boards are created.

For those individuals that believe this is a process that takes weeks, months, or even years, a solid outline of those items can be completed in about 12 hours with a focused and prepared group of individuals. This is true regardless of how difficult or complex the subject matter. Having experience in over a half a dozen institutions of higher learning and dozens of colleges within those institutions, this model has been proven and remained consistently true. Additionally, the same online development teams can develop courses in human services, IT, business, psychology, counseling, lean manufacturing, leadership, criminal justice, public administration, medicine, and nursing at all levels of education: undergraduate, graduate, and professional. What matters the most is not the online team, as their skills are generalized, but the content expertise of the faculty or SME.

While the outline for the course is developed in these two days, this does not happen without research and preparation on the parts of both the online team and the SME. Then after this initial meeting, a timeline and schedule is created for the next 60 days to ensure that a series of agreed-upon deliverables are completed. These deliverables are the details of the course and may include creation of mini-lectures, templates for assignments, resources or books, Internet sites, and so on. These items are accomplished in a series of meetings between the SME and the instructional designer (ID). One of the most important pieces of this process is to understand that the SME has the final word on academic content and the ID the word on what works or meets the conventions of online.

Kettering employs best practice in online development by employing professional instructional designers who are not only degreed but have years of experience in their fields. They are trained in the process of development and given the authority to manage the SME relationship. A set of deliverable is determined with timelines at the summit, and the SME is not required to write specific pieces of the course. Instead, in a series of video and phone meetings with the ID, the SME provides the subject and academic details for the ID to weave into the course using the appropriate writing conventions that allow the course to have universal navigation.

This may appear a nuance and something that initially feels uncomfortable to some faculty; however, in all the years of development, there have only been a few instances where this relationship has not been successful. It is imperative that the SME read, review, and approve everything written in the course to ensure its accuracy and legitimacy. In the end, the SME must make the final determination that the details of content are sound. This is key and goes to the point of allowing the SME to be the expert in content. As a result, this relationship is not contentious, but one where both parties respect the expertise of the other and work from a collegial perspective. The results are an excellent course where students are successful.

After both the ID and the SME are satisfied that the course has met the expectations originally outlined, they must pass the course to a quality assurance (QA) team. The quality assurance check cannot be lightly dismissed. This team runs a series of checks on the course to ensure a variety of items: for example, citations and references are correctly noted according the standards used at the university or college (MLA, APA, Chicago style), grammar is correct, conventions are used, standard language is assured, there is clarity for all items, and the resources selected provide students with enough information to accurately complete assignments. Questions of design typically defer to the ID and academic issues to the SME or the department responsible for the program. In some cases, when significant clarifications must take place, another QA is performed. Once the QA Team is satisfied the course is at its best, it is passed on to the team that builds the course in the Learning Management System (LMS). The course is once again reviewed by the SME in the LMS and then approved to run.

Continuous Improvement

While some institutions and groups may only review courses that are developed online every couple of years (more often for courses in computer science and information technology), the best practice is one of continuous improvement. It is also a Lean technique based on some of the same concepts used in manufacturing. Employing continuous improvement reduces unnecessary items and provides for the course to be reviewed by the online team with the instructor that most recently taught it. This instructor may or may not be the SME that developed the course. The best practice is to have the SME teach the course the first time to note any issues or concerns. Then, as other instructors, who are also experts, teach the course, they can provide additional insights with language, assignments, or resources. These recommendations are noted, and suggestions

or clarifications for students to be able to navigate the course are more easily discussed. These changes, if appropriate, are immediately made to the
course. In some cases, it is necessary to go back to the department or the
original SME to seek further clarification to ensure academic cohesiveness.
This practice keeps materials fresh and up-to-date.

Online Faculty

While the design of online programs and courses is vital to student and
institutional success, even a poorly designed program can limp along if
there are excellent instructors involved. Combine excellent instruction
with high-quality programs and courses and you have the first two parts
of a powerful formula. There are some basis items to consider when developing your model of online Instruction:

- Not everyone who teaches F2F can teach well online.
- Online courses take more teaching time than a traditional class to be done
  well.
- Online faculty must be well trained in online methodologies to be effective.
- Online faculty do not have the same course freedoms they do in the traditional
  classroom.
- Online faculty need to understand policy, standards, and the process for such
  issues as what to do about special accommodations for students, how to han-
  dle a student who does not show up or complete assignments on time, and
  where to go with technology issues, to name only a few potential issues.

Online courses are often taught by adjuncts. While this is a cost-
effective way to teach, and an easily expandable option, the future may
instead hold that institutions provide more opportunities for hiring full-
time online instructors who have other responsibilities to the institution
as a whole, such as committee work. It may seem like a wild idea to have
faculty that live miles away from their home institutions to be fully participating members of the academic community, but this model allows for
the very best instructors to teach regardless of where they live or the time
zone. The model of distance employees is not new, but the idea of full-time
distance faculty for an institution is much less common.

The fourth bullet in the list above may be concerning to some faculty. After all, academic freedom is at the core of what it means to be a
part of the academy. The Association of American Colleges & Universities (AAC&U) recently reaffirmed the principles of academic freedom for
faculty: "Academic freedom is necessary not just so faculty members can

conduct their individual research and teach their own course, but so they can enable students-through whole college programs of study-to acquire the learning they need to contribute to society."[8] While it is a subtle but important caveat in this discussion, the centralized, collaborative online model has courses owned by the university or department as a whole and not individual instructors. Subject matter experts, whether full-time faculty or other recognized experts, are paid above and beyond their normal salary for their development expertise. As a result, courses are not "owned" by individuals but instead "owned" by the institution. This practice is unusual but not unheard of in traditional universities.

There may be some who are questioning why this is such an important caveat. While all academic programs are under intense scrutiny to ensure quality and relevance, no one group is under more pressure than those institutions with online programs. Online programs must be able to demonstrate a level of quality that sometimes exceeds the standards that are required in a traditional campus course. This is due to the scrutiny online programs have from the Department of Education, accrediting institutions such as the Higher Learning Commission, specific accrediting agencies such as ABET and ASCPB, and the faculty, department heads, and deans who must feel comfortable with the quality of rigor of online as equal or exceeding what is taught F2F. The only way to ensure this is to maintain that the course sections taught adhere to the same standards and course outcomes use the same assessments and rubrics and apply the same policies to all students, regardless of who is teaching a course.

As one of the goals of online programs is to expand the current student population, thereby expanding the mission and enhancing revenue for the academic institution, such an undertaking is not possible without ensuring that all sections of a given online course are maintaining the same standards and that students are learning the same material, thereby completing their degrees by meeting program outcomes that have been carefully mapped to course outcomes and weekly learning objectives. In a course owned by individual faculty members, each faculty member may choose a different set of exercises, assignments, and lectures to meet outcomes, which is allowed and supported by academic freedom.

However, if one of the goals of online programs is to increase university revenue, the individualistic model becomes chaotic if there are 15 sections of the same course running with 15 different approaches. That does not mean an online class should be robotic; this kind of development actually allows more freedom for the faculty to share their experiences in discussion forums and provide insights into practical applications of material to work situations instead of worrying about designing a discussion question that can allow for different responses from students and meet the objectives for the week. A course on leadership taught by someone who has been a vice president of a hospital will provide a different set of examples than those from someone who was a manager in a manufacturing plant. Both are valid and valuable for the student. This model also allows for more mentoring and the ability to provide substantive feedback to students on assignments.

Online programs and courses are not just for convenience; they also bring more students to the university. Additional revenue from online programs can enhance a university's ability to continue its mission and expand its vision. This revenue has built an almost entirely new campus at Southern New Hampshire University, as it has for other institutions. If we can agree that increased revenue is one of the primary reasons for beginning to venture into online education, then a few more standards must be noted.

Universal Navigation

In online education, universal navigation means there is one LMS template, and the navigation and organization for the template are replicated for every course in a program. Changing this logic creates undo confusion and difficulty for students. This is one of the major differences between one-off courses developed by individual faculty members and courses and programs developed with a centralized approach.

ADA Compliance

All online courses should meet the basics of the American with Disabilities Act (ADA) compliance regardless of a "request" for accommodations. This minimally entails the following:

- San serif fonts
- Ensuring color contrast at the highest level (black against white, dark blue against white, etc.)
- No images without HTML tags
- No video without transcription
- No flashing or psychedelic-moving images
- No music without transcription

Rubrics for All Assignments

Rubrics are grading supports that are standardized for a program. They allow students to understand the standards, and they enhance academic performance. While the rubric should be generalized to standards, the assignments and all items to be graded must have very specific details.

Standard Timelines for Grade Deadlines

Students deserve to have timely grades, but in online courses, this is even more important. One approach from research on adult learning allows students to build on a previous week's or module's experience to improve upon the next assignment. Without substantive and timely feedback, this is not possible. This is true for both F2F and online courses; the best assignments build on learning from week to week and result in a culminating assignment or practical application of materials. Providing feedback to a student before the next assignment is required allows for some consideration and reflection by the student of ways to improve before the next section or segment of an assignment is due and the opportunity to seek clarification from the instructor.

Standard Timelines for Responses to Student Messages

Online often means accelerated learning, and even if courses are not accelerated, there is a need for communication above and beyond a traditional classroom. Therefore, it is important to establish appropriate deadlines for responses to student messages. This not only ensures that students get the necessary mentoring and help to succeed in their courses, but it aids the relationship between student and instructor, which is a very important nuance as neither will occupy the same space during the learning experience.

Faculty Training

Teaching online requires not only some of the same skills required to teach in the classroom but some additional skills as well. These are not something to "pick up along the way," the way many of us who earned our doctoral degrees began teaching. Online teaching requires a different rhythm and method to be effective, and the institution is responsible for ensuring that everyone who teaches online adheres to these same standards. This requires a standard teaching and evaluation course and regular feedback as an instructor begins and continues to teach. Failure to provide adequate instructor training can lead to a significant negative result from a group of highly motivated students utilizing social media to share their negative evaluations and can permeate an entire online program. The way a course is taught and how it is fairly administered are imperative to an institution's success online.

Online and Higher Education's Future

If you began this chapter thinking online was something that would ultimately save your university and be a bright spot in the future of higher education by providing a much-needed influx of students and cash, you may be thinking twice at this point. Is it possible to create a high-quality set of online programs that will not only expand your organization's mission and vision but reach out to students that never would have considered your institution in the past? Absolutely! Is it a simple, easy, and inexpensive process that anyone can start on a shoestring budget with a little motivation and no background in online learning? Absolutely not! Like all disciplines in academia, online education has an associated set of processes, standards, and expertise. It requires planning, research, and development. It demands a team of highly motivated individuals, academic departments, faculty, and top administrators for success. In today's market, it demands something more—an academic partner.

Academic Partners

Unless an institution has several million dollars to begin a quality online program, it is not likely they will be successful. Although a small institution could grow a program using a grassroots approach 20 years ago, this approach is no longer viable. One of the reasons is the way programs must be marketed and how students search for the perfect program to meet their needs. Today, it requires a thorough knowledge of Google Analytics, search engine optimization, pay per click (PPC), and social media to become a successful online institution. If any of these terms are foreign to you or your institution and you do not understand the concept of keyword searches and keyword "buys," then the best way to venture into online is through the use of an academic partner.

Few institutions realize the costs associated with marketing online programs today, and even fewer are able to quickly create a development team to centralize program development. In addition, the need to respond to student inquiries in less than 24 hours is essential. There are very few admissions teams on traditional campuses that are used to this demand and can ramp up to the level of 24/7 online inquiry.

This is why an academic partner is so important. Academic partners are for-profit companies that work with, or "partner" with, an institution to provide the necessary support (both in terms of human resources as well as financial capital) to launch online programs. This is the quickest and most cost-effective way to get started online. These partnerships use their own capital to market and support an institution and in turn share the tuition from the students they bring into programs.

There are many companies that provide this service, and an institution should perform due diligence to ensure it is working with an appropriate partner who understands the institution and its identity. These are long-term relationships, so this scrutiny cannot be underestimated. Some of the questions to consider when vetting a partner include the following:

- How long as the company been in business?
- Who are they currently working with and can you talk to those partners?
- Who provides the venture capital and how long have they been successfully in business?
- What is the academic experience and pedigree of the leaders and midlevel managers for the organization?
- What is the experience and background of the leadership in regard to online?
- How many individuals will be solely focused on your institutions?
- How many "other" institutions are they working with and plan to work with in the future?
- What is the demonstrated success they can provide?
- Is it possible to terminate the relationship if it is not successful?

When properly vetted and the right partner decision made, the outcomes can be quick to market with high-quality courses and with only a small capital investment from the institution itself.

Several ideas and concepts included in this chapter provide opportunities not only for online departments but for all traditional departments in colleges and universities: employer boards to aid the development of new programs and courses, online companion courses for all F2F classrooms, rubrics for all assignments, and collaborative development, to name only a few. Additionally, a return on investment is not the only reason for an institution of higher learning to run a program. Sometimes a program is mission-driven and part of the institution's identity, for example, a religious studies program in a church-affiliated college. Such determinations are valid reasons if supported by leadership and the board of trustees. By forcing online programs to justify and become rigorous, practices and processes have developed that can support and improve all higher education learning.

In Part II, Faust seeks redemption by trying to gain back his soul from the devil.[9] By creating an entire business model that supports online, with quality standards, processes, and procedures, we are literally trying to seek redemption from the sins of past, when online education required less scrutiny. While not the savior for every institution, it provides a viable option for those institutions willing to give online its due.

Notes

1. J. Goethe, *Faust* (Chicago: William Benton, 1952).

2. Georgie Miller, "History of Distance Education," WorldWideLearn, November 10, 2014. http://www.worldwidelearn.com/education-articles/history-of -distance-learning.html.

3. "Distance Education Professional Development," Continuing Studies, University of Wisconsin–Madison, 2013. http://continuingstudies.wisc.edu/distance -education.

4. William Y. Arms, "Carnegie Mellon and the Andrew Project" *The Early Years of Academic Computing* (published online: Internet First University Press, 2014). http://www.cs.cornell.edu/wya/AcademicComputing/text/andrew.html.

5. Ellen Wexler, "In Online Courses, Students Learn More by Doing Than by Watching," *Wired Campus* (blog), September 16, 2015. http://chronicle.com /blogs/wiredcampus/in-online-courses-students-learn-more-by-doing-than-by-watching/57365.

6. C. Lee, "The Adult Learner: Neglected No More," *Training* 35, no. 3 (1998): 47–48, 50, 52.

7. "Obama Administration Announces Final Rules to Protect Students from Poor-performing Career College Programs," U.S. Department of Education, October 30, 2014. http://www.ed.gov/news/press-releases/obama-administration -announces-final-rules-protect-students-poor-performing-career-college-programs.

8. AAC&U Board of Directors' Statement, "Academic Freedom and Educational Responsibility," Association of American Colleges & Universities, January 6, 2006. https://www.aacu.org/about/statements/academic-freedom.

9. Goethe, *Faust*.

CHAPTER THIRTEEN

Reimagining Higher Education through Entrepreneurship

Miranda Barrett

While his friends are still sleeping off their late night, 22-year-old student entrepreneur Gonzalo Fernandez rises at 6:30 a.m. and immediately checks his e-mail for any overnight crises with his business that might require his immediate attention. He then shifts gears to his studies, putting the finishing touches on his thesis on strategic growth models, preparing for exams, and studying for the GMAT. Then, a few hours later, he's back to CEO mode, holding a morning meeting with his team, reviewing new orders, and checking deliveries. "I can manage my time quite well," he says with a laugh. "We have very fast and effective meetings focused on only relevant information. We don't waste a moment."

The world is full of young entrepreneurs like Gonzalo, who are taking their cities by storm with their innovation, creativity, and drive to solve problems. For Gonzalo, he saw the traffic problems plaguing his home country of Spain; he saw the culture of cycling in the Netherlands, where old bikes are constantly discarded; and he saw the perfect opportunity. His business, BeCiclos, takes abandoned bicycles, repairs them to shiny-new perfection, and delivers them to new customers who carefully choose their new bike "soul mate" through an "adoption" process. Gonzalo is an extraordinary young entrepreneur, and he's not alone.

The Global Student Entrepreneur Awards (GSEA),[1] a program of the nonprofit peer-to-peer learning organization the Entrepreneurs' Organization (EO),[2] has heard hundreds of stories like Gonzalo's, of university students who are not just studying entrepreneurship but living it on a daily basis, taking risks, creating jobs, and changing industries. Some grow to become large businesses with millions of dollars in revenue, while others are discontinued by choice or by failure. But all these extraordinary young people share the same drive to learn, grow, pioneer, and take risks, which makes it easy for GSEA to build a trusted network across cultures, geographies, and backgrounds. By leveraging the same values that have made the Entrepreneurs' Organization successful for years, GSEA is growing a similar network of "studentpreneurs" who are committed to the collective success of the group. The competition program was acquired by EO from Saint Louis University in 2006, and it has been in operation since 1998.

While GSEA is competition for student entrepreneurs, it places far greater scoring value on the strength and character of the entrepreneur over the success of the business. It recognizes that businesses may come and go, but the qualities of the entrepreneur are what endure. To quantify this, the judging sheet asks such questions as, "Is the student seeking out expert advice and wisdom and proactively growing their own knowledge?" and "Does the student have a unique personal identity that he/she brings to the business?" It seeks to identify individuals who are integrating their dual roles as student and business owner, learning quickly from mistakes and innovating for the future.

Moreover, the network-building aspect of GSEA is far more important, and more valued, than the competition. While the competition serves as a reason to bring the group together, the events focus just as heavily on relationship building, learning, and mentorship. At the 2016 final round competition in Bangkok, Thailand, 51 studentpreneurs representing 51 countries came together for three days of speakers, trust-building workshops, and competition. "It was amazing how easily I connected with the other competitors," said Gonzalo. "We all are facing the same struggles; we were all saying the same things. And it was humbling—I thought I was working hard but there were others working even harder and under more challenging circumstances."

The event strives to be a celebration of the student entrepreneurs themselves, which is something they don't always get in their lives, where friends and family don't understand the crazy lifestyles they lead juggling school and a company. From the special name badges they get, to the video interviews and program book accolades, the goal is for them to leave the event feeling recognized for choosing the challenging path of entrepreneurship.

Before the event, they answer questions about their values, obstacles they've overcome, their vision, and so on. Those quotes appear throughout the event on screens and in printed materials, showing just how extraordinary they all are, and how similar. Despite a difference of 51 countries, their journeys as entrepreneurs are remarkably similar. "I knew that I would never want to work for anyone, because these companies that offer 'job security' are companies that were started by individuals just like me. I asked myself, 'Why can't I start a company that will one day offer many South African university graduates job security?" said Tokologo Phetla from South Africa. A similar sentiment is echoed by many of his peers, including the 2016 GSEA Champion Violeta Martinez: "In my country (El Salvador), the opportunities are small. But I'm standing out with new ideas and creativity—I told myself that I was born to be a leader. I dare to dream big, but I am also working hard every day to make things happen."

On the first day, students spent an intense morning together with exercises drawn from the Forum product of the Entrepreneurs' Organization, which EO members rank as their most important benefit of membership. At EO, a Forum is a group of 6 to 10 members who meet monthly for four hours. The meeting is guided by moderator-trained members and emphasizes confidentiality, personal responsibility, and lessons learned. Members speak directly from their own experience rather than giving advice. It allows hard-charging entrepreneurs to speak freely about their deepest challenges, hear similar challenges, and then make their own decisions about the right path forward. Forums hold each other accountable to commitments and are genuinely invested in each other's personal and business well-being. There are plenty of examples of EO members who moved away and are still flying back monthly to attend their Forum meetings, or of a member who suddenly passed away and the Forum stepped in to run the business for an interim period.

Introducing this new way of communicating and sharing to GSEA finalists immediately sets the stage to build trust within the group, changing the environment from one of competition to one of community. They become invested in each other's success as well as their own and build relationships that will outlast their short time together at the event. "We discovered that we can help each other so much," said Gonzalo, recounting his time in Bangkok. "We are at different stages and in different countries, but we are facing so many similar challenges. And the different approaches to problems and perspectives are so valuable to me." Forum exercises may include drawing a "lifeline" of the highs and lows of your life, answering the question, "If you really knew me you would know that ____," or discussing a greatest fear or uncertainty. Certain cultures or individuals struggle with this degree of openness more than others, but, overall, the student rated it as one of the best experiences of the entire event.

GSEA currently receives about 1,500 applications from student entrepreneurs around the world. A few hundred of those attend in-person competitions, and 51 attended the premiere finals event, which was held this year in Bangkok. It has grown from being a North American–focused program to one with a wide footprint reaching into more than 60 countries. In some locations, chapters of EO are deeply integrated into the program, holding large events and connecting their members with students. In others, GSEA has sought support from other schools and organizations to find studentpreneurs and funnel them to an event. All competitors must be undergraduate students who have been running their own business for at least six months, generating at least $500 in revenue or with $1,000 in investments.[3]

The challenges faced by the GSEA program vary greatly by geography. For example, in the United States, hundreds of business plan competitions crowd the marketplace, making some students "professional competitors" who earn thousands of dollars in winnings. In some countries, entrepreneurship is not seen as a desirable career path, where parents would rather see their son or daughter take a traditional professional path over entrepreneurship. In others, students have avoided officially registering their businesses due to complicated government regulations and are hesitant to participate in an event that may draw attention to their success. Despite a desire to rapidly grow its geographic footprint, the program has had to be strategic about which countries' markets it pursues.

GSEA is currently supported largely by EO, which is in turn funded by the dues of members. That brings an obligation to deliver value not just to the students in the program but also back to the chapters and members that keep it operating. On a local level, an EO chapter can opt to host a city or national competition and use the event to generate external awareness, sponsorship, and community engagement for itself. These activities help create a unique experience for their existing members and attract new ones. With a mission to "engage leading entrepreneurs to learn and grow," most EO members are willing to mentor and share their experiences to help the next generation, whether it's just for the day or with a longer-term commitment.

"Here at EO, we have a sense of mission to help budding entrepreneurs, by infusing learning at an early stage to help accelerate their growth," said Vijay Tirathrai, CEO. "It is our hope that EO will be the leader in providing learning, resources, and mentors to studentpreneurs around the world. This is a very important way for us to make a global impact as an organization." As EO celebrates its 30th anniversary of "engaging leading entrepreneurs to learn and grow," the alignment with GSEA is obvious, and the passion shown by EO members serving as mentors is contagious. "It is so amazing to see the impact that EO can have on the lives of others throughout the world," said Gary Bushkin, a member of EO Arizona who recently mentored a studentpreneur on the other side of the world in Sri Lanka.

GSEA has also become a tool to help EO expand its global reach, which currently stands at 52 countries and growing. The GSEA staff team works with a local partner, such as a university or NGO, to hold a competition in a city without an EO chapter. That event lays the foundation to showcase EO to potential members and the external community. This year, GSEA reached into about 15 countries with no EO presence, from France to Vietnam to Peru. This early ecosystem engagement readies local contacts and resources for when EO moves forward with a new chapter launch. In March 2016, a new EO group in Dhaka, Bangladesh, was close to becoming an "official" EO chapter. A GSEA competition was held, which engaged the incoming chapter officers, exposed them to a globally organized program, and attracted local media. It brought energy and excitement to a group that was not yet feeling the connection to the larger global organization.

While GSEA focuses on the needs and journey of the studentpreneur, another EO program, Accelerator, addresses the business learning needs for entrepreneurs with annual revenue of $250,000 to $1 million. Through quarterly learning days, mentorship, and accountability groups, EO Accelerator is poised to catch GSEA students as they graduate and continue their learning and growth. It keeps them connected with the EO community and its resources as they scale their businesses.

Recently, a group of eight EO members from around the world sat down for one hour with a small group of student entrepreneurs at a business incubator in Amsterdam. The EO members were taking a break from a nearby meeting; the students were participants in Team Academy, an innovative academic program offering a BA degree in entrepreneurship. All the students were running their own businesses, most in the early start-up phase. No structure was given beyond a table breakout and asking students to provide a quick description of their business and the biggest challenge they were currently facing. The group came back together after one hour to share outcomes. "I will take that piece of advice my whole life," said one student, who was called out by a young EO member for not taking notes and then given a rapid-fire list of tricks for coming across as professional and serious in a meeting. Another found herself questioning whether her business model was sustainable and was considering a complete pivot in her market. A third learned a new way for discovering customer segments he hadn't considered. All of this came from a one-hour meeting, bringing together like-minded individuals willing to listen, share, and learn from each other.

Any of the 51 country finalists who attended the GSEA finals event in Bangkok would enthusiastically agree that the experience made a profound impact on their lives, bringing global connections and learnings they will leverage on their entrepreneurial journeys. And most of the hundreds who attended local and national events would likely say the same. But this represents a fraction of the exceptional young entrepreneurs out in the world, starting and growing businesses with little guidance or support. What would it take for a program like GSEA to really scale, touching tens of thousands of student entrepreneurs to the same degree?

Ecosystem Partnerships

EO and GSEA are far from being the only quality programs that see the importance of supporting young emerging entrepreneurs. Universities, incubators, NGOs, and government programs are more and more seeing the value in nurturing small businesses as a solution to economic and social instabilities. Many provide practical teachings, connections to local mentors, and even access to funding, all of which are critical to early success. EO and GSEA can complement that business focus with additional resources geared at the totality of the entrepreneur, such as Forum. They also bring an extensive global network of members who all share a deep interest in helping each other succeed. With more and more emerging businesses crossing country borders, having an immediate network in new geographies can make a massive difference in speed of operation. When the day comes that Gonzalo wants to expand BeCiclos beyond Spain and the Netherlands to the United States, he has an immediate network of successful entrepreneurs ready to support him.

But while GSEA continues to build a network of individuals, having a bigger network of organizations would quickly expand its reach and ability to run events. With so many diverse organizations invested in the success of young entrepreneurs, there is little coordination among them with all the different offerings and methods. EO and GSEA excel at focusing on the totality of the entrepreneur and global community, which could compliment the business focus of other organizations. A quick way to source qualifying students in more markets and partners to host competitions would make an immediate difference in the reach of the program. GSEA could then fold those students into the community and continue offering learning, resources, and connections.

Technology

It's hard to imagine a more demanding group to support with technology than student entrepreneurs. If they don't like a particular platform, they move on to the next hot thing or just build their own over a weekend. They want instant connectivity and ease of access and have little patience to wait for it. But the technology must also re-create the trust and intimacy fostered at in-person events and Forum meetings. It must allow for the spark of recognition all student entrepreneurs find in each other after two minutes of conversation. At the moment, the 51 GSEA country finalists are bouncing around various social media platforms, continuing to share challenges and photos of travels and to celebrate successes. But GSEA needs to bring them together under one roof and add some structure to meet their needs.

Sponsors

GSEA is currently operating with the majority of its funding provided by EO, along with a generous donation by Peter Thomas, a successful Canadian entrepreneur, author, and philanthropist with a passion for student entrepreneurship. But scaling the reach of the program would be expedited with financial and in-kind support from corporations, who could provide not just dollars but services needed by studentpreneurs, such as accounting, legal, online services, PR, marketing, and more. And support of GSEA would bring not just access to the student entrepreneur network but to the 12,000 members of the Entrepreneurs' Organization, who all have larger businesses earning at least $1 million in annual revenue.

The prize package currently offered to the overall global winner of GSEA is $20,000, with small prizes to second and third place, and $1,000 awards around Social Impact, Innovation, and Lessons from the Edge. The ability to increase these amounts through sponsorship would raise the awareness of the program and help bring more traction in markets already crowded with competitions.

Mentors

The 2015 GSEA finalists were polled about what they most wanted to help them and their businesses. The answer was mentorship and access to funding. This year, GSEA piloted a six-week mentorship program, matching the 51 country finalists with volunteers from EO. All matches were virtual and very diverse—a member in Arizona mentored a student in Sri Lanka, and so on. Learning content from EO's Accelerator program was provided (which focuses on businesses' growth) as well as best practices from EO's existing mentorship program for members and a video conference tool. Matches were created manually by staff with knowledge of the individuals, personalities, businesses, and languages. Overall, the program was a great success, with a few challenges around technology, time zones, and the short duration (one EO member found himself having to explain what a balance sheet was and the importance of financial reporting in general).

Imagine if this mentorship pairing could be expanded to all student entrepreneurs participating in the GSEA community, with mentors able to select the amount of time they had to contribute and their topics of expertise and mentees automatically matched up. Software already exists for this, and EO is pursuing it as a benefit for both its members seeking their own high-level mentors and for GSEA. There will be a pool of student entrepreneurs ready to dive in the moment it's up and running.

Trust is a commodity in short-supply in the business world today, yet entrepreneurs must be both trusting and trustworthy to be effective leaders. In their book *Becoming a Trustworthy Leader*, Drs. Aneil and Karen Mishra describe the "ROCC of Trust—Reliable, Open, Competent, and Compassionate." They make the case that a successful leader must demonstrate courage, authenticity, and humility to create a "virtuous trust cycle" with their organizations.

Despite how much they stand to lose, entrepreneurs can be incredibly open and trusting with their peers when they are provided with a safe environment. At EO, that environment is created within Forum, with a strict code of confidentiality and nonjudgment. Within GSEA, student entrepreneurs are hungry for a similar environment, where they can share with each other, learn from those more experienced, and have a safe place to talk about their challenges. As peers, they inherently trust each other already, making it easy to build a dynamic and supportive global community. It is this opportunity, together with the immense support provided by the Entrepreneurs' Organization, that allows GSEA to continue to grow and support student entrepreneurs in their inspiring entrepreneurial endeavors. "When I say things that make good business sense, people take me seriously," said Gonzalo. "They see past my age, and it no longer matters."

Notes

1. http://www.gsea.org.
2. https://www.eonetwork.org/about/.
3. All amounts in this chapter are in U.S. dollars.

CHAPTER FOURTEEN

The Next Generation of Higher Education Leaders

Dennis Barden

When my clients inevitably ask me the state of the market for chief executives in higher education, I always give the same answer: the market is de facto irrational for the simple reason that there are still people who want the job. Despite the difficulty of being the servant (leader) of many masters, the discomfort of living in a fish bowl, the stress of financial challenges, the pressures of fund-raising, and the frustrations of shared governance, dedicated, accomplished people still seek to lead the enterprise.

Will they always? I think they will. People drawn to higher education tend to be idealists, compelled by the possibility of changing the trajectory of individual lives (through teaching) and societies (via research). They believe that they can change the world, and thus the vicissitudes of the journey are already built into their thinking. Not all who so aspire have the requisite skills and experience for leadership in these times, but those who do take their positions knowing that the going will be difficult and that success is far from guaranteed.

As he anticipated taking the reins as the president of Hampden-Sydney College, Dr. Larry Stimpert reflected on the genesis of his interest in institutional leadership thus:

> I started thinking about higher education leadership a long time ago. My PhD adviser had gone into administration, and I asked her about her motivation. Her answer resonated with me: You go into a job like this because

you want to make a difference. The people who are going into it for themselves, for the perks, or because they simply don't want to teach any more
are doing so for wrong and terrible reasons. The difficulties and downsides
of leadership are too great to do it for selfish ends. You want to make things
better, to make a difference, for your institution and its people.

The ongoing market correction in higher education is exceptionally
painful for generations of faculty and administrators who came to their
positions, for the most part, in another time and environment. Many leaders find themselves working not to change the world but rather to ensure
the existence of their institutions beyond what is anticipated to be an era
of closures and consolidation among higher education institutions across
the spectrum—non- and for-profit, public and private, large and small,
teaching and research, two- and four-year, generalist and specialist. This
generation of leaders is paving the way for what we can only hope will be
a more rational, more stable higher education marketplace in the future.

One index of the nature and rate of this change can be found in our firm's
history of presidential/chancellorial search criteria. For example, in 1999,
my colleagues and I supported the search for a chancellor of a regional campus of a major Midwestern public university. In that search, engaging productively with external partners was essentially an afterthought, mentioned
only once in the candidate criteria as "[a]n interest in and capacity for fund-
raising," as 22nd out of 29 total desiderata. By the time we supported the
search for that chancellor's successor 10 years later, "to build a track record
of success in creating and maintaining business partnerships and success in
private fund-raising" was a central requirement of the position.

The current disruption encourages boards and legislatures, in particular, to reconsider the very underpinnings of higher education as we have
known them for a very long time. The most sacred of orthodoxies are being
questioned—tenure, shared governance, tuition, traditional pedagogies,
even liberal arts education itself—and governing boards are challenging
structures that have been in place for centuries, in some cases *because* they
have been in place for centuries. It seems entirely likely that the academy
will undergo fundamental change as a result. As of this writing, the future
is not remotely clear, but a few educated guesses are likely to provide a
roadmap for the aspiring higher education leader of tomorrow.

The Evolving Nature of Shared Governance

Perhaps no aspect of higher education, with the possible exception of tenure, is so foreign to those who view the sector from the outside—including

board members—as is shared governance. When it is working well, the natural inclination of faculty to seek and to hold out for the ideal, the perfect, is balanced with the administration's accountability for getting things done in the environment as it exists. This balance keeps the institution from being held captive by the temporary or the utilitarian while at the same time allowing it to conduct its affairs in keeping with conditions on the ground. In good times, the two are symbiotic.

Unfortunately, in dynamic, challenging times, the two forces can all too easily fall out of balance. In the current environment, in which it is extraordinarily difficult to separate fad from fundamental market force, the instinct of the faculty to move deliberately on change is oft perceived by boards to be obstructionist, and faculty view their board partners as being slaves to fashion and finance. Boards fear for the business model—if not the very existence—of the institutions for which they have a fiduciary responsibility, and faculty fear not only for their jobs but for the individual and societal impact of short-sighted decisions made by people they see as marginally informed if not totally misguided.

Notwithstanding the tensions—and sometimes the open animosity—that so often characterize shared governance in the present day, some version of it is very likely to continue for the long run. Many institutions will reconfigure what aspects of institutional operations are subject to shared governance with an increased focus on curricular matters and a diminishment of influence over what are essentially operational decisions, but the CEO of the future will still be balancing the overlapping imprimaturs of governing board and faculty.

Many Masters Demanding Jacks-of-All-Trades

The motivations and complex, interlocking agendas of these two key stakeholders are not all that the president or chancellor of the future must juggle. In individual states, legislatures are also highly likely to continue to attempt to assert control over their public institutions. That they will likely be doing so despite having less and less skin in the game in terms of budgetary support will likely not hold them back. They will continue to conflate the many missions of public institutions—teaching, research, workforce development, economic development, cultural enlightenment, employment, and so on—and to attempt to treat them not as institutions of higher education but as state agencies. It is anybody's guess when it will happen, but at some point, a state legislature is going to give one of its institutions no money at all for its operating budget and yet still assert hegemony over it. That will be a strange day indeed.

In some places, that day is not very far off. As of this writing, Wisconsin is perhaps the most notable example. Its governor recommended devastatingly deep cuts in the state's budget allocation to its public universities for FY2017 (the state's legislature intervened and tempered the governor's initial budget proposal, but the cuts were still extremely substantial) while simultaneously threatening even more draconian reductions should the University of Wisconsin System not enact specific "reforms" to its tenure and promotion policies and other deeply cherished imprimaturs of the faculty. When the system's president, Ray Cross, attempted to find ways to accommodate the governor and legislature while maintaining as much institutional autonomy as he felt possible, he was sanctioned with a vote of no confidence by the faculty of the flagship campus.

Add in the many other constituencies of the average college or university—students, alumni, parents, staff, administration, the local community, funders, consortia, governmental regulators, and, in some cases, sponsoring or legacy religious organizations—and it is clear that the CEO of the future must continue to lead in an environment of many masters. Thus, personal attributes such as integrity, sound judgment, diplomatic skills, political savvy, courage of convictions, and the ability to speak truth to power will be of paramount importance.

Among the issues that divide constituents is the notion of running higher education institutions "like a business." This infuriates faculty in particular. To many on the faculty, running the institution like a business means making decisions on the basis of consumer (i.e., student and parent) demand, essentially becoming vendors providing for their customers what is asked of them rather than what they themselves know to be in those customers' best interests. Board members, most of whom are successful in the world of business, simply cannot understand that an organization that charges for its services can be so unresponsive to the marketplace, so stubbornly willful as to refuse to accommodate the hands that feed it.

There are all too many examples of how extreme these positions can be. The efforts of the University of Virginia's Board of Regents to run off their president, Teresa Sullivan, is only the most notorious. Lesser known are little stories, like the one I heard from a client on the West Coast. It seems that an elected faculty representative to this institution's board was sitting in a budget meeting. The group was struggling to match the revenue and expense sides of the ledger when the faculty rep spoke up: "Why do we have to have a balanced budget? We are a nonprofit organization." Clearly, the gap remains wide.

That gap will likely close, however. Already, institutions are being enormously more transparent with their budgeting processes, inviting faculty and other constituents into the conversation and challenging them to make difficult decisions regarding budget allocations, rightsizing programs and staffs, and articulating institutional priorities. This movement is likely to continue and may well accelerate.

What is certain is that the CEO of the future will have to demonstrate sound business acumen, whether or not he or she ever uses the word "business." The days of tuition increases that surpass the rate of inflation are likely over, at least for as far out as can be reasonably predicted. Cost containment will be the constant mantra in the boardroom. Institutions will be challenged to prioritize their programming on a regular basis, and most institutions will no longer be able to afford to be all things to all people, making the choice of what thing to be and to which people of central importance. The president will play a seminal role in this process and must bring to the table considerable working knowledge of higher education finance, budgeting, debt financing, bond rating, and financial regulation. This is truly the president or chancellor as chief executive officer.

Revenue Streams as Existential Imperatives

Another clear trend of the past 30 or so years is the increased and increasing proportion of the president's time that is devoted to activities beyond the campus. Fund-raising is only the most obvious of these responsibilities. As the imbalance of supply (the number of available slots for undergraduate students) and demand (the number of prospective students, especially those of traditional college-going age) has become more and more evident, the inevitable suppression of cost, that is, tuition, has put institutions in a bind. With enormous, expensive investments in physical plants and traditional, labor-intensive pedagogies, colleges and universities have minimal options to reduce budgetary expenditures, and most will soon have reached the asymptote in those efforts. Thus, even as supply and demand reach a point of stasis (once the sector has gone through its seemingly inevitable consolidation), presidents and their boards will continue to be challenged to diversify revenue streams.

Fund-raising is the traditional external source of both expendable revenue and investment. Philanthropy has become a major factor in American life, and philanthropists have become and are becoming increasingly well informed about and involved with the investments they make in nonprofit institutions. Presidents and chancellors, then, are the shepherds of those investments, engaged not only with cultivating prospects and soliciting gifts but with negotiating increasingly restrictive terms—some of which seem to or actually do conflict with institutional missions, values, and priorities—and stewarding donors who expect their investments to show a return. Back in the day, the fund-raising attribute that separated candidates for presidencies was their ability to "put the number down" in a solicitation. Today and into the future, added to that will be the ability to negotiate terms (despite a complete imbalance in leverage) that provide both what the institution needs and what the donor wants.

Controversies over the designation and intent of philanthropic support abound. Faculties, preternaturally inclined to suspect conspiracies where substantial sums of money from external sources are concerned, have expressed concern over or even outright opposition to such gifts as the Bass family's support of the study and teaching of Western civilization at Yale University, the Koch brothers' support of George Mason University (and particularly the naming of its law school in honor of the late associate justice of the Supreme Court Antonin Scalia), and the naming of a research center at the University of Chicago after the economist Milton Friedman, who was both an alumnus of and former faculty member at the university.

The naming of endowments or facilities long since established are likewise being called into question, with debates over John C. Calhoun's name on a college at Yale University and Woodrow Wilson's associations across the campus of Princeton University (and with such organizations as the Wilson Center for International Scholars) becoming almost daily fodder for reconsideration and retrospective judgment. Presidents are therefore being challenged to not only generate philanthropic income but to generate it from only what are perceived to be acceptable sources—and what is acceptable is very much in the mind of the beholder.

Financial Capital as a Function of Human, Social, Intellectual, and Political Capital

There are other deliverables beyond fund-raising, however. Colleges and universities have assets and produce outcomes that have significant value. Foremost among these are their people, especially their faculty and students. Colleges and universities are among society's most important institutions because the people they educate and the discoveries they generate are the lifeblood of the emerging knowledge-based economy. Over the years, those products of colleges and universities have taken on recognized value, and competitive markets have emerged for them. Presidents and chancellors, therefore, are increasingly positioned to generate revenue in return for access to these critical assets, most productively through win-win arrangements with institutions desirous of that access. A current example—though the jury is still out in terms of the efficacy of the arrangement—is Arizona State University's agreement with Starbucks to provide employee education. The company wants a more educated workforce, a compelling employee benefit, and influence over the mode and timing of delivery; the university benefits financially from the arrangement, presumably by providing a resource that fits well within its mission.

Some institutional assets have long been leveraged to generate revenue. College and university efforts to benefit from the use of their largely vacant campuses in the summer are a good example. Some have emerged over the course of recent decades, such as intellectual property arrangements between the academy and the commercial sector. In FY2015, for example, Stanford University realized $91.5 million in gross royalties from 695 different technologies.[1] Colleges and universities are in a constant—and, in some cases, desperate—search for additional opportunities. The president of the future must set the tone for this entire effort, not the least of which is convincing the faculty of both the importance of the outcome and the mission-centrism of the exercise. Having accomplished that Herculean task, he or she must then engage with external partners, negotiate win-win scenarios, and steward the outcome to no less an extent than is typical with major philanthropic investments.

Governments are another external constituency with which a president must reckon. Whether by controlling budgetary purse strings, enforcing regulation, providing direct support (e.g., funds for research, tuition support, loan guarantees, etc.) or services (e.g., public safety, roads, civic infrastructure, etc.), or actually controlling the governance of the institution by comprising its board, federal, state, and local governments are in the business of colleges and universities. As the nation's body politic has become more fractious, colleges and universities have become easy fodder for partisan politics. While the leaders of public colleges and universities are obviously on the firing line for relationships with political leaders, their private institution counterparts are only slightly less obviously burdened with building and maintaining cordial, supportive relationships with city halls, statehouses, Congress, the U.S. Department of Education, and the White House.

Leaders of faith-based institutions add another major external stakeholder to the mix: the sponsoring organization. Whether formally through reserved rights of governance—which frequently include the final say over the hiring and firing of the president—or because of historical precedent, tradition, or an intrinsic presence within the institutional brand, founding and sponsoring religious organizations can wield tremendous influence over the operational decisions made by a president and a board. Thus, the president of this type of institution is faced with yet another party with which to negotiate its operations, its decisions, and its strategies, one with a very different and difficult-to-quantify level of influence and leverage.

Particularly when those religious organizations are themselves experiencing a period of rapid and fundamental self-reflection and change, their presidents must be particularly sensitive, adept, facile, and yet resolute when maintaining and strengthening institutional bonds. A cogent example is Catholic institutions. As the Church evolves—and, in particular, as Pope Francis expresses increasingly progressive social views on its behalf—Catholic colleges and universities struggle both to keep their values and their brands current while at the same time maintaining productive relationships with their key constituencies, especially alumni whose memories of their collegiate experience are often at odds with current practice.

Alumni with whom the university wishes to build strong, symbiotic engagement to optimize both deliverables—especially philanthropic support—and brand equity have long been a powerful external factor in institutional life. Parents are an increasingly important constituency both for what they pay in tuition and supply in regard to fund-raising. Bond-rating agencies are beginning to have a profound impact on not only institutional business practices but on their brand equity; search firms now routinely cite bond ratings—and particularly changes in those ratings—when recruiting key personnel to institutions, especially including presidents. Banks and financial institutions are central to the financial viability of many institutions, and endowment managers directly impact their financial fortunes. Not last and not least are accreditors, who are playing an increasingly active oversight role in an effort to ensure institutional viability and performance.

In short, a president or a chancellor is now and will increasingly be an outwardly facing leader.

The Higher Education Leader of the Future: Change Agents under Multiple Microscopes

What does this mean, then, for the skill set of the ideal leader of the future? Nothing discussed above speaks at all to such issues as curriculum, general education, pedagogy, student outcomes and success, residential life, promotion and the awarding of tenure, quality of teaching, or the pursuit and fruits of basic and applied research. These are the core pursuits of a college or a university—the work of the faculty and students. They also represent the aspects of the organization with which traditional candidates are most familiar and generally most comfortable. Will they no longer be the province of presidents and chancellors? If not, will the CEO of the future even need to know anything about these fundamental aspects of his or her institution? Are we inevitably headed toward the sorts of presidents and chancellors that boards typically think they want, that is, someone to run a "business"?

Certainly, pressure will increase for many institutions to move in this direction. That pressure will take at least two forms. Boards will look at the litany of external partners and the complexity of the fundamental financial pressures facing their institutions and will decide that they need at the helm not an educator but a person experienced with organizational change. They will also be critical in taking stock of leaders who emerge from the very environment that necessitates the change—that is, the traditional president or chancellor. Leaders with traditional experience from within the academy, especially those that emerge from within the faculty, will likely have very short leashes when being judged on both the extent and the pace of change, with board members taking a skeptical view of the likelihood of fundamental change coming from within the academy rather than being catalyzed from without. This seems to be the gist of the Teresa Sullivan story at UVA.

Nonetheless, it seems unlikely that leaders emerging from other economic sectors and industries will become a predominant model for the president or chancellor of the future, at least in traditional nonprofit four-year colleges and universities. One critical factor will always be the shared governance model. Even if shared governance undergoes significant recalibration in the years to come (as seems inevitable), the engagement of the faculty in the process of creating and managing the core intellectual enterprise of the institution—curriculum, research, pedagogy, outcomes assessment, etc.—will always be so critical as to necessitate its engagement in governance. In fact, given the increasingly external focus of the chief executive, a strong argument may be made that the role of the faculty is actually even more critical than in earlier times when presidents had the luxury to opine upon and to directly influence thinking on such matters.

Tenure, of course, is another delimiting factor when institutions consider candidates from outside the academy. How many CEOs in the commercial sector must contend with employees who regularly question their leadership, their judgment, their intentions, or their authority with the impunity with which that can be and is regularly done by faculty members remarking on their own institutional leaders? Tenure will likely undergo change as this disruptive era continues, but the simple fact of the matter is that academic freedom is so central to the academic and scholarly exercise, so intrinsic to its success, that protecting it must be a fundamental aspect of any future form of faculty appointment and employment. Thus, whatever the form of tenure that emerges from this era, at some very significant level the presidents and chancellors who lead the faculties of the future will still be leading workforces with very few governors on their expression.

It remains to be seen, for example, whether the tenure "reforms" at the University of Wisconsin will result in an environment that tempers the rhetoric of the faculty in regard to university and state leadership, but the sanction for doing so would be so extreme in terms of the system's ability to recruit and to retain outstanding faculty members that it seems a reasonable guess that they will not. The legislature appears to be far more focused on issues of productivity vis-à-vis employment protections. That there has been no legislative response to date to the vote of no confidence in the system's president would appear to support this view.

When added, then, to the simple and oft-proved tenet that organizations are usually best led by people who are steeped in that industry, it seems entirely likely that the preponderance of the college and university presidents and chancellors of the future will emerge from within the sector. The job of the president or chancellor, however, is radically different from that of the people he or she leads, and thus the preparation of candidates for these leadership positions must change, as well. This is likely to become manifest in two important ways. The first is that presidents and chancellors will increasingly emerge not from institutions' academic leadership but from its administrative leadership. Particularly as the role of the chief academic officer becomes more internally focused—in counter-balance to the external role of the chief executive officer—leaders of major administrative units will begin to emerge more frequently as well-prepared and highly valued candidates for the CEO role. This will require the faculty to recognize the central importance of the external and managerial skill sets and to compromise on academic preparation, in return for which they will benefit from leadership that already understands the nature of their work and their imprimatur.

This trend is well begun and is very likely to accelerate. For example, since 1998, fully 20 percent of all presidential or chancellorial searches supported by Witt/Kieffer have resulted in a placement with leadership experience in higher education but outside of academic affairs. Only 5 percent of such placements over that same period came to the position from outside the academy altogether.

The other way in which preparation for leadership will change involves its intentionality. In the past, leaders emerged from within the academy somewhat organically. Whether because someone was viewed as *primus inter pares* among the faculty or because he or she was successful in leading a smaller subunit of the whole, presidents and chancellors very frequently ascended to their posts with strong bona fides within a discrete portion of the overall institution but very little frame of reference on the entirety. When costs—and expectations for an immediate return on the investment—were lower, these folks had time to get up to speed on the requirements of the position and to learn the necessary skills on the job. That time no longer exists.

Today's and, especially, tomorrow's leaders must hit the ground running, especially in terms of engaging with key constituencies in productive ways. Thus, the preparation these emerging leaders receive must be more purposeful, more focused, and more intense. Such preparation means not only the availability of training and education in formal settings but in the experiences with which they are provided during their journey to institutional leadership. So that these experiences may be meted out in efficient, productive ways, this also means seeking, recognizing, and nurturing people and their talents from an early point in their career so that they will be prepared when their time comes. Identifying the potential for institutional leadership, valuing it, and augmenting it will therefore become a more highly focused and purposeful exercise in the future.

In fact, there is something of a growing cottage industry in the identification and training of leaders for higher education. Several higher education associations (the American Council on Education's Fellows Program is the best known), some consortia, and even one of our search firm competitors offer such services. While it would not be completely unfair to speculate that there are revenue objectives in these offerings—colleges and universities are not the only organizations seeking to diversify their revenue streams—most if not all sincerely attempt to provide both theoretical and experiential lessons in the present and future challenges facing college and university leadership. Given the demand for such training, on the part of both emerging leaders and the institutions seeking them, it seems logical to expect additional programs to emerge over time.

It is indeed irrational that people want these jobs and that they actually seek to lead such large and complex enterprises with so many stakeholders with such different points of view and motivations. They do, though, and they still will as the future unfolds, cloudy though the view of it seems today. The important thing, then, is not whether there will be people for these jobs in the future but rather whether those people will have been properly prepared for these roles as they exist, rather than as they have existed. If higher education as an industry accomplishes that task, it will have taken an important step toward becoming a more rational, more stable enterprise.

Note

1. "Stanford Office of Technology Licensing Annual Report: 2014/15," Office of Technology Licensing, Stanford University. http://otl.stanford.edu/documents /otlar15.pdf.

CHAPTER FIFTEEN

Restoring Trust in Higher Education

Aneil K. Mishra and Karen E. Mishra

This book represents the beginning of our effort to champion for changes to restore trust in higher education. Countless other books, research, and popular press articles and op-eds have been published over the past several decades with suggestions about how to reform it. Nonetheless, the endemic problems with higher education, especially its failure to fulfill its promises to students, parents, and employers, have only multiplied. This is despite decades of price increases above the inflation rate as well as significant increases in federal subsidies through research grants, student loan guarantees, and federal student grants. Indeed, on a per full-time equivalent (FTE) student basis, Pell grants have increased from $871 in 1994–1995 to more than $2,000 in 2014–2015, and total federal aid, including loans and work-study, has increased from $4,800 to $10,800 over the same time period.[1]

One reason for the lack of true reform in higher education that we have not discussed in the book so far deserves mentioning. It is the paradox of the demand on greater research productivity for faculty while hiring ever more adjuncts and clinical faculty whose responsibilities typically do not include publishing research. This has resulted in tenure-track faculty devoting increasing amounts of time to research at the expense of teaching or service activities. In the social sciences in which we publish, our top journals now typically have rejection rates between 90 percent and 95 percent. One reason for the high rejection rates is that as faculty have postponed retiring, even with the increase in the number of publication outlets, there are simply more faculty competing to publish in top journals.

At a typical "R1" institution, that is, a school that focuses on research and has PhD programs, tenure-stream faculty members typically devote 50 percent of their time to research.[2] In essence, that means that by the standards of their own peers (i.e., peer blind-reviewed research), they spend 45 percent of their total time on research that is not publishable in top-tier journals (0.9 rejection rate × 50%). To the extent that research time is not paid for by government or private-sector grants, then either tuition dollars and, in the case of public universities, state taxpayer dollars are directly paying for that research effort. In addition, time spent on research, unless it is pedagogic research aimed at improving teaching, is not likely to lead to insights into how to reform higher education.

At the same time, the number of adjunct (or contingent) instructors hired at universities and colleges has risen to almost 50 percent of all faculty appointments.[3] This increase has occurred because of the high cost of those active research professors and the fact that as they do more research, they do less teaching. The only way to make up the difference is to hire adjunct instructors, who may or may not have a doctorate, to teach at a much lower rate of pay. If students and their families are expecting to get the benefit from the tenure-track professors that the school claims teach, those stakeholders may be disappointed to find out that they are being taught by less-qualified instructors. This is not to say that adjuncts are unqualified, as one of us started our academic life as an adjunct instructor. Many adjuncts are passionate, enthusiastic, and eager to teach. But they are not treated as equal faculty members and are marginalized, even as they are expected to have a major impact on large numbers of students.

We have resolved the conflicts among devoting time to research, teaching, or service; to achieving scholarly rigor versus practical relevance; and to developing new knowledge versus helping our students become more adept with the demands of the workplace through a research program involving several key elements. First, we focused our research on significant real-world problems and opportunities, which we have identified by building trust with leaders, managers, and employees in a wide variety of contexts. Second, we've conducted our research largely in field settings, although we have also conducted experiments with students. Third, we have often involved our students in our research, in real time, using field projects and service learning in our courses.

In our longitudinal research, sometimes spanning decades, students get to read case studies about the leaders and organizations we are studying, meet top leaders through guest speaking in our classes or keynote events on campus, and, in semester-long group projects in which the students identify problems and opportunities through their interviews with leaders

and surveys of employees, provide the organization with recommendations for improvement. Through this approach, we have found that it is
possible to produce research that is both theoretically and methodologi-
cally rigorous while also useful for the classroom and the improvement of
business practices.

We have also chosen to collaborate with adjuncts and clinical faculty on
research, having learned how to do this as a couple starting out together in
academia. We published several articles together while the first author was
an adjunct and the second author an assistant professor at Penn State. We
now include adjuncts and even students in our research and publishing.
Aneil invited a former colleague and current clinical professor to contribute a chapter to this book, and Karen has coauthored a textbook with an
alumna of Michigan State who's an advertising executive. Great coauthors
do not have to have PhDs, and our collaborations with them are far richer
as a result.

The contributors and interviewees in this book provide a variety of
perspectives as well as innovative, transformative, and lasting solutions to
revitalize and restore trust in higher education that have not received the
attention they need or deserve. They were invited to provide a more varied
and broader view of the challenges and opportunities in higher education
than is typical of most books about reforming this institution. What is
needed now is pressure from "consumer stakeholders," that is, students,
parents, alumni, and employers, to vote with their feet and their pocket-
books so that these efforts can be scalable and sustainable. Based on our
experience, change will likely not be forthcoming from academic administrators, faculty, or staff. Some would say that's because these "supplier"
stakeholders benefit from the status quo, and that is certainly the case in
many instances. However, many of the people we've worked with more
than 25 years in academia are as frustrated as we are at the inability to
improve higher education's processes and outcomes. But the ever-present
need to increase financial resources that has turned academic leaders
outward instead of inward, and the erosion of governance systems that
have historically helped faculty and staff shape institutional strategies and
missions, means that change will be much harder to initiate from within.
We have witnessed true reformers within the universities at which we've
worked, but their efforts have not been sufficient to make real, lasting
changes take place.

Higher education will only fully enrich society both economically and
socially if those who benefit when it works and those who suffer when
it doesn't take responsibility for demanding that it rebuild the trust they
have lost. However, rebuilding trust requires that those demanding that

trust be restored themselves act in a highly trustworthy manner. This will require greater investments from the consumer stakeholders, but not in the form of additional money, which they probably don't have or don't want to spend. Instead, it will require them to expend more effort and time in evaluating whether they are getting what they deserve for their already considerable investments of time and money.

To build and rebuild trust, institutions and stakeholders must focus on four ways to build trust: build the ROCC of Trust. The ROCC of Trust includes being reliable, open and honest, competent, and compassionate (Mishra and Mishra).[4] Any one of these trustworthy actions is a good place to start, but to be considered trustworthy overall, all four dimensions of trust must be in place. For each of the consumer stakeholders, we first outline their responsibilities and some suggested actions if they are going to be effective in restoring trust in higher education. We then provide a set of questions each stakeholder should be asking when evaluating a particular college or university, or, in the case of alumni, their own institution. Some of these questions are deliberately repeated across the set of four stakeholders, as it has been my experience that the answers to these questions, if there are answers, often depend on who is asking the question and who is answering it.

Students

For students, this first means showing up for all of their classes and appointments with advisers, and showing up fully prepared, that is, demonstrating the reliability and competence dimensions of the ROCC of Trust. Reliability can also be developed and demonstrated by actively seeking out academic advisers after the initial meeting to select courses at matriculation or before each new semester. By developing a strong relationship with an adviser early in one's academic career, students can also develop more competence, as they will be better informed about the requirements for graduation, appropriate electives, and prerequisites. Being in control of one's own final result, that is, successful, timely graduation, should be the goal. Advisers are there to help plan for what happens after graduation, whether it is full-time employment, seeking a promotion at one's current job, or graduate or professional school. It also means demonstrating openness by communicating transparently.

Specifically, demonstrating the openness part of the ROCC of Trust by providing course feedback in an identifiable way, either through formal course surveys or simply e-mailing the professor, can be incredibly helpful in fostering continuous improvement. This can still be done after the course so that their feedback can in no way influence their course grades.

As professors who have read the results of thousands and thousands of course surveys by our students, 99 percent of whom report their satisfaction or dissatisfaction anonymously, we can honestly say that the feedback is mostly worthless. That's precisely because it's anonymous. We need to know what our *best* students think about our course content and delivery, whereas feedback from students who skipped a lot of classes or who didn't put their full effort into individual or group assignments is worthless. But we don't know who's who when it comes to that feedback. Because of the limitations of most student surveys, we consistently seek out our best students after the course is over (and sometimes during the course) to get as much feedback, negative or positive, as possible.

Finally, students can demonstrate the compassion dimension of the ROCC of Trust in a number of ways. Compassion-based trust first requires understanding another person's needs or interests and then finding ways to further them. At a minimum, it means not taking advantage of another person. In academic settings, this includes refusing to shirk any group project responsibilities, the bane of all professors who assign significant group work in a course. It can also mean providing thoughtful input when asked how to improve a course or suggestions for guest speakers or taking advantage of cocurricular opportunities that advisers or professors recommend.

Getting involved in cocurricular activities, especially student clubs or even research projects led by a professor, not only enriches the life an institution but also helps the student better prepare for life after college. Interacting with professionals who are often guest speakers at student clubs or learning how knowledge is produced through research develops both cognitive and interpersonal skills that can be useful throughout one's life. Here again, the idea is to build *relationships* with people outside the classroom in ways that make college life more interesting. Even getting a group of students in one of your classes to ask one of your professors to lunch can provide invaluable insights that they simply don't have time to fit into their formal teaching. It also provides them with another window into who you are, which will be critical if you need a recommendation letter or reference for a job or for graduate school.

Key Questions Students Should Be Asking about Colleges

- What is the true four-year graduation rate for this college?
- What is the average salary upon graduation? After five years?
- What percent of students are admitted to their chosen graduate or professional programs?
- How do average salaries differ by major?

- What is the average percent of time spent by a tenure-stream faculty member on
  o Research?
  o Teaching?
  o Service?
- What percent of your faculty members are not tenure stream? How does their workload differ in terms of research, teaching, and service?
- How many office hours are professors required to hold each week?
- Will I be assigned an adviser to help me with course selection?

Parents

Parents will have to invest more time by identifying trustworthy information sources that can be used to evaluate institutions during the search process, asking tough questions of advisers, professors, and other staff who directly work with students. They must also be prepared to use the full power of social media when an institution consistently fails them, as we all often do when it comes to other providers of products and services, whether in highly vulnerable contexts (think health care, home energy, and transportation) or less vulnerable ones (hotels, cable service, restaurants). They should also consider attending a few classes (not the ones their children are in) or even enrolling in an online or face-to-face class that meets after work hours. Participating directly in what other students are experiencing would provide better information than what a college provides in its marketing materials or what they learn secondhand from their kids. After all, they are the ones cosigning the student loans, thereby affecting their credit scores and ability to borrow for other reasons. They are also often the ones subsidizing, partially or completely, the room and board costs as well.

Key Questions Parents Should Be Asking about Colleges

- What is the true four-year graduation rate for this college?
- What are the best predictors for a successful graduation rate at this school?
- What are advisers responsible for, and how do they help students make the most of his or her time with an adviser?
- What early warning systems are in place in case a student struggles with depression, bad grades, or homesickness?
- Beyond grades, how do you measure whether what a student is learning will be useful later on?
- What is the average percent of time spent by a tenure-stream faculty member on
  o Research?
  o Teaching?
  o Service?

- What percent of your faculty members are not tenure stream? How does their workload differ in terms of research, teaching, and service?
- How does this institution interact with external communities (for-profits, non-profits), and how does it facilitate interactions between these communities and students?
- What opportunities exist for students to become world citizens through this institution?

Alumni

Alumni need to be proactive about giving feedback to their institutions, the good, the bad, and the ugly. They will undoubtedly have perspectives shaped not only by their experience as students but also by how their educations have helped or limited their careers and life satisfaction. They will also have learned how other institutions have influenced the lives of their colleagues and friends, which can be used as a form of benchmarking. Providing feedback will be more useful and influential to the extent that alumni are actively involved in the institution's activities, and not just fund-raising. Providing career development and mentoring, for example, by participating in mock interviews for students or serving as guest speakers, will enhance the two-way communication that is essential to building trust and fostering lasting change. Being advocates for their institutions with the employers is also critical and helps alumni learn how well their alma maters are preparing students for the world of work. Finally, getting involved in alumni networks, either officially sponsored by their colleges and universities or developed independently of them, not only builds the social capital and trust within the networks but also provides additional resources for institutions, including ideas for improvement as well as human and material wherewithal to implement those ideas.

Key Questions Alumni Should Be Asking Their Schools

- What is the percentage of alumni who provide unrestricted financial support each year? What is the average amount they give?
- What infrastructure exists, including social media, for alumni to network with one another? Who is responsible for developing and maintaining this infrastructure?
- What is the four-year graduation rate for our institution?
- What has been the trend since I graduated in terms of employment rates upon graduation and starting salaries?
- How have alumni's incomes changed over time?
- What percentage of students choose either public service or working in non-profits upon graduation?

- What can I do to help our students in their career development?
- What topics are you looking to fill for guest-speaking opportunities or on-campus conferences?

Employers

As a key consumer of one of higher education's outputs, educated students, employers are in an excellent position to help rebuild trust by demanding excellence in the form of cognitive and interpersonal skills. Cognitive skills include analytical skills, literacy, and numeracy. Interpersonal skills include both oral and written communication as well as the ability to lead and work effectively in teams. All of these are required in employees for organizations to succeed in the 21st-century global environment. Unfortunately, according to a survey in 2016 by PayScale and Future Workforce, employers are reporting that college graduates are often lacking these and other skills.[5]

Employers are in a unique position to offer advice and counsel to a school where they recruit students for internships and full-time positions. Many schools of business, engineering, communication, hospitality and restaurant management, and other schools that have direct relationships with employers would appreciate having employers on their advisory boards. This would give them an inside perspective on what is most important in their hiring process and what skills and trends are important to keep up with in their industry. Forging relationships with a school can also give an employer first pick of top students for internships and full-time jobs.

Key Questions Employers Can Ask Schools Where They Recruit

- May I come to a class (or two) and speak about how the skills in that class are useful for a career at our company?
- Do you have an advisory board for your campus that could use our expertise?
- Can we create an intern program?
- What cocurricular program can we fund to help your students become better prepared for a career with our company?

All stakeholders have a reason to speak up and challenge the status quo at their beloved alma mater. We all want our institutions to get radically better for the next generation of college students. The only way to improve is to courageously challenge the status quo, humbly admit our shortcomings, and authentically attack the challenges head-on with our strengths.

By making the significant investments worthwhile again, higher education will restore the trust that will enable it to transform a society that truly needs it.

Notes

1. "Trends in Higher Education: Federal Student Aid per Student by Type over Time, 2016," The College Board. https://trends.collegeboard.org/student-aid/figures -tables/federal-aid-student-type-over-time.

2. "Basic Classification Description," The Carnegie Classification of Institutions of Higher Education, accessed 2016. http://carnegieclassifications.iu.edu /classification_descriptions/basic.php.

3. "Background Facts on Contingent Faculty," American Association of University Professors. https://www.aaup.org/issues/contingency/background-facts.

4. Aneil K. Mishra and Karen E. Mishra, *Becoming a Trustworthy Leader: Psychology and Practice* (New York: Routledge, 2013).

5. "2016 Workforce-Skills Preparedness Report," PayScale, accessed 2016. http://www.payscale.com/data-packages/job-skills.

About the Editor and Contributors

Editor

Aneil K. Mishra is the Thomas D. Arthur Distinguished Professor of Leadership at East Carolina University's College of Business. Dr. Mishra earned his AB in economics, cum laude, from Princeton University, and his PhD in business administration from the University of Michigan. His previous roles include associate dean for academic affairs at North Carolina Central University, and VP of curriculum and faculty relations for 2U Inc., where he helped lead the successful development and launch of UNC–Chapel Hill's Kenan-Flagler School of Business's online MBA program, MBA@UNC. He has also served as a management professor at Wake Forest, Duke, Penn State, and Michigan State. Prior to earning his PhD, he worked for the General Motors Corporation as a human resource specialist and manufacturing engineer. He is the coauthor of two books on leadership as well as numerous scholarly and practitioner articles and writes for both Entrepreneur.com and IvyExec.com.

Contributors

Dennis Barden is senior partner at Witt/Kieffer, which he joined in 1998 after 20 years in academic administration. Dennis works extensively with boards, senior institutional leaders, and search committees in support of searches for presidents/chancellors, chief academic officers, deans, and advancement and other leadership in both public and private institutions. Dennis began his administrative career at his alma mater, St. Lawrence University in Canton, New York. He went on to serve on the staffs at Georgetown University and Northwestern University and subsequently served 11 years at the University of Chicago, first as assistant dean of its law school and then as an assistant vice president. Dennis has written extensively on the search process in higher education, with a focus on the work of boards and search committees in times of change. Dennis is a past chair of the American Council on Education's Executive Search Roundtable and is a regular contributor to the Chronicle of Higher Education. He earned a BA in English literature, magna cum laude, from St. Lawrence University.

Miranda Barrett is vice president of strategic engagement for the Entrepreneurs' Organization. She earned a BA in political communications from George Washington University. Before completing her degree, she dropped out of college to work for the White House during the Clinton administration, coordinating the details of presidential travel around the world. She has worked for the Entrepreneurs' Organization for nearly 10 years on a wide range of functions, from member recruitment, chapter launches, and external engagement. She loves collaborating with high-energy entrepreneurs around the world, especially the college students in the Global Student Entrepreneur Awards program. She is a certified association executive (CAE).

Laura Graham is a faculty member at North Carolina Central University, in Durham, North Carolina, where she leads the Business Communication area. Her focus is on teaching today's business students to find their authentic, professional voices. Professor Graham holds an MA in communication studies from the University of North Carolina at Chapel Hill, where she studied the rhetoric of corporate communications. Her varied teaching career includes stints in community college, women's college, HBCU, and large public university classrooms. Her professional career includes employment recruiting, directing the marketing and admissions function for the WEMBA program at Duke's Fuqua School of Business, and many years in advertising and public relations for a variety of clients. Whether in academic or professional positions, her goal is to help people tell their stories so compellingly that others will want to write themselves into those narratives.

Austin L. Hollimon is CEO and founder of CommitU, which works with high schools and universities to increase retention and help students exploit their potential. Mr. Hollimon earned his AB in history from Princeton University. A 2012 U.S. Olympic Trials participant and a 2013 NCAA track champion, he has turned his passion for performance into a passion for performance through education. Mr. Hollimon is also a work-study coordinator at Cristo Rey Atlanta Jesuit High School and a former Teach for America Houston Corp member.

Leah Katell is pursuing a PhD in business administration with a concentration in management at Virginia Commonwealth University. She holds a bachelor's degree in mathematics from East Carolina University and a master's degree in economics from the University of North Carolina at Charlotte. She worked for the East Carolina University College of Business (COB) from 2011 to 2016, first as an applied economic research associate and then as the director of assessment from 2013 to 2016. As the director of assessment, she coordinated all of the assessment for the departments in the COB. The coordinated assessments were based on the guidelines from both the Association to Advance Collegiate Schools of Business (AACSB) and the Southern Association of Colleges and Schools Commission on Colleges (SACSCOC).

Vin McCaffrey is the founder and CEO of Game Plan, a unified student-athlete development platform. Mr. McCaffrey earned a BA in international relations from Lehigh University and an MBA from Indiana University. A former Lehigh University basketball player, Vin believes that the student-athlete experience can be a powerful tool for professional development that prepares student-athletes for life beyond college. Vin is well-known within college athletic circles as a leader in student-athlete development and has been a speaker on student-athlete development and successful identity transitions for student-athletes at the National Association of Collegiate Directors of Athletics (NACDA), National Association of Academic Advisors for Athletics (N4A), Major League Soccer (MLS), and many other colleges and organizations.

Karen E. Mishra is a member of the marketing and supply chain faculty at East Carolina University's College of Business, where she teaches marketing and international business. Dr. Mishra earned her BA from Albion College in economics and music, her MBA is from the Ross School of Business at the University of Michigan, and her PhD in integrated marketing communications is from the University of North Carolina at Chapel-Hill. She is a Gallup-certified strengths coach, and has been awarded MBA Professor of the Year for her strengths coaching and advising. Her research interests include internal communication, trustworthy leadership, and digital marketing. She is the coauthor of three books, including, most recently, *The Beginner's Guide to Mobile Marketing*. She writes about marketing for small business for Entrepreneur.com.

Christopher P. Puto is president of Spring Hill College in Mobile, Alabama. Dr. Puto holds a PhD in business administration from Duke University, an MBA from the University of Miami, and a BS in economics from Spring Hill College. He has served on the faculties of the University of Michigan, the University of Arizona, Georgetown University, and the University of St. Thomas (Minnesota). He was professor of marketing and business dean at Georgetown and St. Thomas. Prior to earning his doctorate at Duke, Puto spent several years as a marketing and sales executive at Burger King Corporation and in the Quaker State Oil Company distribution network. He has consulted with General Electric, Kodak, Bank of America, and various other corporate and nonprofit organizations.

Linda Quick is a member of the accounting faculty at East Carolina University College of Business. She is a native of eastern North Carolina and a graduate of the East Carolina University undergraduate and masters of accounting programs and the honors program at ECU. Dr. Quick spent three years working in public accounting as an auditor for KPMG, with clients in the manufacturing, communications, retail, and banking sectors, and then completed her PhD in business administration from the University of South Carolina. Her research interests include behavioral research in international accounting and auditing, issues related to the implementation of IFRS and principles-based standards in the United States, auditor litigation, and auditor judgment and decision making. Her teaching interests include financial accounting and auditing.

Kellie Sauls serves as the executive director of the office of student and alumni affairs at the Lyndon B. Johnson School of Public Affairs at the University of Texas at Austin. She has a BA in sociology from the University of Texas at Austin and an MS in counseling and psychological programs from Columbus State University. She has over 16 years of higher education experience both in career services and admissions. Prior to Batten, Ms. Sauls worked for the Darden School of Business as an associate director of admissions and as the director of diversity initiatives and programming. Her higher education career began at Wake Forest University's MBA program, where she spent over seven years. She is active in her community and has served on local and national advisory boards and boards of directors. Her career also includes teaching, community-based advocacy, and psychotherapy. Kellie most values her family and friendships developed across the globe as she has traveled to and lived in over 30 countries.

Christine M. Wallace is the vice president of Kettering Global for Kettering University in Flint, Michigan, where she leads the development of online programs and courses for Kettering University Online as well as continuing education and corporate training efforts. She has held numerous roles in higher education, including assistant professor of organizational and healthcare leadership at the University of St. Francis, program manager at the University of Illinois Global Campus, and the executive director of product strategy and development for laureate education. Dr. Wallace received her PhD in public administration from Western Michigan University, a master of education in community counseling from Georgia Regents University in Augusta, and her BA in psychology from the University of Michigan.

Brian M. Welke is an attorney in Washington, D.C., and is a founding member of RenegadeWorks, a business technology company. He enlisted in the Marine Corps in 2003 at the age of 17 and deployed with I Marine Expeditionary Force to Ramadi, Iraq, in 2005 through 2006. Upon discharge from the Marine Corps Reserve in 2010, he had attained the rank of sergeant, having been a platoon sergeant leading 90 marines. He earned his BA in history and political science from the University of Iowa and his JD from the Regent University School of Law.

Index

National Association of Intercollegiate
  Athletics (NAIA), 134
National Collegiate Athletics Association
  (NCAA), 134; noncompliance penalties,
  138
National Junior College Athletics
  Association (JuCo), 134
National Survey of Student Engagement, 12
Native American students, 57–58
NBN sports, 116
Neal, Anne, 5
Networking, 114–115, 127, 130, 143;
  and entrepreneurship, 178; and student
  entrepreneurs, 174. *See also* Alumni
  networks
New America Foundation, 147
New Jim Crow, The (Alexander), 59–60
No Child Left Behind, 105
North Carolina Central University
  (NCCU), 1, 3, 93, 110
Notre Dame University, 94, 109–110

Obama, Barack, 124
Ohio State University, 59, 141–142, 144
Online courses, 157–160; accreditation for,
  167; ADA compliance, 168; continuous
  improvement, 165–166; course
  development, 163–165; determination
  of costs, 162; faculty for, 166–168;
  faculty involvement in, 158–159; faculty
  training for, 169–170; and the future
  of higher education, 170; goals of, 167;
  marketing of, 170–172; market research
  for, 161–162; program development,
  160–163; timelines for grade deadlines,
  169; timelines for responses to student
  messages, 169; universal navigation in,
  168; use of rubrics, 168–169. *See also*
  Online degree programs
Online degree programs, 9–10, 80n8.
  See also Online courses
Openness, 6–7, 148, 196
Oral communication, 116
Organizational communication, 96–97
Orientation programming, 127
O'Rourke, James, 94, 109–110
Our Kids: The American Dream in Crisis
  (Putnam), 4, 153

Page, Scott E., 58
Parents: as constituents, 188, 198–199;
  evaluation of institutions by, 198–199;
  as stakeholders, 195; trust needed by,
  12. *See also* Families
Paul Quinn College, 14
Penn State University, 2, 158, 195
Peregrine Academics, 42n3
Personal growth, 151
Persuasion, 113
Peter, Mohan, 88, 150
Phetla, Tokologo, 175
Philanthropy, 185–186, 188
Positive psychology movement, 82
Posse Foundation, 63
Posttraumatic stress disorder (PTSD),
  73–74
Pratt School of Engineering, 110, 114
Pre- and posttesting, 37–38
Predominantly white institutions (PWIs),
  56–57; difficulty recruiting Native
  American students, 57–58; efforts to
  enhance diversity in, 63–64
Preferential admissions, 60
Preschool education, 67
Primary school education, 67
Princeton University, 3, 7, 124–126, 150,
  186
PRISM program (Meredith College), 104
Professional careers, preparation for, 11
Professional education, 15n7
Professional organizations, 114
Professionals, demand for, 66
Profit, 23
Program of study (POS), 162–163
Program Summit, 163
Public speaking, 113–114
Purpose, 126–127, 130; loss of, 75–76; in
  the university experience, 77–78
Putnam, Robert, 4, 153

Quality assurance (QA) team, 165
Quest Bridge, 63

Race-conscious admissions, 60
Raleigh Coaching Academy, 89
Recruiting, deceptive, 14
Relationship building, 197